The Chinese Economy into the 21st Century

— Forecasts and Policies

Chief Editor Li Jingwen

FOREIGN LANGUAGES PRESS   BEIJING

First Edition   2000

Chief Editor: Li Jingwen
Deputy Chief Editors: Lü Zheng   Liu Shucheng
Wang Zhenzhong   Liu Rongcang
Editorial Committee: Zhao Jingxing   Chen Dongqi
Han Shengjun
Writers: Mao Liyan, Wang Zhenzhong, Bai Zhongyao, Jiang Xiaojuan, Yu Ping, Qi Jian'guo, Lü Zheng, Liu Shucheng, Liu Rongcang, Chen Naixing, Chen Dongqi, Yang Shengming, Li Zhou, Li Jingwen, Zhang Ping, Zhang Jun, Zhang Lingguang, Shen Jiru, Zhao Jingxing, Zhao Zhao, Han Shengjun and Wei Houkai

Translated by Zhang Tingquan

Home Page:
http://www.flp.com.cn
E-mail Addresses:
info@flp.com.cn
sales@flp.com.cn

ISBN 7-119-02029-3
©Foreign Languages Press, Beijing, China, 2000
Published by Foreign Languages Press
24 Baiwanzhuang Road, Beijing 100037, China
Distributed by China International Book Trading Corporation
35 Chegongzhuang Xilu, Beijing 100044, China
P.O. Box 399, Beijing, China
Printed in the People's Republic of China

Foreword

Mankind will soon bid farewell to the calamities and difficulties of the 20th century to enter a new century replete with hope and uncertainty. What's to come for China's 1.2 billion people in the 21st century? In which direction will China with a population of 1.2 billion and a vast territory develop during this historical period? How will this vast and sprawling nation change? And how will these changes affect the rest of the world? These are of vital interest not only to the Chinese, but to statesmen, economists, business people and others all over the globe. This book has been written and is now published in an attempt to answer these questions.

The work combines academic analysis with medium- and long-term forecasts for economic development and policy proposals. In the spring of 1993 the State Council asked the Chinese Academy of Social Sciences to research the intellectual superstructure supporting economic development in China until 2010. The scholars were to precede their colleagues in the various governmental departments in beginning this analysis. The Chinese Academy of Social Sciences instructed me to invite a number of scholars from relevant research institutes to form a research group. The experiences gained since the initiation of the reform and opening policy provided the foundation for determining projected developments over the next 15 years. Qualitative and quantitative analyses were the tools whereby we derived our opinions and designed proposed policies. In the spring of 1994, as reported in the press, the group presented a report entitled "Intellectual Foundations of and Policy Selection for the Ninth Five-Year Plan and a Long-Term Program for Until 2010" to the State Council and relevant governmental departments. Subsequently, the group continued its work, finishing the book in March 1995 when it was published to much favorable notice both at home and abroad, including a national book award in 1996. The report delivered to the State Council received the 1997 Sun Yefang Award for Economics.

This book recognizes China's enormous achievement in economic development since the initiation of the reform and opening policy and holds that the years leading up to 2010 will continue this achievement. Using a macroeconomic model, the writers provide economic forecasts for 2000 and 2010 and effect a penetrating illumination of the goals and basic characteristics of China's economic development. Coming trends of changes in the industrial and consumption structures, are explored and detailed description and analysis provided concerning the rural economy, industry, rural enterprises, the building industry, tertiary industry, investment, income distribution, foreign trade, use of foreign capital, regional economies, scientific and technological advances, population, employment, ecological environment and international economic relations. The results of this thoroughgoing research are put forward in ideas and policies for alleviating present and future contradictions in the economic system and sustaining steady, rapid economic growth. The result is a comprehensive outline for future development, one that identifies the obstacles on the road ahead and proposes how they may be overcome.

After publication, some of the book's content was adapted for use in various government documents. Forecasts presented in the book are already beginning to be proven true.

As a service to those abroad concerned with the Chinese economy, the Foreign Languages Press has distilled the most essential portions of the book and translated them into English. My colleagues and I extend our heartfelt thanks to the Press and its translators for their painstaking work. I believe that this English edition will surely play a positive role in helping the world to better understand China and strengthen economic, technological and culture exchange and cooperation between China and other nations.

Any questions or comments inspired by this book will be

gratefully received. We look forward to further academic discussion concerning China's economic future.

Chief Editor: Li Jingwen
September 1997

Contents

Chapter One   General Trends in Chinese Economic Development

Section One   A Brief Overlook of Economic Development in China Since the Initiation of the Reform and Opening Policy

In the 16 years between 1979, when China began its policy of economic reform and the opening to the outside world, and 1994 the Chinese economy grew at an average annual rate of 9.8%, the fastest rate worldwide during this time. The growth rate in primary industry averaged 5.2 percent, secondary industry 11.4 percent, and tertiary industry 9.8 percent. Total import / export volume increased by 16.5 percent annually, (exports 17 percent and imports 15.9 percent). The nation's composite strength increased markedly. The standard of living improved substantially and China's international status and influence climbed.

China's achievement drew attention from all over the globe. Such remarkable progress was predicated on adhesion to the principle of seeking truth from facts, mental emancipation, the concentration of all effort toward economic construction and persistence in the policy of reform and opening under the guidance of Deng Xiaoping's theory of building socialism with Chinese characteristics.

Several key points came to be understood from this experience:

(1) The relationship between reform, development and stability must be balanced appropriately to insure that they are well integrated and mutually promoting. Stability is the foundation, reform the driving force and development the goal. Stability is a prerequisite for

development and development requires reform. Persistent reform, opening and development are essential to the maintenance of social stability. Indeed, only through reform and opening and accelerated economic development, is it possible to achieve enduring social stability. Accordingly, the policy of "seizing opportunities, deepening reform, opening wider, promoting development and maintaining stability" must be continuously upheld.

(2) The old idea of closing the door to the outside world needed to be reversed, opening doors to opportunities in all directions. Economic contacts and cooperation between China and other countries have become closer and deeper than ever, and this opening has vitalized economic and technological development domestically. Total import/export volume as a percentage of GNP rose from 11 percent in 1978 to 38 percent in 1993. The opening process will be further accelerated in the future. The coastal regions will open still further, along with hitherto un-open areas in the hinterlands, border regions and along the Yangtze River. China will actively pursue foreign capital and advanced technologies, at the same time actively expanding the range of projects with responsibilities apportioned among international partners entered into.

(3) Overall equilibrium must be maintained as the industrial structure is optimized. The development strategy must recognize the nation's limits and capabilities, achieving a positive balance and pursuing progress while maintaining stability. Most importantly, revenues and expenditures must be balanced, credit and foreign exchange balances maintained and inflation avoided. In the future overall control will be effected primarily through regulating the money supply, availability of credit, interest rates and other financial measures. In adjusting the industrial structure, the leadership role of the national industrial policy, economic plans and programs for the various trades and industries must be given full play, adopting preferential and supportive policies where necessary. At the same time and still more importantly, the fundamental role of the market in the

allocation of resources must be given free rein, optimizing this process as competition allows the best to rise to the top.

(4) Relations between the central government and the local governments as well as inter-regional relations must be handled properly. China is a vast country with an enormous population; widely varying historical conditions, distribution of resources and level of productive forces have produced substantial imbalances in economic development. The eastern coastal regions have a sounder economic foundation and their economic development has far exceeded that of the central and western regions. This gap can only be narrowed through the development of the productive forces. While the eastern coastal regions should be encouraged to further accelerate economic development, policies necessary to bolster the central and western regions should be implemented, strengthening their transportation capacities and the ability to exploit natural resources. China's primary production bases for energy and raw materials are in the central and western regions. With this in mind, in the future reforms in the pricing, financial, tax and commodity circulation systems should be effected so that these regions are justly compensated for their resources.

China continues to work hard to deepen reform and open still wider, seizing every appropriate opportunity to accelerate the development of the new socialist market economic system. Reform, opening and development have all entered a new period. The 15 years from 1995 to 2010 will see rapid economic growth in China. This period will be the most crucial in the historic drive to modernization. The difficult tasks before the nation will require enthusiasm and conviction.

Rapid growth has perhaps inevitably brought with it problems and contradictions that have tended to accumulate with the passage of time.

(1) Development of the different industries has been uncoordinated, resulting in a less desirable industrial structure. First, increases in agricultural production have been irregular and structural upgrading of the agricultural system has been slow in coming. Labor

productivity is low. Development will require both increased production and modification of the agricultural structure. Second, growth in the basic industries and processing industries has not been in concert. The infrastructure continues to be plagued with bottlenecks in transportation, communications, supplies of energy and raw materials and urban construction. Third, tertiary industries are insufficient in number. The incremental value produced by such industries amounts to only 28 percent of GDP, far below the average for low and medium income countries. Moreover, the sector suffers from irrational structuring. Fourth, the growth of new high technology industries is not fast, and they account for too small a proportion in the national economy.

(2) Industrial quality and technological levels are not high. Few Chinese products or services are top-grade; most are of medium quality. High quality goods are in short supply while inferior products proliferate. Shortages and overstocks coexist. Large quantities of goods are imported while new domestic operations remain unopened. Many enterprises have high production costs and low profit margins, hamstringing their ability to accumulate capital. Technological progress is slow and comes mainly through imported technology and equipment. Creativity and assimilation of new ideas are inadequate. As a result, fewer new products are developed and the enterprises sag in the international market. Technological advances account for about 30 percent of economic growth.

(3) There is an increasing disparity in regional economic development. This imbalance has been aggravated since the initiation of the reform and opening policy, and the gap between the east and the west continues to widen. Moreover, this trend seems likely to continue and possibly worsen in years to come if steps are not taken. Such a result would be detrimental to comprehensive economic development and long term social stability.

(4) Population pressures on resources and the environment are growing heavier and heavier. Positive economic results up and down

the production chain still await improvement. The state-owned enterprises in particular are lackluster, many operating at a substantial loss, with low profit margins, lacking the capacity to effectively expand or renovate their operations.

(5) A system advantageous to healthy, rapid and sustained economic development is not yet fully in place. Frictions between the old and new systems occur often, directly affecting economic growth and increased returns.

Section Two   Essential Conditions Affecting Economic Development and Factors Restrictiong Economic Development

I. Population and the Human Resources

China's abundance of human resources, the greatest in the world, provides a tremendous motive force to drive economic development. At the end of 1994, China (exclusive of Taiwan, Hong Kong and Macao) had a population of 1.1985 billion, 51.3 percent of whom, 614.7 million, were employed. Whether measured in terms of population, total employment or employment rate, China leads the world. (By way of comparison, the employment rate in the United States in 1987 was 46.1 percent, Britain 43.9 percent, former West Germany 41.6 percent, France 38.3 percent, Canada 46.6 percent and Japan 48.1 percent.) Bear in mind that the Chinese population is younger than that of these more economically developed countries. China's employment rate should climb still higher in the next decade and beyond.

This higher ratio of employment to total population is partially the result of the large population, rich labor resources, low wages and government policies encouraging fuller employment, but a more fundamental cause is a labor employment system wherein supply restricts demand. Experiences in social and economic development throughout the world have demonstrated that unskilled, low-quality human resources are hardly assets, indeed may prove a heavy burden in less developed countries. Only high-quality human resources, that is to say a well educated, healthy populace with good work skills, can be considered an asset.

Since the founding of the People's Republic, China has done much to limit population growth and improve the quality of the population, improving education, training and public health. As a result, the natural growth rate dropped from 27.64 per thousand in 1964 to 11.21 per thousand in 1994. Nonetheless, China's population is so enormous that even a reduced growth rate produces a great increase in population in real numbers. Full use is not being made of today's human resources. Skills are not being developed and training will fall short of that required in the coming century. Overall, the quality of human resources is not high. There is an unbalanced structure with, on one hand a comparative handful of top scientists and other talents and on the other vast numbers of illiterates and semi-illiterates. There is more than one reason for this state of affairs, but one important factor is the irrational human resources management system.

Today, most Chinese work in primary industries, far fewer in secondary and tertiary industries. A 1990 general survey of employment in different industries showed 72.3 percent of the work force working in farming, forestry, animal husbandry, or fishery, 13.38 percent in industry, 0.1 percent in geological surveying or prospecting, 1.84 percent in construction, 1.83 percent in the transportation or communications, 3.96 percent in commerce, food and beverage or materials supply, 0.95 percent in real estate or utilities, 0.79 percent in public health, sports or social welfare, 2.33 percent in education, culture, arts, broadcasting or television, 0.23 percent in scientific research or comprehensive technical services, 0.33 percent in finance or insurance, 1.94 percent in government organs, political parties or mass organizations, and 0.02 percent working elsewhere. Briefly put, 72.3 percent of laborers work in agriculture, forestry, animal husbandry, or fishery and 13.38 percent in industry. The percentage of the work force working in all other fields is very low. These figures clearly indicate that in the future the labor needs of secondary and tertiary can and will be filled from the ranks of those currently working in primary industries.

The age composition of the work force is also advantageous to economic development. Workers younger than forty account for 70.02 percent of the total work force compared to 48.9 percent in Japan (in 1982). China's work force is much younger than that of Japan. In the coming decade these young workers will gradually rise to preeminence in China's economic construction. On the other hand, 12.04 percent of those employed in China are between the ages of 15 and 19 as compared to 2.45 percent in Japan, indicating that people enter the work force at an earlier age in China, missing out on the opportunity to complete their basic education or receive specialized training. This problem is particularly salient in the countryside.

China has a gigantic supply of labor force which continues to increase rapidly. In numbers, duration and degree of pressure, it presents a situation unprecedented in Chinese history. According to the 1990 census, there were 334.848 million people under the age of 15. Over the next 20 years beginning in 1991, an average of 21 million Chinese will reach working age every year. The working population aged 15 to 59 is projected to reach 812.51 million by 2000, 926 to 961 million by 2020 and 846 to 979 million by 2050. The working population aged 15 to 64 will reach 844.75 million by 2000 and 983 million to 1.018 billion by 2020, before tapering off around 913 million to 1.047 billion in 2050. Excluding those enrolled in school and those whose mental capacities bar them from the work force, the actual working population should be 731.26 million in 2000, 833 to 866 million in 2020 and 761 to 881 million in 2050.

The rural workforce is expected to grow by 100 million between 1992 and 2000. Adding existent surplus rural labor and subtracting natural depletion, there still will be approximately 200 million able workers to be transferred out of the countryside. Currently, rural enterprises absorb an additional 4 to 5 million rural workers every year. The large number remaining will flood into the urban areas in search of job opportunities. Many will join the ranks of the urban unemployed ensuring that the question of labor supply exceeding demand will continue for years to come. Providing non-agricultural jobs for surplus rural labor will be the most pressing employment problem in the future, seriously affecting economic development.

II. Natural Resources

Broadly speaking, China's enormous land mass abounds in natural resources, but they are not evenly distributed, and because of the size of the population and over exploitation, per capita resources are low, most below the world average.

Farmland: China has 1.431 billion mu (15 mu=1 hectare) of cultivated land, 1.22 mu per capita, 200 million mu of farmland is in reserve, far below the world average of 4.57 mu per capita. Even if all available farmland is returned to cultivation from other uses, per capita cultivated land will drop to 1.11 mu by 2000 and 1.02 mu by 2010 as a result of increased population pressures. Moreover, the quality of arable land is poor and cannot be improved without great difficulty. Nearly 700 million mu of farmland is subject to drought, 160 million mu in the south is erosive red soil, 100 million mu is immersion land, 130 to 210 million mu is long term water-logged, and 120 million mu is marshland. Nationwide, there are 500 million mu of saline-alkaline soil, including 100 million mu of cultivated land. As has been made clear, China must deal with a forbidding land resource environment in its quest for sustained agricultural development.

Forests: China currently has 128.63 million hectares of forest, two mu per capita, compared to the world average of 12 mu per capita. Forest coverage is 13.4 percent, also well below the world average of 22 percent.

Water resources: Water resources (combined surface and ground water less double counted circulating water) total approximately 2.8

trillion cubic meters, ranking sixth after Brazil, the former Soviet Union, Canada, the United States and Indonesia. However, China has only 2,710 cubic meters per capita, about one quarter the world average and only 1,770 cubic meters per mu of farmland, about three quarters the world average. China's water resources are by no means abundant. Moreover, these water resources are distributed unevenly, frequently unadvantageously in respect to population, farmland, and mineral resources. The south has more water but less farmland; the north has more farmland but less water. This shortfall is particularly pressing in the north where industry and agriculture each vie for limited water supplies. Energy production is hampered by insufficient water supplies and many cities suffer water shortages.

Mineral resources: Total proven mineral reserves rank third in the world in conversion value, but per capita reserves rank 80th, coming in at less than half of the world average. Reserves of more than 10 major minerals are inadequate. Supplies of petroleum, natural gas, gold, copper and iron ore are insufficient to sustain rapid economic growth.

Thus, shortages in the supply of natural resources will become even more acute between 1995 and 2010, potentially shackling continued economic growth. A solution may be found in scientific and technological advances that allow deeper exploitation and more efficient use of resources. Every effort will be made to produce more with fewer resources, lessening economic development's dependence on the earth's limited resources.

III. Financial Conditions

China will require enormous financial input over the next 16 years. The principal source should be domestic accumulation. Since 1978 China has maintained a high investment rate, particularly during the ten years from 1985 to 1994, when the annual investment rate exceeded 34 percent; the rate exceeded 36 percent in eight of these years, reaching a high of 43.3 percent in 1993. This high investment rate was accompanied by notably increased levels of consumption, great improvement in the people's standard of living, and a substantial increase in personal savings. Overall, while the high investment rate sometimes led to price rises, these did not come at the expense of consumption levels.

The next 16 years will be a golden age for economic development in China. Comprehensive industrialization and urbanization will require large scale investment to finance a large number of infrastructure projects to take the nation into the new century, including the Three Gorges Project, diverting water from the south of China to the north, a high-speed railway line linking Beijing and Shanghai, a tunnel under the mouth of the Yangtze River, airports, harbors, expressways, telecommunication networks, as well as projects involving the raw materials, motor vehicle and electronics industries. The financial resources required will be tremendous, but these projects will inevitably produce accelerated growth throughout the economy. An average annual investment rate of 32-34 percent will be necessary to ensure that the funding for these projects will be available. Such a rate is feasible for three main reasons: first, as production levels increase and incomes rise, public savings will presumably continue at relatively high levels; second, capital will become available from a greater variety of sources, as collective, private and individually held enterprises gradually accumulate more capital; third, foreign capital will play an important role in accelerating economic development. While significant sums will continue to flow into the Middle East, Eastern Europe, Russia and Southeast Asia in the future, China's skyrocketing economy and huge market potential will still attract large quantities of foreign investment.

Section Three   Future Changes in the Chinese Economy

For the next 15 years and beyond a robust Chinese economy will thrive as never before, as summarized in the following ten points.

I. The 20 Years Bridging the Millenium Will Be a Golden Era of Economic Growth as China's Growth Continues to Be the World's Most Energetic

By 2010, China will stand in the front ranks internationally in composite economic power. Although per capita income is currently at the level of a developing country, it is expected to rise to that of a middle income country. The annual GNP growth rate between 1991 and 2010 is projected to be around 8.25 percent; the GNP in 2010 is expected to nearly quadruple that of 1994.

This high growth rate is sustainable for several reasons.

1. China will maintain long term political stability and unity domestically and will benefit from a comparatively relaxed international environment conducive to development. While there certainly will continue to be many disputes in the world, the general movement will be toward peace, cooperation and development, as all nations work hard taking domestic economic development as their first goal, thereby promoting international stability. This international atmosphere of cooperation will be advantageous to the further development and opening of China. Moreover, the return of Hong Kong and Macao will inject new economic vigor.

2. The foundations laid since the initiation of the reform and opening policy will provide the necessary material conditions for further development. Primary industries and infrastructure have been strengthened. Transportation and energy supply bottlenecks are gradually being alleviated.

3. The experience gained and many lessons learned since the early days of the reform and opening policy have taught planners to understand and consciously employ economic laws, avoiding deadends and unnecessary detours and reducing unwelcome fluctuations. Step by step, the establishment and optimization of the socialist market system will provide a new, more effective systematic foundation for rapid high quality development of the Chinese economy.

4. China has an enormous domestic market and total supply and

demand and the scale of consumption will grow enormously. In particular, a tremendous impetus to economic growth will be created by increased consumption if Chinese living standards are raised beyond subsistence to comfort levels.

5. China is vast, but regional development is extremely imbalanced. In the future regional growth will form in a recurrence pattern, with the shifting balances stimulating reciprocal waves of economic growth.

II. The Industrial Structure Will Change Significantly as It Is Progressively Rationalized

Between the present and 2010, primary industry as a portion of GNP will drop substantially as secondary and tertiary industries increase as a result of industrialization and attendant urbanization. In 1990 primary industry supplied 28.4 percent of GNP; in 2010 they will account for only 12.7 percent, as secondary industry increases from 43.6 to 52.8 percent and tertiary industry from 28 to 34.5 percent, (in 1990 prices).

Every industrial sector will undergo significant structural change. Crop cultivation, which has traditionally dominated agriculture, will give way as forestry, animal husbandry and fishery gain considerably in importance. Advances in agricultural science and increased investment in agriculture will lead to increased efficiency, higher yields and better quality. The internal structure of secondary industry will be adjusted and upgraded. While both light and heavy industries will grow rapidly, heavy industry will grow at a faster rate. Comparatively, greater increases will be seen in the transportation equipment, electronics and telecommunications and large-scale, complete sets of equipment manufacturing, and in the power industry and construction industries, these sectors leading the pack during this period of rapid economic expansion. Finance, insurance, commerce, telecommunications and transportation will be at the forefront of tertiary industry, growing by leaps and bounds.

III. The Quality of Technology and Equipment Throughout Industry Will Be Substantially Improved, with Industrialization and Initial Modernization Fundamentally Achieved by 2010

China has already established a complete and inclusive industrial system. Scientific and technological advances will become increasingly essential for further development. The completion of the "863" Project, the Torch Project, the Spark Project and the Golden Bridge Project for the development of new and advanced technologies will further raise the technological level. The active acquisition of advanced technology and equipment from abroad will go a long way to closing the current gap in such areas between China and the developed countries. China will use and assimilate imported technologies to greatly improve its capacity for independent research and development, raising that capacity to the level of the middle rank developed nations. In this way, a complete system of advanced technology reflecting the qualities of the Chinese people will be formed.

IV. Public Consumption Will Reach New Heights as Great Changes Come to the Consumption Structure

Per capita individual consumption is expected to rise from 723 yuan in 1990 to 1,712 yuan in 2000, (up 140 percent) then to approximately 3,530 yuan in 2010, (up 390 percent), (in constant 1990 prices). As the economy grows and the people's incomes increase the consumption structure will be characterized as follows.

1. The income portion spent on food will decrease substantially, with the Engel's coefficient expected to drop to approximately 0.48 by 2000 and approximately 0.35 by 2010.

2. The public housing system will move away from free or semi-free housing to market system. As a result, rural and especially urban expenditure on housing will rise by a tremendous margin, reaching a projected 20 percent of total expenditure of income by 2010. Reform

of the medical system will also bring an increase in the proportion of income spent on medical expenses.

3. Leisure spending as a portion of income will also steadily increase. As the market system is optimized and the people's cultural levels rise, more and more time and money will be spent on adult education, books, audio and video products, theater, tourism and entertainment.

V. China Will Continue to Be the Most Populous Nation on Earth

China will have 1.4 billion people by 2010. The population will grow very rapidly during this period creating social pressures, notably regards employment, that will be difficult to alleviate.

As the government increases spending on education and intensifies educational reform, levels of education throughout the whole population will rise. The percentages of people with higher, senior middle school, junior middle school and primary education will continue to increase. However, providing universal education in the old revolutionary base areas, those inhabited by ethnic minorities, border areas and underdeveloped areas will remain an extremely arduous task.

China is also faced with the problem of an aging population. Even by 2000, 6.8 percent of the population will reach 65 or older, as the nation approaches the model of an "aged" society.

VI. China Will Become Increasingly Urbanized

Urban population is likely to rise to 40 percent by the end of this century and 50 percent by 2010, a figure lower than the projected world average of 60 percent. The mushrooming of rural enterprises has promoted rural industrialization. By itself, the "leaving the soil without leaving the land" policy, encouraging peasants to find non-agricultural work locally, falls far short of solving the problem of surplus rural labor. Increasingly, jobs are in the city and this trend will fuel an unprecedented pace of urbanization in the coming years.

China's large and medium-sized cities have absorbed nearly all the new citizens they can take. Accordingly, most surplus rural labor will flow into newly emerged medium and small-sized cities where they will do non-agricultural work. At the same time, government policies will help consolidate and rationally distribute non-agricultural industries in rural areas, providing leadership and support for the accelerated development of rural tertiary industries. A high tide of urbanization will sweep the countryside by the end of this century, providing the capacity to absorb a great deal of the surplus rural labor.

VII. Ever Increasing Pressures on Natural Resources and the Environment

Although, taken en masse, China has huge reserves of a wide variety of natural resources, per capita reserves are very small, many far below the world average. Natural conditions and current levels of technology prevent the effective exploitation of many newly verified reserves. Shortages of natural resources will certainly hamper economic development to some degree.

Generally speaking, environmental conditions are stable, perhaps even showing some improvement. However, there is no reason for optimism. Growth is impinging more and more negatively on environmental quality.

VIII. Regional Economic Growth Is Imbalanced; Income Discrepancies Between Different Groups and Different Regions Will Widen for a Period of Time, Then Stabilize Before Beginning to Narrow Around 2010

Rapid growth will aggravate regional economic imbalances. For a considerable period to come, the coastal regions will grow at a rate roughly 1.3 times that of the interior. However, intervention by the central government and the accelerated economic growth in the interior should step by step help forestall a number of otherwise expected economic and social problems.

With the development of the market economy, income distribution in China has become increasingly market driven. This will first serve to increase differences in income. But with the implementation of market competition and the ready flow of essentials, income gap will narrow, coming down the far side of the bell curve.

IX. The Socialist Market Economic System Will Be Optimized Step by Step

By 2000, the framework for socialist market economy will be in place, with the market playing the fundamental role in resource allocation. By 2010 a comprehensive market operation mechanism will have been step by step put into place and optimized. During this process changes in the management systems of state-owned enterprises, particularly large and medium-sized enterprises, will be crucial. Most large and medium-sized state-owned enterprises will take the form of companies. The establishment of a modern enterprise system will make these enterprises genuinely a major part of the market.

A unified, open, competitive and orderly market system will be established throughout the country. The markets for capital, labor, technology, information and real estate will gradually be made more orderly and a system based on market defined prices will be fundamentally established.

X. Ties Between China and the Rest of the World Will Become Still Closer, as Economic, Political and Cultural Exchanges Increase

Foreign trade will continue to grow. Export volume is expected to rise to over US$ 400 billion by 2010. The export product mix will also change greatly. As the quality of products and management improve, an export structure dominated by labor-intensive products and those with low added value will be increasingly turned to high value added exports and those containing a greater component of advanced technology.

The return of Hong Kong and Macao will positively effect the Chinese economy. The Hong Kong Special Administrative Region will continue to thrive still stronger as an international center of finance and entrepot trade, buttressed by the strength of the entire Chinese mainland. By 2010, the two sides of the Taiwan Straits may well have reunified under the prerequisite of "one China" and in accordance with the principle of "one country, two systems." Complementary economic relations across the Straits will be extremely beneficial mutually.

Production is by the day becoming more internationalized. The need to actively join in the international division of labor and heighten international competitiveness, as well as immediate self interest will bring common understanding that may hold the embryonic form of an East Asian common market centered on China, Japan and the Republic of Korea.

Section Four   Future Directions in Economic Development Policy

The principles governing future economic policies will be outlined below.

I. The Idea That Economic Construction Should Be at the Center of All Work Will Be Adhered to; Sustained, Rapid, High Quality Economic Growth Will Be Maintained

"Rapid" here means maintaining a comparatively high rate of economic growth, 8.25 percent per annum. Once China entered into the process of comprehensive industrialization, rapid growth is the inevitable pattern. Urban dwellers have already begun to move from a consumption structure characterized by light industrial products to a modern consumption structure principally characterized by rapidly increasing demand for housing, telecommunications and automobiles. This phenomenon has combined with the rapid development of primary industry and infrastructure facilities to help drive the nation's rapid economic growth. Moreover, this rapid growth allows full use of the abundant labor available, and, as an essential measure to reduce the pressing problem of unemployment, is of great significance in ensuring economic and social stability.

Rapid growth is preconditioned on the maintenance of ever better quality growth. Better quality growth may be summarized as follows: (1) Rapid growth will be characterized by sustained, steady development over the long term, particularly avoiding peaks and valleys. (2) Inflation will be kept within acceptable limits. (3) Development will not be through excessive investment or low outputs; neither resources nor environmental quality will be sacrificed. (4) The industrial structure will be continually improved.

II. The Formulation and Putting into Practice of Complete and Complementary Industrial Policies Promoting Coordinated Development and Unremitting Optimization

In the future, industry will remain the leading sector in economic development, with transportation and post and telecommunications and other infrastructure facilities sectors taking the lead. Agriculture will be further strengthened, continuing to play a major role.

Policies for each industry will be customized. Some will only need the government to create the conditions necessary for their maturation, the establishment and optimization of a market system domestically, otherwise requiring no special supports. Other industries that do not attract non-governmental investment but directly affect public welfare will be targeted for government support and investment.

III. Economic Growth Will Increasingly Rely on Scientific and Technological Advances to Transform the Old Production Model Hitherto Crippled with Redundant, Ineffectual Management and Wasteful Use of Resources; Problems Will Be Solved by Improving Production Efficiency and the Economical Use of Resources; Intensified Production Will Ensure Low Expenditures and High Outputs

Technological advances will be the key driver pushing economic development during this period. In the light of its relatively limited financial power and material resources, China will adopt the principle of "grasping key areas to accelerate reform." This strategy calls for making breakthroughs in a limited number of new and advanced technology sectors. Technological progress in the broad range of industries will come through accelerated reform of the economic system, advances spurred on by market competition. The government will use a policy of "appropriate intervention and combined rewards and punishments" to guide technological progress and standardize business conduct. A variety of policies of specified duration will be formulated to spur enterprises to intensification. Administrative, economic and legal measures will be directed toward enterprises, punishing them for inefficient resource consumption and environmental pollution, forcing them to stress technological improvement.

IV. The Gradual Shifting of the Regional Development Policy Toward the North and West

In the wake of the prosperity first engendered in the economic zones of Southern China and Eastern China, a new wave of growth will emerge around the Bohai Gulf and in the Yangtze and the Yellow River basins. Recognizing this trend, during the early years of the coming century the government, while continuing to support economic development in the south and east, will shift its developmental focus to the north and central west. Drawing on the economic momentum already present in the east and south, best use will be made of central west's comparative advantage in resources. Development of the energy and raw materials industries will be stressed, and, building on this base, the processing chain will be extended, continually increasing the depth of processing and added value of resources, developing a comprehensive path to development. Appropriate policies, as well as material and financial support will be used to encourage development in the north and central west. The inland regions will receive a larger portion of total investment, in particular investment in nationwide transportation and telecommunications networks and large scale energy and raw materials production bases. In this way, these regions' backward infrastructure will be brought up to speed. At the same time, the entire country will gradually be opened up in all directions and differences in regional policies will be lessened as a policy of regional preferences is replaced with a policy of industrial preferences. Special measures will be taken to help less developed areas and those inhabited by ethnic minorities and to renovate old industrial bases. Temporary preferential policies will be adopted to accelerate development in the northern and central western regions.

V. A Distribution Mechanism Giving Equal Consideration to Fairness and Efficiency Will Be Established, Encouraging More Rationality and Stability In Income Distribution

Regions that have the conditions that enable them to develop more quickly will be allowed to do so and people will be encouraged to rely upon their intelligence and diligent work to gain wealth before others, thereby driving overall development. For the short term and on the individual level, increased disparity in income can be encouraged, but, in the larger view, the goals of fairness and efficiency will be given equal weight.

Regional disparities in income will not lessen in the normal course of things. Accordingly, the central financial administration will transfer payments and use other measures to increase incomes in impoverished areas, border areas, those inhabited by ethnic minorities and old revolutionary base areas. Helping these people to rise out of poverty will be a long-term task.

Urbanization and the marketization of the economy will be accelerated to help lessen income differences between the city and the countryside. The greatest problem limiting this process remains the question of surplus rural labor.

A social security system will be more quickly put into place and the establishment and optimization of unemployment and old age insurance will be actively promoted. Income differences will adjusted through taxes and other measures. Every effort will be made to lessen great disparities in income between different social strata, gradually rationalizing the mechanism whereby it is defined.

VI. Population Growth Will Be Strictly Controlled and Population Quality Will Be Stressed

China will comprehensively strengthen its capacity to limit population growth. Number of births will be included in regional development plans. Organizational setups of population management departments will be strengthened at every level with personnel, materials and financial support. While population is limited in quantity, comprehensive thought will be given to improving the quality of the population and adjusting its overall composition. Population management departments will coordinate their actions with departments responsible for civil administration, administration of justice, finance, education, public health and other relevant departments, expanding their roles beyond simply limiting population growth.

Great importance will be attached to investment in education, particularly elementary education and education in impoverished areas.

VII. The Country Will Continue to Open Still Wider, Stressing Participation in the Greater World, Actively Exerting a More Substantial Influence on International Affairs

China will continue its policy of attracting foreign investment. Foreign capital not only provides the funds necessary for China's construction, it is also beneficial to industrial upgrading and heightened international competitiveness. In the future, more attention will be paid to placing foreign capital where it can be best used so as to achieve better results.

China will also actively engage in international competition. Taking active upgrading of industry and heightened international competitiveness as prerequisites, it will keep in step with changes in international markets in order to produce competitive export products, organizing production to meet demand side's needs. Relying on quality and high value to win reputation and market share, it will move away from the old practice of relying on increased export volume to increase foreign exchange earnings.

China will with all possible speed establish a unified national market, by accelerating necessary legislation. Particular attention will be paid to getting on track with international business practices, training a new generation of lawyers, accountants and financial and foreign trade specialists well acquainted with the world of international business.

Importance will be paid to the increasing internationalization of production within overall international economic development and the tendency toward regional economic integration. The optimum allocation of key production factors will be promoted in the Asian-Pacific and East Asian regions, strengthening the international division of labor, each country increasing its own competitiveness on the basis of mutual support, each aiding the other with other complementary strengths.

VIII. The Market System Will Be Optimized as It Is Developed, Driving Still Faster the Construction of a Socialist Market Economy

China faces no easy road over the next ten years and beyond of ever deepening reform. Difficult problems include reform of the state-owned enterprises and the financial system, breaking down local barriers to free trade, expeditiously establishing a unified national market, setting up a new employment system, allowing the market mechanism to play its role in the allocation of the labor resources, putting in place a distribution system characterized by both fairness and efficiency, establishing and optimizing the social security system and speeding up work to improving unemployment and old-age insurance systems. On a still broader scale, the functions of government will be transformed, with indirect management replacing direct management as the mainstay, and government providing society with services and inspection and supervision.

Reform of the state-owned enterprises is the key link in the restructuring of the economic system. A modern enterprise system clearly specifying property rights, defining rights and responsibilities, separating government administration from enterprise management and adopting scientific management will be established with all possible speed in the coming years. Currently, existing state-owned enterprises will be divided into different administrative levels, with different enterprises dealt with in different ways. Smaller enterprises will have greater independence than presently, while closer attention will be paid to large enterprises. Large and medium-sized enterprises will undergo reform to standardize their corporate and stock systems to enable their transformation into competitive, legal entities suited to the market. Small and medium-sized enterprises will be reformed using a wide variety of techniques, including reorganization, merger, take over, leasing, contracted management, stock cooperatives and sale. Reform will take many shapes in establishing mechanisms to ensure effective self control and self motivation in the enterprises, and, in particular, solving the problems of surplus manpower and overstaffing.

IX. The Legal System Will Be Promoted and Continually Improved as Political Reform Moves Ever Forward

The legal system will be strengthened so that laws that truly can be relied on, indeed must be relied on. Laws will be strictly enforced and investigation of violations of the law rigorous. At the same time, a variety of regulatory and supervisory mechanisms will be put into place, so as to uphold the dignity of the law, and bring to a halt all illegal practices, particularly to root out emergent corruption in the legal system. China will continue political reform, expanding the people's democracy, strengthening the role of the People's Congress, consolidating and developing the system whereby democratic parties, people's organizations and patriotic individuals engage in democratic consultation. Policy decisions will be reached more scientifically and with more democracy, so as to fully arouse the activism of the nation's billion plus people. At the same time, government will be simplified and the role of government changed as suits the changes in the economic system. Control on the macro level will be strengthened and direct control over enterprises reduced, giving substance to the concept of "small government for a greater society, small organizations providing much service."

X. Stress Will Be Placed on Synchronizing Cultural Work and Economic Construction, With Cultural and Ethical Progress as Well as Material Progress Advancing In Step, so as to Realize Coordinated Social and Economic Development

Chapter Two   Fundamental Characteristics of the Chinese Economy and Development Targets

This chapter will first address overall economic targets for the next 15 years, then explain the attendant economic implications, the historical background, and the supply and demand factor.

Section One   Targets for Economic Growth and Attendant Economic Implications

According to the macroeconomic model we have developed, (Table 2-1) the Chinese GNP will grow 9 percent per annum on average during the 1990s. The GNP in 2000 is expected to be 4.18 trillion yuan RMB (here and subsequently in 1990 constant prices), and per-capita GNP 3,270 yuan. In fact, as GNP grew 11.65 percent per annum between 1991 and 1994, the above target for the decade can be reached if the average annual growth rate does not fall below 7.2 percent for the remaining years before 2000. Given the Chinese economy's current momentum, achieving this target seems a foregone conclusion.

Growth in GNP is projected to continue at the relatively high annual rate of 7.5 percent for the decade 2001-2010. GNP in 2010 should climb to 8.62 trillion yuan, nearly five times the 1990 figure. If the natural population growth rate can be limited to within 7 per thousand, per-capita GNP in 2010 will come to 6,250 yuan, about four times the 1990 figure.

Growth in GNP would then average approximately 8.25 percent per annum over the 20-year term, 1991-2010.

The economic implications of the above-described growth pattern are best displayed through comparisons with other nations. Comparison between Tables 2-1 and 2-2 makes clear that the gap between China and the developed nations will be significantly narrowed. Whether expressed in terms of total or per-capita GNP, China's status within the international economy will have risen. By 2010, China's per-capita GNP, while still at the level of the developing countries, is expected to be positioned to enter the rank of medium income countries, while its economy will be among the front runners worldwide in total scale.

Table 2-1 1990-2010 Economic Forecasts for China and Selected International Comparisons

Year	1990	2000	2010
GNP (billion RMB yuan in 1990 prices)	1,770	4,180	8,620
(annual growth rate over 10 years, %)		9.0	7.5
Population (billion)	1.14333	1.28	1.38
(annual growth rate over 10 years, %)		1.13	0.75
Per-capita GNP (RMB yuan)	1,540	3,270	6,250
GNP in US dollars US$ 1=1.2 RMB yuan (US$, trillion)	1.47	3.5	7.2
World rank	3rd	2nd	2nd
GNP in US dollars US$ 1=5.2 RMB yuan (US$, billion)	340	800	1,650
World rank	10th	7th	7th
Per-capita GNP in US dollars US$ 1=1.2 RMB yuan	1,280	2,720	5,200
Worldwide level	lower-middle	lower-middle	upper-middle

Per capita GNP in US dollars US$ 1=5.2 RMB yuan Worldwide level	297 low income	630 low income	1,200 lower middle
Minimum per-capita GNP for high income countries (US dollars)	7,620	9,650	12,240
Minimum per-capita GNP for upper-middle income countries (US dollars)	2,466	3,250	4,280
Minimum per-capita GNP for lower-middle income countries (US dollars)	611	700	820

Table 2-2   GDP Forecasts for Selected Countries (US $ billion)

	Country	Average Annual Growth Rate 1980-1991, %	Exchange Rate Computation			Country	Purchasing Power Computation		
			1991	2000	2010		1911	2000	2010
1	U.S.	2.6	5,610	7,060	9,130	U.S.	5,610	7,060	9,130
2	Japan	4.2	3,360	4,860	7,340	Japan	2,370	3,430	5,170
3	Germany	2.3	1,570	1,920	2,410	China	1,660		
4	France	2.3	1,200	1,470	1,840	Germany	1,250		
5	Italy	2.4	1,150	1,420	1,800	France	1,040		
6	Britain	2.9	1,010	1,300	1,730	India	1,000		
7	Canada	3.1	580	760	1,030	Italy	980		
8	Spain	3.2	530			Britain	900		
9	Brazil	2.5	450			Brazil	790		
10	China		430			Mexico	600		

27

China	GNP (RMB billion yuan in 1990 prices) (Ten year annual growth rate, %)	(1990) 1,770	4,180 9.0	8,620 7.5			
	GDP (US$ 1=5.2 RMB yuan) (US$ billion) World rank	(1990) 340 10th	800 7th	1,650 7th			
	GDP (US$ 1=1.2 RMB yuan) (US$ billion) World rank				(1990) 1,170 3rd	3,500 3rd	7,200 2nd

Notes: 1). 1991 exchange rate based and purchasing power parity based GDPs computed by the International Monetary Fund (IMF) as reported in *Time*, (U.S.), (5/31/93).

2). Average annual GDP growth rates (1980-1991), taken from the World Bank's 1993 World Development Report. 1991-2010 GDPs computed using these growth rates, using 1991 as base year.

3. The Chinese GNP is expressed in US dollars using two methods. The first uses the official exchange rate, US$ 1=5.2 RMB yuan. The second uses purchasing power parity as calculated by the IMF, US$ 1=1.2 RMB yuan. World ranks in each instance are computed using the same method that was respectively used to calculate GNP. China holds that the IMF's purchasing power parity method overvalues the RMB.

Different methods of comparing different countries serve different purposes and are of varying economic significance.

Per-capita income can provide a general comparison of living standards in different countries. Consequently, purchasing power analysis of per-capita income can be used to estimate the living standard which Chinese may achieve in the future, and objectively demonstrate China's economic growth and improved standard of living. This improvement will be manifested in levels of expenditure for and consumption of food, clothing, housing, travel and other purchases, as well as the amount of savings. Examples would include per-capita grain consumption, per-capita fruit and vegetable consumption, per-capita consumption of meat, eggs and milk, per-capita cloth consumption, per-capita durable consumer goods expenditure or per-capita housing expenditure. The weighted average of this set of indicators is ultimately expressed in concentrated form as per-capita income. Of course, other factors also affect a country's citizen's living standard and welfare, including the distribution structure, consumption patterns, availability of leisure time and environmental conditions.

However, using purchasing power parity to make gross comparisons between international economies has its limitations. These limitations are exacerbated by the IMF's purchasing power parity method which overvalues the RMB. The economic significance of comparisons of the gross scale of national economies can for the most part be found in measuring a nation's capacity for international competition and then to ascertain its position in international trade and the distribution of the world's economic resources through international trade. The exchange rates used in import / export trade are the best tool for achieving this goal.

The difference between the actual exchange rate and purchasing power parity arises for the most part from differing levels of industrialization. International trade can only take place in goods that are commonly traded, which is to say, for the most part, products produced by primary and secondary industries. Over the course of economic development, products produced by secondary industry, especially manufactured goods, have come to dominate trade. As a result, actual exchange rates are principally decided by manufacturing productivity. The discrepancy between actual exchange rate and purchasing power parity emerges because changes in efficiency in tertiary industry come about more slowly in the overall industrialization process. With increased industrialization, this "gap" will gradually close, perhaps eventually becoming "inverted."

This makes clear why actual exchange rates rather than purchasing power parity should be used to compare different national economies.

Computed using actual exchange rates, China's economy will

probably be the seventh largest in the world by 2010. Of course, this does not mean that China will be included in the ranks of the developed countries, as developed and developing countries are not distinguished on the basis of the overall size of their economies. The two terms are intended to acknowledge a country's level of economic development, and thus is best expressed in per-capita income, its citizen's level of well being.

Section Two   The Background of China's Rapid Economic Growth

Beginning with the first Opium War in 1840, the ancient empire of China entered a period of successive reversals in its confrontations with the world powers. These defeats inspired a generation with the lofty ideal of raising the nation to the same level as the great powers and beyond. However, their plans for "national salvation through education," "national salvation through industry," "national salvation through science and technology" and so on all came to nought, not primarily for economic but for political reasons. It was impossible for a nation still colonial or semi-colonial, divided against itself and politically corrupt, to initiate the necessary economic buildup.

As this lesson shows, China's strength and prosperity first requires a politically independent, efficiently forceful state apparatus. The founding of New China in 1949 laid the foundation for the realization of this goal. New China was faced with all the tasks neglected by its semi-feudal, semi-colonial country predecessor, beyond doubt the first of which was to build a strong national defense and then establish a comparatively independent industrial system.

During the years from the founding of the People's Republic to the 1970s the nation succeeded in developing a reasonably independent and complete industrial system operating at such a level that China could explode atomic bombs and launch its own satellites into space.

However, improvements in the people's livelihood were disproportionate to industrial growth, most noticeably in the agricultural sector which continued to occupy 80 percent of the population, producing a serious dislocation between the proportional employment of the labor force and proportional output value within the nation's economy. Obviously, this has implications for differentiation in developmental economics and industrialization in the different nations today. This is because, in essence, industrialization is a historical process wherein major industries satisfy the people's material and cultural needs while at the same time changing people's modes of production and life styles. By this criterion, the hard work of New China's first 30 years of industrialization can only be regarded as initial industrialization or state industrialization in the narrow sense. In terms of function, this industrial system was primarily built to thoroughly shake off the bondage suffered in old China and establish the nation's political independence by outwardly strengthening national defense while inwardly strengthening efficient governmental administration. This was not only reasonable; it was essential. This stage of the establishment of the industrial system by no means marked the completion of the task of industrialization. Quite to the contrary, it marked the historic prelude to comprehensive industrialization.

During the course of the initial industrialization described above, given the singular goal, only the state can serve to mobilize resources and manage the economy. Once this stage of economic development is passed, this method of mobilizing resources and economic management will no longer meet the requirements of economic development, because the objective goal of comprehensive industrialization can then only be to satisfy the material and cultural needs of the people as a whole. For this reason, China only really began comprehensive industrialization characterized by satisfying the material and cultural needs of the people following the market guided reform of the economic system in the eighties. Only in this period did a series of patterns of relationships revealed through the industrialization experiences of various countries begin to show their compelling force in China; per-capita income steadily rose following comprehensive implementation of structural change, impelling rapid economic growth.

Section Three   Changes in Demand and the Demand Structure During the Course of Comprehensive Industrialization

From the sixties through the eighties, economists all over the world studied the experiences of many countries undergoing industrialization, bringing to light certain basic relationships governing the course of the industrialization. First, economic growth results from change in the economic structure. The core of the economic structure is the industrial structure. Second, changes in the economic structure are in proportion to per-capita income levels. Growth comes in a set succession of stages, with different products emphasized in each: first consumer goods, then heavy chemical industry, then advanced technology products and value added products. The heavy chemical industry stage begins with stressing raw materials, and later stressing processing. Third, during this process, economic growth tends to accelerate. Finally, once the economy matures and industrialization is realized, the growth rate will show a pronounced return to the slower growth rate displayed before the process began.

As productivity in large-scale industry is higher than in traditional production, the people's income rises in step with increased industrialization. Higher incomes mean more purchasing power, spurring further industrial development. Expanded production in turn further raise incomes and the cycle continues refueling itself. It is precisely this process of self-support and self-promotion that have created the strong impetus of growth in the stage of industrialization.

There is an income transition point before which this cycle will not be entered. After this point, people's incomes can do more than satisfy their basic survival needs; they allow the accumulation necessary for economic development, creating more and more demand for industrial products, promoting industrial growth. Study of the course of the economic growth in many industrialized countries, has determined that this transition point comes at approximately US$ 300 (1970 exchange price). For larger countries (with populations over 20 million), the figure is lower, around US$ 250.

China reached this point between the late seventies and early eighties as was demonstrated by a variety of indicators and calculation of per-capita income using different methods. During the Sixth Five-Year Plan period (1981-1985), the Chinese economy developed to the point where the people's needs for food and clothing were fundamentally satisfied, quickly passing into a new stage characterized by comprehensive industrialization. Large-scale industry was the tool whereby the people's mode of production and way of life were greatly changed. During this period, a radical change took place in the nation's economic structure, both in popular patterns of consumption and the industrial structure, moving economic development on to a growth "fast track."

Economic development since the eighties has proven this conclusion. During the eighties, the public's consumption expenditure underwent a very significant structural change. Expenditure on food expenses as a portion of total consumption expenditure dropped by a substantial margin, dropping from 56.66 percent in 1981 to 48.56 percent in 1992 for urban dwellers, down 0.74 percentage point annually. In the countryside, the proportion dropped from 61.77 percent in 1980 to 52.77 percent in 1992, down 0.75 percentage point annually. Using the same method of calculation, expenditure on food consumption as a portion of GNP fell from 35.26 percent in 1980 to 30.65 percent in 1992. It should be pointed out that as the pricing system and urban housing system have yet to be rationalized, the

33

consumption structure described above, particularly that of urban residents, is not entirely rational. Food expenditure and levels of nourishment are markedly higher than in countries with market economies at the same level of income. As the reform of the system deepens, changes in the above structure will come still more quickly.

As this consumption structure changes and per-capita income increases, consumption as a portion of earnings clearly decreases. The amount of earnings directed to individual savings rises by a substantial margin year after year, maintaining a high rate of investment.

Under the influence of these factors, on the one hand, with changes in the public consumption structure and increases in income, consumer demand quickly turned to manufactured goods best represented by household appliances and other consumer durables, providing the spark for the development of these industries; on the other hand, the high rate of investment has supported investment in fixed assets and rapid growth in investment grade industries, bringing about manifest change in the industrial structure.

Between 1978 and 1992, China's GDP increased by 333 percent. Agriculture based primary industry, increased by only 200 percent, while manufacturing based secondary industry increased by 420 percent and tertiary industry 370 percent. Primary industry as a portion of GDP fell from 28.4 percent in 1978 to 17.3 percent in 1992, a decrease of 11.1 percentage points, while secondary industry skyrocketed from 48.6 percent to 60.8 percent, with manufacturing similarly rising from 44.8 percent to 56.2 percent. Expansion in tertiary industry came more slowly, rising from 23 percent to 25.7 percent. It is clear that the most rapid increase was found in manufacturing added value, 11.4 percentage points.

Changes in the industrial structure produced corresponding changes in the employment structure. Between 1978 and 1992, employment in primary industry dropped from 70.5 percent to 58.5 percent, a decrease of 12 percentage points. Change in the employment structure slightly outpaced change in the industrial structure. Previously, from the founding of the People's Republic in 1949 to 1975, the portion of national revenue created by industry reached as high as 46 percent, but employment in primary industry as a portion of total employment dropped by only 6 percentage points over the 25 years. In other words, change in the employment structure in the 14 years between 1978 and 1992 came at a rate four times as fast as during the previous 25 years. Thus, beginning in the 1980s, comprehensive industrialization rapidly changed the people's way of life as well as their modes of production.

Rapid industrial growth spurred rapid growth in the total economy. China's GDP grew 9 percent annually from 1978 to 1992, half of this coming directly from industrial growth.

In the late 1980s, as a result of economic growth and the rise in income levels, a number of new structural contradictions began to emerge in the nation's economic life and a turning point in growth was reached. More and more household appliances and other consumer durables were coming into urban homes. In the city, a consumption structure characterized by light industrial products was in place allowing a more comfortable life. The move to a consumption structure characterized by private residences, automobiles and other heavy industry consumer goods, in other words, a better living standard, was already beginning. Still, even by the mid-eighties, sluggish outputs of key industries and underdeveloped infrastructure were manifest, a situation eminently unsuited to new consumer demands. At the same time, surplus rural labor created the urgent need to expand industry to create more employment opportunities and raise income levels.

It can be anticipated that this round of structural transformation will be accompanied by the rapid development of key industries and infrastructure and urbanization. At the same time, rural surplus labor will be relocated in great numbers and rural incomes rise significantly. This will create still greater demand and purchasing power than in the eighties, providing the motive force for a new round of rapid growth in the consumer goods industries.

Section Four Analysis of Supply Factors During the Course of Comprehensive Industrialization

Whether an economic growth rate is high or low, can be said to hinge on demand conditions, but it also is governed by supply conditions. Supply conditions refer to availability of capital, labor, and resources. Resources include land, water and minerals, including coal, petroleum and natural gas, as well as environmental resources.

China's future supply conditions may be characterized briefly. Available capital will increase relatively quickly. Labor resources will be extremely abundant, indeed huge numbers of jobs need to be created every year. Acute shortages of other resources, especially farmland, water and environmental resources will continue and worsen for an extended period.

China accumulated approximately 5.5 trillion yuan in fixed assets between 1951 and 1990, (in 1990 prices). Calculated at the same rate, another 6.7 trillion yuan in fixed assets will be accumulated between 1991 and 2000, over one trillion yuan more than in the previous 40 years. Another approximately 15 trillion yuan in fixed assets is expected to be acquired between 2000 and 2010, making a total of nearly 22 trillion yuan for the 20 year period, 1991-2010, nearly four times the total for the preceding 40 years. This will accomplish more than simply increasing fixed assets, equipment and so on; it will fundamentally alter the nation's infrastructural backwardness.

Basically, the scale of fixed asset accumulation depends on the national income accumulation rate. Beginning in 1949, New China effected a thoroughgoing transformation of the old wealth distribution pattern, raising the accumulation rate to over 20 percent. This rate rose to 33 percent during the Fifth Five-Year Plan period (1976-1980), far higher than in other countries at comparable income levels. This historic foundation will allow China to sustain a high level of accumulation. Moreover, during the course of consumption structure transformation stages will be gone through and time lags underwent, are also important factors raising the accumulation rate. Individual income levels rise gradually and individual consumption levels are realized through a certain consumption structure, in some stages jumping ahead. This creates a time gap between rises in income levels and rises in consumption levels. This is particularly evident when income levels rise quickly, but changes in consumption practices come relatively slowly, creating a still greater time gap between the two levels. These all may lead to high levels of individual savings. In addition, the Chinese people have long been frugal, another contributor to the continuation of a high rate of accumulation. These factors have kept the average accumulation rate in China in the 1980s around 33 percent, a state of affair unlikely to change greatly in the future. This will become a powerful motive force behind rapid economic growth.

According to the Harold-Dorma growth model,

$$G = \frac{S}{V}$$

In this formula, G represents the economic growth rate, here the national income growth rate. S represents the accumulation rate and V the capital-output ratio. As can be seen, the economic growth rate varies with changes in accumulation and capital-output rates.

China's capital-output ratio dropped notably in the 1980s, from 4.4 to 3.7 during the Fifth Five-Year Plan period. Here may be found the exact cause for this decade's rapid economic growth. It increased the annual economic growth rate in the 80's by 1.5 percentage points. This sort of change, it can be said, marked the real beginning of comprehensive industrialization.

According to the law defined by the Harold-Dorma growth model, a balanced growth line can be achieved only when the growth rate satisfies the condition that investment equals savings. Otherwise, there will be unemployment, idle production capacity and widespread economic depression. Using the above calculations, China will require a huge average annual investment of one trillion yuan. If the economy fails to sustain a fairly high growth rate and corresponding scale of investment, this portion of product value cannot be realized and it will be impossible for reproduction to follow its normal cycle. Therefore, maintaining a fairly high national economic growth rate is not only necessary in order to satisfy the people's ever-increasing material and cultural needs, but also to maintain economic stability.

Assuming an accumulation rate of approximately 33 percent and a 3.7 capital-output ratio, China should maintain an economic growth rate of approximately 9 percent during the 1990s. During the subsequent decade, 2000-2010, a growth rate above 7 or 8 percent will be necessary, even if the capital-output ratio increases, because of restraints imposed by limited resources, particularly environmental resources.

Future increases in the labor supply will likewise call for a high rate of economic growth. According to the 1990 census, 756 million Chinese were between 15 and 64 in age, 66.9 percent of the total population. This number is expected to rise to 858 million by 2000, 66 percent of the total population, and to 956 million by 2010, 68.3 percent of the total population. Subsequently, the total number of people in this age group may continue to increase, but that number as a portion of total population will begin to decrease. During this same period, elderly as a portion of total population will increase rapidly, from an estimated 7.7 percent in 2010 to 16.5 percent in 2040. Given these expectations, China must make full use of current human resources to accumulate for the future, to make the necessary material preparations for the "silver wave" coming after 2010. If not, the next generation will face enormous difficulties. China's current age structure is at an optimum level for production and accumulation. This valuable opportunity should not be missed. Proper use must be made of it. China will add an average of 14.5 million people to its labor force every year from 1990 to 2010. In addition, 120 million surplus rural laborers need jobs. If they are all to be transferred to non-agricultural industries, an average of 6 million new jobs will need to be created each year. These two items alone will necessitate 20 million job openings annually. This provides tremendous pressure, but also a powerful impetus for economic growth.

The most egregious factors restricting economic growth are resource related. Whether calculated on a land area or per-capita basis, most resources are below world average levels. The worst shortfalls come in farmland, water and environmental resources.

Only 7 percent of the world's arable land is to be found in China, where it must support 20 percent of the world's population. Constant economic growth will cause this fact to exert an ever-increasing influence on all aspects of the national economy. (1) Importation of farm products, principally food grains, is an irreversible trend. (2) Given China's natural resource endowment, its employment structure will deviate from the "standard model," with more people necessarily employed in primary industry than in other countries, increasing agriculture's share in the national economy. (3) Secondary and tertiary industries, especially secondary industry, must have a higher productivity level than in other countries at similar income levels so as to compensate for the greater presence of primary industry. Otherwise it will be difficult to raise the overall income level. All these influences when concentrated will hamper industrialization in its role as a driver behind economic growth and cause agriculture and the output of agricultural workers to claim a relatively high proportion of GDP for years to come.

China has an even greater shortage of water resources than farmland. The nation's water resources account for only 5.8 percent of the world total, per-capita level less than a quarter the world average. Even worse, these water resources are unevenly distributed. This is an irreplaceable resource. China must use engineering projects to store water and control flooding. Water from southern China must be diverted to northern China. In the Northeast, water must be diverted from the north to the south. In this way, water can be supplied throughout the nation throughout the year. At the same time, technological improvements must be used to raise water utilization rates. Both types of measures will require massive investment, clearly increasing the cost of economic growth.

Important environmental issues also threaten future economic growth. Whether proceeding from the nature of a socialist country or from international environmental protection, China must decide to pursue both development and environmental protection. The cost of environmental management is very high. The costs for a given project will on average increase by about one fifth if measures for environmental management are added, leading to a corresponding rise in the capital-output ratio. Beyond doubt, this will slow the rate of economic development.

The question remains how best to deal with these problems. In particular, the question of how to use innovations in the system and in technology to lessen the restrictions on long term economic growth imposed by resource problems will remain, from beginning to end, extremely important.

Chapter Three   The Basic Pattern of Industrial Structure Transformation

This chapter will build on the information presented in the preceding chapter analyzing basic pattern of industrial structure transformation, noting key characteristics.

Section One   Analysis of the Present Industrial Structure

Change in the industrial structure mainly comes about through the evolution of the two factors: per-capita income levels and the supply of key elements (capital, labor and natural resources). Increased income leads to changes in the demand structure while changes in the supply of key elements lead to changes in trade and corresponding technologies. As income levels rise, the industrial structure changes in accordance with a regular pattern. Industry's contribution to GNP increases, as agriculture's decreases, and that of services changes slowly. Agriculture's position in labor structure is reduced and that of industry changes slowly, with most of the labor force displaced from agriculture being reabsorbed by tertiary industries. Table 3-1 is based on statistics from more than 100 countries.

Table 3-1 Per-Capita GNP and Change of Industrial Structure

Per-capita GNP (US dollars)	100	200	300	400	600	1,000	2,000	3,000
Primary industry's portion in GNP, %	46.4	36.0	30.4	26.7	21.8	18.6	16.3	9.8
Secondary industry's portion in GNP, %	13.5	19.6	23.1	25.5	29.0	31.4	33.2	38.9
Tertiary industry's portion in GNP, %	40.1	44.4	46.5	47.8	49.2	50.0	50.5	51.3
Workforce in primary industry, %	68.1	58.7	49.9	43.6	34.8	28.6	23.7	8.3
Workforce in secondary industry, %	9.6	16.6	20.5	23.4	27.6	30.7	33.2	40.1
Workforce in tertiary industry, %	22.3	24.7	29.6	23.0	37.6	40.7	43.1	51.6

Source: "Industrial Structure and Macro Control" and "Studies of Quantitative Economy and Technical Economy" by Li Changming, 12th issue, 1994.

Since the initiation of the reform and opening policy, the Chinese economy has entered into a stage of comprehensive industrialization and significant changes have taken place in the industrial structure. From 1978 to 1992, secondary industry, primarily industrial manufacturing, maintained an average annual growth rate of 10.7 percent, double the rate for primary industry. In comparable prices, secondary industry's contribution to GDP rose from 48.6 percent in 1978 to 59.2 percent in 1992, with industrial manufacturing rising from 44.8 percent to 55.4 percent over the same period, a striking increase in the rate of industrialization, (see Table 3-2).

Table 3-2   The Composition of GDP by Industry (in comparable prices)

Year	GDP (billion yuan)	Primary industry (billion yuan, %)		Secondary industry (billion yuan, %)		Tertiary industry (billion yuan, %)		Per-capita GNP (yuan)
1978	358.81	101.84	28.4	174.52	48.6	82.45	23.0	375
1992	1,194.84	193.92	16.2	707.05	59.2	293.87	24.6	1,025.6

Note: *The Chinese Statistical Yearbook* (1993).

This characteristic structural change is the main source of China's rapid economic growth. Of the added value, 836.03 billion yuan created between 1978 and 1992 63.7 percent was generated by secondary industry, and 92 percent of that came from industrial manufacturing.

As secondary industry's contribution to GDP rose quickly, primary industry's dropped 12 percentage points over the 14 years.

Even more illustrative of this structural change is the fact that the portion of all workforce working in primary industry dropped from 70.5 percent in 1978 to 58.5 percent in 1992 (see Table 3-3), down 12 percentage points over 14 years. Workforce in tertiary industry increased by nearly 8 percentage points from 1978 to 1992, from 12.1 to 19.8 percent.

Table 3-3   The Distribution of the Workforce Within the Industrial Structure

Year	Total workforce (million)	Workforce in primary industry (million, %)		Workforce in secondary industry (million, %)		Workforce in tertiary industry (million, %)	
1978	401.52	283.13	70.5	69.7	17.4	48.69	12.1
1992	594.32	347.69	58.5	129.21	21.7	117.42	19.8

Note: *The Chinese Statistical Yearbook* (1993).

Research has proven that the structural changes expressed above match the regular pattern generally experienced by all industrializing countries. However, if China's industrial structure is observed in stasis, a snapshot at a certain time and space, distinguishing characteristics may be discerned.

1. Calculated in terms of the same year's prices, secondary industry produced only 48.2 percent of GDP in 1992, (see Table 3-4). This figure is higher than that found in countries with similar income levels and in developed countries. However, it was 11 percentage points lower than it would be if calculated in terms of comparable prices. Correspondingly, primary industry's share of GDP was 7.7 percentage points higher when calculated in current prices rather than comparable prices.

Table 3-4   GDP Output Value by Industrial Sector (in current prices)

Year	GDP (billion yuan)	Primary Industry (billion yuan, %)		Secondary Industry (billion yuan, %)		Tertiary Industry (billion yuan, %)		Per-capita GNP (yuan)
1978	358.81	101.84	28.4	174.52	48.6	82.45	23.0	375
1992	2,402.02	574.4	23.9	1,157.52	48.2	670.1	27.9	2,063

Note: *The Chinese Statistical Yearbook* (1993).

2. Examination of the employment structure shows that while the proportion of the workforce in primary industry dropped significantly from 1978, the figure still remained as high as 58.5 percent, nearly double that of countries at similar income levels.

A thoroughgoing analysis of the above data is of great importance to the understanding of the coming changes in the industrial structure.

1. Per-capita farmland in China is far below the world average. China is a huge country with a population of 1.2 billion. The basic supply of agricultural products must be produced domestically.

Accordingly, China must devote more labor power to agriculture in order to overcome this shortage of farmland. On the other hand, China is only a newly developing country. Industrialization cannot proceed gradually; it must advance in leaps and bounds learning through the experiences of other nations. This has produced a significant gap in productivity and earnings levels between the modern and traditional economies. This, in turn, has made a portion of the rural workforce redundant, created a major oversupply of agricultural workforce, a second factor explaining the greater proportion of workforce in primary than secondary industry. Surplus labor will gradually be redistributed during the course of industrialization. However, the employment structure will continue to be determined by the availability of resources, and employment in primary industry will continue to exceed that in other countries at similar income levels.

2. The above resource factors will also influence the proportionate shares of output value in current prices through the workforce employment structure, resulting in the added value in GDP created by primary industry being correspondingly higher than in other countries with similar income levels. This added value consists of three parts: wages, profit and depreciation, with wages supplying the greatest part. In a market economy, the equal quantities of production demand equal pay. Therefore, the wage rate for agricultural labor measured in terms of other equivalent labor will keep up with wage rates in secondary and tertiary industries. Thus, when the portion of the workforce employed in primary industry is higher, the proportion of added value created by primary industry will be correspondingly higher. The increase in added value is chiefly the result of redistribution, the transfer of a portion of the income of other industries, primarily secondary industry, to primary industry. This is achieved for the most part through price levers.

For a long time, the relative prices of industrial products and agricultural products in China have been irrational, with agricultural products' prices lower than their actual value. This phenomenon substantially results in peasants' incomes being lower than those of workers. This has given rise to China's unusual industrial structure. On one hand, industry accounts for more than 46 percent of the national income; on the other, 80 percent of the population is engaged in agricultural production. In a narrow sense, this is precisely the essence of China's state industrialization. A relatively independent and complete industrial system has been built on backs of the low income peasant majority with the support of the scissors differential between the prices of industrial and agricultural products.

Since the initiation of the reform and opening policy, China has used a variety of methods to raise rural incomes, allowing contracting of farmland, establishing rural enterprises and raising the purchase prices for agricultural and sideline products. During the Sixth Five-Year Plan period, increased agricultural production contributed 41.03 percent of the newly created rural income, non-agricultural production 37.83 percent and adjusted prices for agricultural and sideline products 21.14 percent. During the Seventh Five-Year Plan period (1986-1990), non-agricultural production supplied 38.54 percent of the growth in rural income, adjusted prices 34.49 percent and agricultural production 26.79 percent. Increases in agricultural production were responsible for much less of the rise in rural income than during the Sixth Five-Year Plan period, with adjusted prices playing a far greater role. Overall, between 1978 and 1992 prices for agricultural products went up more quickly than did those of secondary or tertiary industry. Accordingly, primary industry as a portion of GDP is higher when calculated in terms of current prices than in comparable prices.

However, higher prices for agricultural products is not the only means of raising rural income. In order to raise peasant's income and avoid the excessive price rises, it is necessary, first of all, to effectively raise the productivity of agricultural labor. First, a large portion of surplus rural workforce must be transferred to non-agricultural production to increase its utilization rate. Second, high-quality, highly efficient agriculture must be developed to best take advantage of the strengths of a large rural workforce: labor-intensive and land-intensive agriculture must be developed. Third, in order to avoid a return to former pricing inequities and lessen overall price rises, prices for goods produced by secondary industry should be kept stable. This will require a still faster pace of industrialization and improved efficiency, necessary for a still faster growth rate and in order to create the material conditions for earnings transfers to primary from secondary industry. At present, on the basis of the current exchange rate, the prices for major farm products in China approximate international market prices. However, the quantity of agricultural products necessary to exchange for industrial products of equivalent value is still far higher than in developed countries. Prices of agricultural products and industrial products remain inequitable. Addressing this irrationality in pricing will remain an important long-term task in the course of industrialization.

As demonstrated above, China's industrial structure can be viewed through two different lenses. Viewed dynamically, with calculations in constant prices, primary industry's share of GDP grows smaller, while that of secondary industry increases sharply. However, viewed at specific points in time, with calculations in current prices, primary industry's share of GDP seems relatively stable and that of secondary industry will even decrease.

Regards the employment structure, employment in primary industry as a percentage of total employment will drop substantially as a result of the economic development, but the comparable gap between China and other countries will become bigger and bigger. This process will continue at least until the middle of the next century and will be reversed when total population clearly decreases.

Section Two   Change Tendencies in the Industrial Structure

Change in the demand structure is the intermediate link between increased income levels and change in the industrial structure. The regular pattern of change in the demand structure resulting from rising income levels is the exact cause of changes in the industrial structure. Changes in the demand structure resulting from increased incomes are manifested in three ways:

1. Changes in the ultimate demand structure. First, food's share of total consumption demand decreases; to wit, the Engel coefficient falls, and the demand for manufactured goods rises. The gist of the Engel coefficient is that when income levels reach a given point in time, the income elasticity of demand for food is less than one. During the latter part of the Sixth Five-Year Plan period, a historical turn came in the Chinese people's income elasticity of demand for food, as the elastic price dropped significantly, beginning to fall below one, while demand for manufactured goods rose quickly and the corresponding income elasticity was much greater than one. Second, changes are manifested in the apportionment of consumption and investment. The portion of earnings devoted to investment rises steadily as income increases. The accumulation and investment rates in China have always been higher than in other countries with similar income levels. Fixed asset investment has maintained its strong momentum. Coming into the 1990s, investment as a driver behind growth has become a still more prominent characteristic of economic growth.

2. Demand for intermediate products, (used in the manufacture of other goods), as a portion of total product demand rose significantly. This demonstrates that the ratio between total output and added value is a comprehensive indicator of increases in demand for intermediate inputs as a portion of total demand. If the total value of output is taken for gross output and GDP for added value, this ratio increased from 1.9 to 2.4 during the 1980s. Agricultural production may be taken as an example. Consumption of chemical fertilizers in 1992 was 3.3 times that in 1978; rural power consumption was 4.4 times that over the same period. However, in comparable prices, added value rose only 100 percent. The acute shortages of energy, raw materials and transport facilities since the 1980s all point to the fierce demand for intermediate inputs.

3. Comparative advantages changed. This was primarily manifested in changes in the export structure, with the share of primary products decreasing and manufactured goods increasing. Manufactured goods accounted for 49.7 percent of export volume in 1980, but 79.9 percent in 1992, a gain of 30 percentage points in 12 years; the share of primary products dropped from 50.3 percent to 20.1 percent over the same period.

Clearly, all the above factors will greatly spur the demand for manufactured goods, further accelerating industrial growth, increasing industry's proportion in the national economy.

Model forecasts indicate that growth in secondary industry, primarily manufacturing, will still take the lead in China in the coming years. Moreover, the urbanization accompanying industrialization will lead to rapid growth in tertiary industry. In this way, secondary and tertiary industries' shares in the GDP will increase by substantial margins, as that of primary industry drops. Table 3-5 outlines this forecast in comparable prices.

Table 3-6 shows the proportion of primary, secondary and tertiary industries in GDP in 2000 and 2010 in prices for those years. These projections were made in consideration of China's historical starting point for industrialization, natural resources and development experiences during the 1980s. Table 3-7 shows the employment for the same years.

The figures shown in Table 3-6 and Table 3-7 are only estimates. They are provided to serve as a framework for addressing the following issues. (1) Millions of surplus rural manpower will be transferred to secondary and tertiary industries over the next decade. How can development in secondary and tertiary industries be promoted so as to create the capacity to absorb this surplus labor? (2) History and availability of resources make changes in the price structure and general price rises inevitable. This raises the question of how to successfully change the price structure and keep price rises within tolerable limits, another issue that needs to be addressed timely and directly.

Table 3-5   Projected Changes in the Chinese Industrial Structure (1990-2010)

		1990	2000	2010
Primary Industry	Growth rate (%)	(1981-1990) 6.2	(1991-2000) 4.0	(2001-2010) 4.0
	Absolute volume (billion yuan)	501.7	742.6	1,099.2
	Proportion (%)	28.4	17.7	12.7
Secondary Industry	Growth rate (%)	(1981-1990) 9.5	(1991-2000) 11.0	(2001-2010) 7.3
	Absolute volume (billion yuan)	771.7	2,191.2	4,425.6
	Proportion (%)	43.6	52.6	51.3
Tertiary Industry	Growth rate (%)	(1981-1990) 10.9	(1991-2000) 9.7	(2001-2010) 9.5
	Absolute volume (billion yuan)	497.4	1,251.9	3,102.1
	Proportion (%)	28.0	30.0	36

Note: Calculated in 1990 comparable prices.

Table 3-6   GDP and Industrial Structure (in current prices)

Year	GDP (billion yuan)	Primary Industry (billion yuan) (%)		Secondary Industry (billion yuan) (%)		Tertiary Industry (billion yuan) (%)	
1990	1,768.13	501.7	28.4	771.74	43.7	494.69	28
2000	7,060.32	1,835.68	26	2,894.73	41	2,329.91	33
2010	22,673.65	5,441.68	24	7,935.78	35	9,296.2	41

Note: *The Chinese Statistical Yearbook* (1993).

The underestimation factor in the tertiary industry has not been included in the calculations; tertiary industry may account for as much as 45 percent of GDP in 2010.

Table 3-7   Employment Structure

Year	Total workforce (million)	Workforce in Primary Industry (million) (%)		Workforce in Secondary Industry (million) (%)		Workforce in Tertiary Industry (million) (%)	
1990	567.4	340.49	60	121.58	21.4	105.33	18.6
2000	640	320	50	153.6	24	166.4	26
2010	717.51	287	40	179.38	25	251.13	35

Note: *The Chinese Statistical Yearbook* (1993).

Table 3-6 shows projected GDPs for 2000 and 2010 calculated in prices for the respective years, assuming a 1 : 0.65 ratio between the economic growth rate and price growth rate. This assumes an average annual reduction index of 105.36 percent between 1991 and 2010, approximately the same as between 1978 and 1992.

Table 3-8   Annual Price Increase Rate (1990-2010)

GDP	Primary Industry	Secondary Industry	Tertiary Industry
5.36	8.66	3.96	9.16

Table 3-8 shows that price increases in primary and tertiary industries are the principal factors in overall price increases. Given that prices in the transportation industry and other industries are currently low, average wage levels and prices for farm products are rising and tertiary industry's relatively low capacity to digest price rises in other industries, price rises will be difficult to avoid. In order to forestall excessive increases in general price levels, any price rise for the products of secondary industry, particularly manufactured goods, must be much lower than price rises for products of primary

51

and tertiary industries. This necessitates increases in productivity in secondary industry to outstrip those in primary and tertiary industries (see Table 3-9).

Table 3-9   Annual Per-Capita Output Growth Rate (1990-2010)
(incomparable prices)

Unit: %

GDP	Primary Industry	Secondary Industry	Tertiary Industry
6.99	4.89	7.02	4.93

As a result of these price changes, primary, secondary and tertiary industries' shares of GDP will be completely different if they are calculated in current prices as opposed to constant prices. Primary industry's share will remain basically stable, but secondary industry's share will drop. The substance of this structural change is the change in the personal income structure, mainly as the result of the role of price levers. Behind the price levers is the effect of industrialization. If secondary industry can not create enormous material wealth, the above results will be impossible to achieve.

Can this structural change be achieved while keeping general price levels essentially stable? Generally speaking, this will be difficult. Prices have a strong and inflexible tendency to rise. Price adjustments can only be effected by raising prices of relatively low priced products. This will push general price levels up.

Table 3-7 shows projected employment structure for 2000 and 2010. Estimates of total workforce are based on projected population increase and population between the ages of 15 and 64. Workforce in primary industry assumes the continuation of the average annual decrease of one percentage point seen from 1982 to 1992. It should be noted the figures used are optimistic, requiring finding new jobs for seven million agricultural workforce per year, obviously a formidable task. However, even so, the percentage of the total workforce employed in primary industry in 2010 will still be far higher than in other countries with similar income levels.

If the figures projected in Table 3-6 and Table 3-7 can be achieved, the income differential between workers and peasants can be narrowed from 2.37 : 1 at present to 1.35 : 1 in 2010, basically achieving income equality between the two. It can be said that this is the material foundation for the establishment of a socialist market economy and also the material prerequisite for further economic growth without inflation. Conversely, if these goals cannot be achieved, two scenarios are presented. Either the portion of the total workforce working in primary industry will remain high, despite the narrowed income gap between workers and peasants, greatly encumbering national economic development, manufacturing in particular, or the irrational income disparity between workers and peasants will continue, discouraging agricultural development and reducing the market for manufactured goods, hindering development of secondary and tertiary industries.

Section Three   The Relationship Between Industry and Industrial Development in China's Expanding Economy

As China's economy grows, radical changes in the industrial structure have an important influence on the relative positions of different economic sectors and their interrelationships. Below, brief analyses of agriculture, manufacturing, infrastructure and the financial industry are provided and the relationship between urbanization and the development of tertiary industry explained.

I. Agriculture

The position of agriculture varies during different stages of industrialization. Generally speaking, increased industrialization brings lesser dependence on agriculture for economic development. When industrialization was being prepared for and during the initial industrialization period, industrialization was dependent on agriculture. Agriculture provided food and raw materials for industry and generated the accumulation necessary for industrial development. As industrialization has progressed, this dependence has gradually weakened, with the situation regards accumulation actually being reversed. Agricultural development has become dependent on industrial development for increased intermediate inputs, financial support and cheaper manufactured goods. Moreover, the manufacturing sector will be needed to absorb surplus rural labor.

However, this does not mean that agriculture can be neglected. China is a large country with a population of more than one billion. There is a huge demand for farm products, and China needs to rely almost entirely on itself for their supply, although this does not forbid importation of farm products. China's particular circumstances, enormous rural population and an inadequate supply of farmland, call for special attention to be given to agriculture.

For a fairly long time to come, China's agricultural problem will actually consist of three issues: the development of the agricultural production, rural incomes and the so-called rural industrialization.

1. The question remains how to maintain and increase agricultural production. In this sense, agriculture, like energy, communications and transportation, raw materials and other industries, is a basic industry and as such important. Efforts should be made to promote its development.

The contradiction implied by undersupply of agricultural products will continue to worsen. Given limited agricultural resources and huge population, this problem cannot be solved merely by raising agricultural output. While the agricultural structure is being optimized, some farm products will need to be imported.

Maintaining an average annual growth rate of 4 percent in agricultural output value will be a major achievement. This will be accomplished primarily by adjusting the internal structure of agriculture and developing high-quality, high-efficiency agriculture. China's potential for the development of basic farm crops such as grain are limited. Per-hectare yields are already among the highest in the world. An annual growth rate of 2 percent would be no small accomplishment. A relentless drive to raise agricultural output so as to achieve complete self-sufficiency while ignoring limitations on agricultural resources would not make economic sense and would probably be doomed to failure. Losses will outweigh gains if the nation's overall growth rate is retarded. With this in mind, China will increase agricultural input while giving full play to policy measures and technology. On the one hand, the state, collectives and peasant households will increase their input of capital, materials and labor power in farmlands and water conservancy works and other public facilities, and on the other, building on the basis of the further revamped social organization in the countryside, gradually realize scale operations in agriculture. At the same time, China will steadily expand agricultural imports according to plan.

2. The problem of rural incomes involves both labor productivity and prices for farm products. There are different ways to solve this problem. (1) Transfer surplus rural labor to non-agricultural industries so as to increase the utilization ratio in farm work. This is the prerequisite for raising the productivity of agricultural labor. (2) High-quality, highly-efficient agriculture can be developed. High added value agriculture will raise the per-capita output rate of agriculture. (3) Prices of farm products can timely and appropriately be adjusted or subsidies given to peasants. A rational distribution mechanism would check excessive increases in urban incomes.

3. Rural industrialization entails transferring peasants to non-agricultural industries. Its core is urbanization. Understood in this sense, the formulation of rural industrialization is not truly accurate. The village remains as the unit of social organization in the agricultural economy. The transfer of peasants to non-agricultural industries should proceed in step with urbanization. Progress in

urbanization in China lags far behind the industrialization. Rural enterprises have mushroomed all over the country. This problem has aroused the government's attention and appropriate measures have been proposed.

The three problems are both distinct and inter-linked. Raising peasant incomes is a powerful lever for developing agricultural production. Finding peasants jobs in non-agricultural industries is the first step in raising rural incomes. The common goal pursued in all three problems is rural modernization.

II. Industry

Industry will continue to lead development in China for the next decade and beyond. It will provide increased material input for agricultural development, exactly what is needed for future growth in the agricultural sector. At the same time, industrial development create jobs for surplus rural labor. This is an effective means of raising rural incomes. With the development of industry, a larger portion of the national income will be transferred to the countryside through price levers and rural incomes raised. Such an increase in income is an important pre-condition for future agricultural development. Industry will supply the capital goods necessary in tertiary industry infrastructure and also create demand to fuel the development of tertiary industry. Fundamentally speaking, only when secondary industry provides more material goods is there the material foundation for the expansion of tertiary industry.

Industry is a major producer of goods. Accordingly, it must properly coordinate its relationship with other economic sectors and within its own sector.

The industrialization experiences of other countries have shown that in the course of its development, industrialization is marked by different stages: first the development of a consumer goods industry, then the development of the heavy chemical industry. This latter stage is also demarcated into stages, principally raw materials industry and processing and assembly industry. Given China's current situation, heavy chemical industry, principally processing and assembly, is expected to gain in prominence during the Ninth Five-Year Plan period (1996-2000). At the same time, light industry and the raw materials industry will continue their strong momentum.

Light industry developed more quickly than heavy industry in the 1980s. Light industry expanded by 790 percent between 1978 and 1992 and heavy industry 530 percent. The average annual growth rate of the light industry was 14 percent and that of the heavy industry was 10.6 percent. Since 1992, growth in heavy industry has outpaced that in light industry. Today, China's steel production capacity exceeds 100 million tons a year and its power generating capacity one trillion kilowatt hours. This demonstrates that industries with intermediate inputs typified by raw materials have the capacity for rapid development. The subsequent stage of development should concentrate on improving quality and results rather than quantitative expansion of scale. This will inevitably call for considerable development of production capacity for large and complete installations. Development of transportation facilities and telecommunications is being accelerated. Residential telephones are quickly becoming commonplace. Demand for automobiles will reach two million by 2000.

Developmental trends indicate that China is currently focusing on speeding development in processing and assembly, as typified by the machine-building industry.

However, industrial development comes in overlapping stages in China and light industry and the raw materials industry will continue to hold important places in future industrial development. Heavy industry needs to be greatly developed, but, at the same time, importance must be attached to the development of light industry. The processing industry must be greatly developed and development in the raw materials industry stressed. Prominence should be given to improving quality and economic returns in light industry and the raw materials industry.

III. Tertiary Industry

The main problems restricting development in tertiary industry are inadequate infrastructure, the underdeveloped financial sector and insufficient urbanization.

1. Infrastructure. In a broad sense, infrastructure not only includes roads, railways, harbors, waterways and telecommunications that provide the "hardware" necessary for production and daily life, but also includes necessary "software" such as education, culture and law. Here we are discussing "hardware."

Infrastructure construction generally requires enormous capital input. The capital stock in infrastructure exceeds the combined capital used in basic and manufacturing industries, accounting for nearly one half of all capital stock. Infrastructure returns are mostly to be found in the external economy created. This characteristic often makes enterprises and individuals unwilling to invest in it. During rapid economic growth, this often leads to underdevelopment of infrastructure, thus reducing the efficiency of direct production capital, reducing the efficiency of the national economy and a lack of material foundation for the development of the tertiary industry.

In order to correct this situation, China will work to increase the portion of national income going to state revenues and expand the scale of such revenues, at the same time gradually adjusting prices for use of infrastructure facilities that market services. At present, state revenues in China claim only around 14 percent of GDP, not only less than in developed countries, but less than in other developing countries. This is an important cause behind the backward state of China's infrastructure.

2. The financial sector. An important factor behind the present sluggish circulation of capital, irrational fund allocations and inefficient use of capital is the underdeveloped financial industry. In addition to problems inherent in the current system, personnel shortages, poor quality, insufficient networking and outdated

equipment also plague the industry. In recognition of these problems, China is strengthening efforts at improvement.

3. Urbanization and the development of the tertiary industry. The share of total employment working in tertiary industry is markedly low. A basic factor contributing to tertiary industry's underdevelopment is delayed urbanization. On one hand this describes a lack in quantity and scale of cities, on the other, a lack of quality in existing cities. If tertiary industry is to be developed more quickly, urbanization must be combined with industrialization.

Chapter Four Development of the Rural Economy

Section One Changes in the Economic Structure and the Fundamental Status of Agriculture

A precipitous transformation is taking place in the Chinese economic structure. The most outstanding feature of this change is the rising of overall economic productivity based on the increased productivity ratios of agricultural labor and resources leading to a marked drop in the agricultural sector's share of the total capital and employment structures. This decrease is the beginning of the fundamental change taking place in the economic structure.

Table 4-1 shows the increases in agricultural resources productivity and the agricultural labor productivity.

Table 4-1 Agricultural Resources Productivity and Agricultural Labor Productivity

	Unit	1978	1980	1983	1984	1990	1995
Wheat	ton/hectare	1.84	1.89	2.80	2.97	3.19	3.54
Maize		2.80	3.08	3.60	3.96	4.52	4.92
Rice		3.98	4.13	5.09	5.37	5.72	6.03
Cotton		0.44	0.55	0.76	0.91	0.81	0.89
Agricultural labor productivity	yuan/annum per-capita	490.9	644.8	869.0	1,014.4	2,298.8	6,290.6

Note: Calculated in current prices on the basis of *The Chinese Statistical Yearbook* (1996).

As can be seen, outputs rose substantially between 1978 and 1984. Average annual per-capita rural income also rose from 133.57 yuan to 355.33 yuan, providing the foundation for rural industrialization since 1985.

The sudden rise of non-agricultural industry in the countryside as exemplified by the township enterprises beginning in 1985 raised the curtain for the structural transformation of rural industry. The rapid development of non-agricultural industry has overturned agriculture's overwhelming dominance of the rural economic structure (see Table 4-2), abruptly shifting the focus of rural development from agriculture to non-agricultural industry.

Table 4-2   Output Values of Different Rural Economic Sectors (1978-1995)

Unit: %

	1978	1985	1991	1992	1993	1995
Agriculture	68.6	57.2	42.9	35.8	26.9	23.9
Industry	19.4	27.6	43.5	50.1	56.4	57.4
Construction, transportation and commerce	12.0	15.2	13.6	14.1	16.7	18.6

Source: Based on *The Chinese Statistical Yearbook* (1978-1995) of the Chinese statistics in the previous years. Total rural output value equals 100, calculated in prices for the given year.

In the 17 years between 1978 and 1995, non-agricultural industries' share of total rural output value rose by 44.7 percentage points, an average of 2.63 percentage points a year. This near reversal of shares of total output value between agriculture and non-agricultural industry demonstrates the rural economy's switch from agriculture promoted growth to growth promoted by non-agricultural industry. In 1993 agricultural growth was responsible for 7.8 percent of the actual national economic growth rate. A far greater contribution came from rural industry, construction, transportation and commerce. Agricultural growth's contribution to the actual national economic growth rate is likely to continue to fall. That contribution was 0.47 percentage point less in 1993 than in 1992, a 3.2 percent drop in proportion. This change in the pattern of economic growth does not mean that agriculture is no longer fundamental to the national economy. Agriculture's role as the foundation of the national economy cannot be shaken. It should be strengthened for a fairly extended time to come for the following reasons.

1. China's demand for farm products will steadily increase for the next 10 to 20 years for two main reasons. First, a growing population will increase demand. According to census data, China will face a third birth peak period during these years when the population will increase by an average net of 17 million a year. By 2010, the Chinese population will have grown from 1.2 billion to 1.4 billion. An ever-growing, already enormous population will pressure the supply of farm products, creating demand. Second, demand will come from manufacturers and other producers. China is a late comer to industrialization. Comparative advantages found in economic development at the present stage have determined industry's, especially much of light industry's dependence on deep processing of farm products. Moreover, this period will also see the level of per-capita consumption moving from concerns for sufficient food and clothing to a more comfortable lifestyle and even to minor affluence. The people's diet once based on grains revolve more around animal protein and high fat products, and the demand for meats, poultry and eggs will grow rapidly. Rapid increases in the production of feed grains will be key to sufficient supplies of meat, poultry and eggs. China's grain supply is projected to reach at least 560 million tons by 2010. To achieve this goal, grain production must grow by an average of 1.5 percent per annum for the next 15 years, nearly one percentage point above the annual average growth rate between 1990 and 1993.

2. Agriculture is an important producer in the national economy and will remain an important source of employment and income for

the peasants for a fairly long period of time. At present, 330 million people are employed by agriculture, 75 percent of the total rural workforce and 56.4 percent of the total workforce. Agriculture is currently the largest employment sector in China and will inevitably remain so through the beginning of the next century.

Agriculture will play an active role in employing the rural workforce for a very extended time and, moreover advances and retreats in agricultural production will directly affect the income of most of China's rural population. In 1995, 49.13 percent of rural household per-capita net income came from agriculture. Rural incomes directly affect the ability to exploit the 900 million strong rural market, thus affecting the development of the national economy throughout.

3. The supply of agricultural production resources that cannot be regenerated is decreasing day by day. China's farmland has decreased by about 10 million hectares over the past 10 years and longer, an average of 870,000 hectares a year. If these figures are continued, farmland can be expected to decrease by another approximately 15 million hectares by 2010. The supply of the agricultural production related resources will be under supply for years to come. Ever growing demand for farm products and relative shortages of agricultural production resources combine to create the obstacles to easing contradictions between supply of and demand for farm products. The tight supply of farm products predicted over the coming period gives evidence that while agriculture is no longer the engine driving the nation's economic growth, its fundamental role in the national economy is beyond dispute. More than other countries, given its enormous population cannot depend mainly on the international market to solve its food supply problems. Moreover, China has not yet achieved the level of industrialization that would allow it to disregard the support of agriculture. Agriculture's position as the foundation must not be weakened, rather strengthened. Otherwise, economic development will be thrown into chaos. The inflation rate in China in 1994 was 21 percent, and 60 percent of that inflation was a result of problems in the agricultural sector. This alone gives proof to the above conclusion.

Section Two   Structural Change and Agricultural Development

I. The Problem of Agriculture's Decreasing Comparative Advantage

Agriculture's rapidly decreased and non-agricultural industries' rapidly increased share of total rural output value makes clear that the comparative advantage of the former is less than that of the latter. Three points may be gleaned from this. First, the comparative advantage of grain crops is low compared to that of cash crops. Second, it is low compared to that of forestry, animal husbandry and fishery. Third, it is low compared with that of non-agricultural industry.

Cash crops generally require more labor input than grain crops. With cash crops, there is a strong positive correlation between land productivity rate and the amount of labor provided. Accordingly, the marginal return for labor input does not fall as quickly with cash crops as it does with grain. The comparative advantage is higher than with grain crops. In the course of actual production, the net output value for each day worked raising cash crops is higher than that for the grain crops (see Table 4-3).

Table 4-3   Net Output Value Per Workday for Different Crops (1991)

Unit: yuan

	Cotton	Bluish dogbane	Cured tobacco	Sugar cane	Sugar beet	Averaged national price for six food grains
Net output value for each workday	9.37	9.43	6.27	12.69	10.30	6.98

Source: *Total Nationwide Revenues from Farm Products Compilation*, 1992, China Prices Publishing House.

During the transformation of the industrial structure, workers' incomes will experience a period of rapid growth with the shift in predominance from agriculture to the non-agricultural industry. More money in the workers' pockets will facilitate the switch from a diet chiefly composed of starch products to one chiefly composed of animal products. The income elasticity of demand for animal husbandry and fishery, the sources of animal products, is higher than that for growing crops, a relevant factor during this time of change. The comparative advantage in animal husbandry and fishery is higher than that of crop growing. As a result the former has a significantly higher growth rate than the latter (see Table 4-4).

Table 4-4   Crop Growing, Animal Husbandry and Fishing Industries Growth Rates (1993)

	Crop growing	Stock breeding	Fishery
Increase over previous year (%)	4.1	6.1	11.6

Source: *1993 Annual Report on Chinese Rural Economic Development*, 1994, China Social Sciences Publishing House.

An examination of the development experiences of other industrialized countries and medium- and long-term individual income growth trends evident in China, indicate that the transition from basic sufficiency in food and clothing to a more comfortable life characterized by a broader range of consumption and then to moderate affluence will keep the consumption elasticity of demand for animal products at a fairly high level. As a result, such production will have a greater comparative advantage than that for growing crops (see Table 4-5).

**Table 4-5   Past and Future Income Elasticity of Demand
for Different Food Products**

Food Product	1995	2000	2020
Grain	0.335	0.249	0.231
Meat	0.580	0.540	0.426
Eggs	0.936	0.673	0.553
Milk	1.400	1.189	1.100
Aquatic products	0.468	0.606	0.472
Fruit	0.710	0.819	0.974

Source: *Strategy for Medium- and Long-Term Food Development in China*, p.14, 1993, Agriculture Publishing House.

**Table 4-6   Changes in the Comparative Advantage Index for
Chinese Agricultural and Industrial Products**

Year	Agricultural products	Fuels, mineral products & metals	Textiles & garments	Other manufactured goods
1965-69	2.1	0.3	3.3	0.44
1970-74	2.3	0.3	3.4	0.48
1975-77	2.2	0.7	3.9	0.46
1978-80	1.9	0.8	4.6	0.48
1981-83	1.6	1.0	5.0	0.47
1984-86	1.4	1.1	5.1	0.47
1987	1.3	0.7	6.5	0.49

Source: Kym Anderson: *Changing Comparative Advantages in China: Effects on Food, Feed and Fibre Markets* (1990).

Non-agricultural industries have a higher comparative advantage than agriculture. This is the third implication of agriculture's low comparative advantage. Agriculture's decreasing comparative advantage is intimately connected to the economic growth rate, the supply of agricultural resources and population density. Generally speaking, the faster the economic growth rate, the shorter the supply of the agricultural resources and the larger the population, the earlier agriculture's comparative advantage begins to decrease and the faster the rate of decrease. China has a relative shortage of land resources and an enormous population, and it has seen rapid economic expansion since the 1980s. As a result, agriculture's comparative advantage has dropped quickly. In the 22 years between 1965 and 1987, the agricultural products comparative advantage index dropped from 2.1 to 1.3. During the first 12 years of the period this index figure decreased by only 0.2. In comparison, during the first seven years of the 1980s included in the chart, the index figure dropped 0.6, 75 percent of the decrease over the 22-year period (see Table 4-6). Given medium- and long-term macroeconomic development trend and changes in the environmental conditions for agricultural production, agriculture's comparative advantage will continue to fall as a result of economic growth.

II. Small-Scale Production and Efficiency

Traditional Western economic theory holds that, once a certain level of economic development has been reached, the only way out for small-scale farmers is expanding the scale of production and only this will raise efficiency. There is some truth to this theory, but it does not hold true for all countries and situations.

A peasant household in the Chinese hinterland had an average of 0.41 hectare of farmland in 1993, a smaller scale of production than in Taiwan (1.5 hectares) or Japan (0.8 hectare). It has become more and more difficult to raise the productivity of Chinese farmland. Per-hectare grain yield was 4,659 kilograms in 1995, surpassing the 1980 level for developed industrialized countries. If there is no major substantive breakthrough in biotechnological genetic engineering, it will be very difficult to continue to raise productivity. Farmland productivity and economic scale of production have no obvious correlation. On the contrary, in a country like the United States which has adopted intensive large-scale farm production, farmland productivity is lower than in China. The notion that small peasant operations are less efficient, clearly refers not to farmland productivity but to productivity per unit of labor. The sweeping statement that small scale farming is inefficient is misleading.

The notion that small scale farmers refuse to accept technical innovations is not supported by the East Asian example of farmers in Japan, the Republic of Korea and China's Taiwan, all of which continue the small scale farming model. The Chinese olive transport and marketing cooperative in Taiwan took only two or three years to develop a new variety and popularize its cultivation over a large area. Taiwanese fruits have rapidly improved in quality, becoming very competitive in the international market, thanks to the highly efficient development and popularization of new varieties. This demonstrates that while the small scale farming is one factor contributing to agriculture's low comparative advantage in China, it is by no means the only factor. The promotion of agricultural development in a country with limited resources like China, requires the gradual promotion of agricultural operations of appropriate scale, the introduction of different forms of scale production levels and the elevation of the scale of returns from scale production, all with the peasants' voluntary participation. In addition, different measures will need to be taken to raise agricultural productivity, such as increasing agricultural inputs, putting more new technology and equipment to use and raising peasants' educational levels and their understanding of science and technology.

Section Three   Rural Economic Organization: Innovation and Development

Innovation in the double-level agricultural production system, combining unification and separation and recognizing peasant households' rights to use farmland, has made positive and important contributions to the rapid rural development since the 1980s. However, innovation in the production system alone cannot ensure the peasants' smooth access to the market. Peasants simply do not know how to access the market in the absence of innovative reorganization of that access when dealing with the "invisible hand" of the market economy. The agricultural production fluctuation cycle has been sped up and the amplitude of that fluctuation increased, creating more risks for peasants and eventually making them understand that they must respond with organizational innovation. This innovation involved not only production, but also circulation or even the integration of production and circulation.

The main forms this organizational innovation took in the middle and late 1980s: (1) Specialized households emerged on the basis of expanded scale of production. A large number of households sprang up each taking a specialized share of the labor process whether in production, transportation or sales, each operating on a household basis. These households are bigger and more specialized than other peasant households both in scale of production and income. They produce more commodities and receive more income than other households. (2) New rural economic alliances. Seeking to overcome the contradictions presented by diffuse production and concentrated processing, transportation and marketing centers and to make up for inadequate scientific knowledge, technology, funding and managerial experience, peasants have created many forms of economic alliances at different levels on the basis of specialized production. These new economic alliances bring together different stages and portions of production, transportation and marketing or production, transportation and marketing. This cooperation may be between individual peasants, individuals and collectives, individuals and state-owned enterprises. Some are regional, others trans-regional. Industries involved include crop growing, forestry, animal husbandry, sideline occupations, fishery, manufacturing and commerce. There were 1.368 million rural economic alliances in 1993, 93.5 percent of all specialized rural cooperative organizations. (3) Rural specialized technical associations.

Specialized technical associations are a new type of cooperative organization established by peasant households on the basis of specialized production taking technology for such production as its core. These associations are mostly for fish breeding and poultry raising and the cultivation of non-grain crops involving relatively complicated growing techniques. As these do not touch upon fundamental household operations and present very attractive technologies, they have been warmly welcomed by peasant households. There were 94,960 rural specialized technical associations in 1993, approximately 6.5 percent of all rural specialized cooperative and joint organizations. (4) Company / peasant household cooperative organizations. This sort of organization centers around specialized producers or sellers, making use of their respective strengths in funding, technology, equipment, scientific research or marketing to organize the diffuse production of peasant households, and providing access to the market. As the companies have complete pre-production, in-production and post-production service systems, they can help peasant households solve problems cropping up in the course of production. Keeping in mind where the profit ultimately to be reaped by their operations comes from, the companies look out for the peasant households' economic interests. Bearing in mind their own weaknesses regarding production and marketing, peasants in turn look out for the interests of the companies insofar as they wish to develop their production and raise their incomes. This form of organization is even more welcomed by peasant households because it links the peasant households' and the companies' interests in production, supply and marketing. Shandong's Zhucheng County model was created in this way.

These organizational innovations have some shortcomings:

1. Some cooperative economic organizations are hampered by not yet having completely separated government administration from enterprise management. Over half of the cooperative economic organizations and village committees share the same leadership. Involvement in economic activities allows administrative organizations to overcome the underfunding for administrative expenditure and to effectively join in the development of community welfare work. However, this interference will significantly distort the organizations'

locus of operations, increase operating costs and sap the cooperative economic organizations' vitality and creative energy.

2. These organizations are far from meeting rural economic development requirements both in range of cooperation and numbers involved. The 1.46 million cooperative economic organizations are not enough to provide for 220 million peasant households and 910 million peasants. Most cooperation and association comes in production operations, far fewer in production services. The range of regional cooperation is likewise limited. In short, rural cooperation has not to date broken through regional administrative boundaries. In 1991, for example, of the 120,000 cooperative economic organizations in the form of rural specialized associations, only 1,700 are established above the county level, only 1.42 percent of the total; 30 trans-provincial associations account for only 0.025 percent of the total.

3. Rural cooperative economic organizations were established without necessary legal guidance with the result that when participants have differences regarding their interests, some could not receive the necessary and lawful protection for those interests. Needless to say, this facilitates the organization's disintegration.

Practice has shown that household operation needs well-organized, standardized economic cooperative organizations more urgently than do large scale operations. Accordingly, an upsurge in the development of cooperative economic organizations can be expected in the Chinese countryside. This is a requirement for the development of agricultural production and the rural economy.

Section Four   Relocation of the Agricultural Workforce Under Structural Change

The greatest and most profound influence of national economic restructuring on economic development is the change of the employment structure resulting from the transfer of surplus agricultural workforce to non-agricultural industries, and the consequent advance of the modern economy.

I. General Characteristics of the Relocation of the Agricultural Workforce

Relocation of the agricultural workforce between 1952 and 1995 occurred within two different economic environments, each demonstrating its own distinctive characteristics. Before 1980, under the highly centralized planning system giving priority to heavy industry, decreases in agricultural workforce as a portion of all workforce came much more slowly than decreases in agricultural output value as a portion of total output value. According to the World Bank's *1982 World Development Report* and data from the International Labor Organization, agricultural output value as a percentage of total output value in 92 developing countries and low income countries dropped by 13.6 and 12 percentage points respectively during the years between 1960 and 1980, while agricultural employment as a percentage of total employment dropped by 13.5 and 5 percentage points respectively. During this same period in China, agricultural output value as a percentage of total output value dropped by 5.48 percentage points, but agricultural employment as a percentage of total employment rose by 3.2 percentage points. That changes in the employment structure are lagging behind corresponding changes in output value is further demonstrated by the fact that decreases in primary industry's portion of total output value have exceeded decreases in primary industry employment as a portion of total employment, while non-agricultural secondary and tertiary industries' portion of total output value has increased more quickly than their respective shares in total employment. The relationship between changes in shares of total employment and output value can be expressed by the difference between share of total employment and share of total output value (see Table 4-7).

Table 4-7   Lagging Structural Change in Three Industries
(1952-1995)

Year	1953	1957	1970	1978	1980	1985	1988	1993	1995
Primary industry	32.6	40.2	44.2	41.6	37.7	32.0	31.7	35.19	32.32
Secondary industry	-13.8	-20.8	-29.9	-30.5	-29.8	-23.7	-24.4	-29.38	-25.36
Tertiary industry	-18.8	-19.4	-14.3	-11.1	-7.9	-8.3	-7.8	-5.92	-6.96

Source: Calculations based on figures taken from various editions of *The Chinese Statistical Yearbook*.

Differential = employment as a percentage of total employment – output value as a percentage of total output value

Theories of the correlation between change in the industrial structure and change in the employment structure indicate that if the two changes are approximately the same, resultant friction and loss will be minimized and the period necessary to effect the change shortened. In China, change in the employment structure has lagged behind change in the industrial structure, distorting resource allocation, quickly raising the organic formation of industrial capital and irrationally shortening the time during which labor-intensive industries are developed. Moreover, this lack of coordination also offset the gains of many years of investments in modern agricultural equipment intended to raise technological levels and labor productivity. Distinct differences in level of development were created between two economic sectors: traditional agriculture and modernized industry, a model dualistic pattern in the national economy. Thus, the economic growth momentum released through structural change became imbalanced. This did more than constricting the overall operation of the national economy. Peasant incomes grew slowly and the rural market became sluggish, incapable of supporting industrialization. At the same time, hidden unemployment created by the delay in transferring agricultural workforce to industry, increased the difficulty of raising national labor productivity.

In three respects, the reform of the rural economic system begun in 1978 created the necessary conditions and opportunities for the transfer of portions of the agricultural workforce to non-agricultural industries. (1) On policy level, the dismantling of the people's communes and the rebirth of small scale production groups gave peasants a relative independence to make decisions concerning production. Optimizing resource allocations insofar as policy allowed, including transferring surplus workforce out of agriculture, peasants have responded to market demand, moving into non-agricultural activities. (2) On the material level, successive good harvests from 1979 to 1984 laid the foundation for the accumulation of funds and the supply of materials for the development of non-agricultural industries. (3) On the level of agency, following the good harvest of 1985, there was an oversupply in low level consumables. The good harvest did not translate into increased income. For the first time, peasants came to realize that the decrease in agriculture's comparative advantage resulted in stagnant incomes. Increased incomes have become the primary goal for peasants moving into non-agricultural industry, the prime agency behind that move.

After 1985, non-agricultural industries, primarily township enterprises, suddenly sprang up as a force in the countryside, quickly absorbing tens of millions of surplus agricultural workforce. This was something never encountered in the past.

1. Large numbers of workers were transferred in a short time. In the 15 years between 1978 and 1993, rural non-agricultural industries created 98.417 million new jobs, an average of 6.561 million a year, an average annual transfer rate of 11.9 percent. The quickened transfer of surplus agricultural workforce reduced the formerly broadening differential between agricultural employment as a portion of the total employment and agricultural output value as a portion of the total output value (see Table 4-7). On an annual basis, the decrease in the agricultural workforce as a portion of the total workforce exceeded the decrease in agricultural output value as a portion of the total output value for the first time or the differential was reduced (see Table 4-8).

Table 4-8   Changes in Agriculture's Portion of
Total Output Value and Total Employment
(1952-1993)

Unit: %

Year	1952-65	1965-77	1977-88	1989-93
Agricultural output value as a percentage of the total output value	45.42-30.91	30.91-20.87	20.87-19.65	26.40-21.22
Average annual rate of decrease	1.12	0.84	0.11	1.036
Agricultural workforce as a percentage of the total workforce	83.5-81.6	81.6-74.5	74.5-59.5	59.95-56.40
Average annual rate of decrease	0.14	0.59	1.36	0.71

Source: Figures taken from various editions of *The Chinese Statistical Yearbook*.

2. Transfer of agricultural workforce from region to region has been clearly restricted by the system, first, by the cities' strict regulation of residency permits and, second, by the resource supply mode for non-agricultural industries. The rigidity of the urban and rural residency permit system was an important factor contributing to urbanization's lagging behind industrialization during the course of economic modernization. It has been very difficult for peasants to rely on their own to break through the barriers of residency registration control, to move independently and freely into the cities. Moreover, the priority in allocation of resources given to the cities under the traditional planned economy has made it difficult for the peasants to have their fair share of the "pie" in the division of resources. Under these circumstances, peasants had to build up non-agricultural

industries by obtaining resources in the easiest way at the least cost within the limits prescribed by policy. This has resulted in a situation quite unlike that in other developing countries where workers stream from one region to another. In China, former peasants leave the soil but not their native homes and go to the factories without going to the city.

3. Combining transferred agricultural workforce with labor-intensive non-agricultural industries has formed an industrial structure with a comparative advantage. Restricted by the resource supply system and limited by their low accumulation capacity, the transfer of the surplus agricultural workforce in China has to proceed with a low capital-labor ratio. For example, from 1978 to 1984 in comparison with state-owned enterprises, for every 10,000-yuan increase in output value, rural enterprises substituted 0.8 workers in place of 3,360 yuan of fixed assets. This substitution for key production elements in the countryside, undersupplied with capital and oversupplied with labor, promoted the transfer of surplus agricultural workforce and the formation of industries with their own comparative advantages. For example, at the beginning, the surplus agricultural workforce found work for the most part in labor-intensive industries like coal mining, food processing, textiles and farm machinery and building materials manufacture.

4. Regional differences in the transfer of the surplus agricultural workforce are fairly distinct. This transfer differs greatly from region to region in terms of number, speed and stability. Generally speaking, in the more developed eastern coastal provinces and the rural areas around the large and medium-sized cities, surplus agricultural laborers found jobs in larger numbers, more quickly and their job situation was more stable. This process was less successful in the central and western regions, with better progress in the former than the latter. The west lags behind the other two regions in terms of numbers, speed and stability (see Table 4-9).

Table 4-9   Rural Agricultural and Non-agricultural Employment in Three Major Regions (1992)

Unit: %

	Eastern region	Central region	Western region
Agriculture	69.5	81.5	85.8
Non-agriculture	30.5	18.5	14.2

Source: *The 1993 Annual Report on Rural Economic Development in China*, p.120, 1994, The Chinese Social Sciences Publishing House.

The transfer of surplus agricultural workforce and the development of non-agricultural industries in the countryside has contributed greatly to China's economic growth. Of the national income's 4.9 percentage points increased increment speed in 1992, nearly 4.8 percentage points were contributed by increased increment speed in the rural economy, with accelerated speed in rural non-agricultural industries contributing 4 percentage points to the total. As this makes clear, the great majority of increased increment speed in 1992 came from rural non-agricultural industries. (See *The 1992 Annual Repoon Rural Economic Development in China*, P.167, 1993, The Chinese Social Sciences Publishing House.)

II. Trends in the Transfer of Surplus Agricultural Workforce

Agricultural portion accounted for only 25.39 percent of the national income in 1993; agriculture is no longer the principal driver behind economic development. However, China still has a rural population of 910 million and 332 million agricultural workers. It is still a distinctly agricultural country. Of the 332 million agricultural workers today, 120 million are redundant, 36.15 percent. Moreover, every year between 1994 and 2000, 13 million new workers will be added to the rural workforce. If as over the last 15 years an average of

6.561 million rural workers are transferred to non-agricultural industries annually, the number of surplus workforce in the countryside will rise from 120 million today to 180 million or more by the end of century. This huge number of surplus agricultural workforce will constitute a powerful shock wave rocking the transfer of workforce to non-agricultural industries through the close of this century and the first half of the next century. (1) This effect will be felt as a motive force within agriculture. First, agricultural resources are in short supply. Land resources are overloaded in 12 of the 30 provinces, municipalities or autonomous regions and this situation has reached a critical state in eight. Together, this describes 80 percent of China by area or 60 percent of available farmland. Second, agricultural labor productivity will rise with increased input of machinery and improved quality of intermediate input. More labor power will be released as a result, providing a powerful motive force within agriculture. (2) Under the influence of income elasticity of demand, agriculture's comparative advantage decreased, income from agriculture fell far behind that of non-agricultural industries. This widening gap, (see Table 4-10), gave rise to a force drawing surplus agricultural workers, accelerating their transfer to non-agricultural industries.

Table 4-10   Growth of Workers' Wages in Different Industries (1990-1993)

Unit: yuan/year

Year	Agriculture, forestry, animal husbandry, sideline industries, fishery	Manufacturing	Wholesale and retail trade, and foodstuffs	Nationally
1990	1,541	2,073	1,818	2,140
1991	1,652	2,289	1,981	2,340
1992	1,828	2,635	2,204	2,711
1993	2,042	3,348	2,679	3,371

Source: *The 1994 Chinese Statistical Yearbook*, p.122.

Non-agricultural industry's capacity to absorb surplus agricultural workforce is falling, despite the pressure. Employment in the rural industry rose by an average of 7.1 percent a year in the years between 1985 and 1992, but this figure dropped to 5 percent in 1993. Employment in the building industry, transportation and commerce rose by an average of 15.4 percent between 1985 and 1992, but dropping to 7.8 percent in 1993. These figures demonstrate that rural non-agricultural industry has a diminished capacity to absorb new workers. Indicators of elasticity of output value and employment show that employment elasticity in rural non-agricultural industries in 1993 was only 0.13, lowest annual figure in the 15 years between 1978 and 1993 and 50 percent lower than in 1992. Low employment elasticity in rural non-agricultural industries meant achieving the same employment as in the past required still higher growth in output (see Table 4-11). The reason behind the drop in the output value and employment elasticity index was the density of industrial capital in the rural areas. Investment in industrial fixed assets in the countryside came to 72.06 billion yuan in 1992, 42.06 billion yuan more than in 1991, an increase of 140.2 percent. Employment grew only 8.99 percent over the same period.

Table 4-11   Elasticity of Output Value and Employment in Rural Non-Agricultural Industries

	1985-92	1993
Rural manufacturing	0.24	0.12
Rural building materials, transportation and commerce	1.20	0.15
Rural non-agricultural industry	0.39	0.13

Source: *The 1993 Annual Report on Rural Economic Development in China*, p.237, 1994, The Chinese Social Sciences Publishing House.

**Table 4-12   Comparison of Urbanization in China and
Abroad at Different Levels of GNP**

Year	GNP (US dollars)	Urban Population in China (%)	Level of urbanization internationally at corresponding level (%)	Differential between Chinese and international urbanization levels
1980	300	19	20	-1
1991	647	26.7	33	-6.3
1992	719	27	34.2	-7.2

Data taken from *The 1992 Annual Report on Rural Economic Development in China*, p.173.

Employment elasticity has fallen faster in the building materials industry and transportation and commerce than in industrial output value. This presaged rural tertiary industry, following its relatively rapid development from 1985 to 1992, encountering restraints imposed by the lagging pace of urbanization (see Table 4-12). Accordingly, China is faced with two problems to be solved in the course of future economic development, excessive increases in industrial capital in the rural areas and lagging of urbanization. The failure to solve these problems is bound to affect the transfer of the surplus agricultural workforce and distort the rural industrial structure.

Uneven economic development as resulted in an undersupply of labor power in the developed eastern coastal provinces and an oversupply in the underdeveloped western provinces, has exacerbated the flow of surplus agricultural workforce from the underdeveloped to the developed regions. In 1993, 49.242 million peasants left their home villages to work elsewhere; 38.655 million going to the cities and towns. Cities were the destination of 78.5 percent of those leaving their native place. (See *The 1993 Annual Report on Rural Economic Development in China*, p.174, 1994, The Chinese Social Sciences Publishing House.) For the most part, they went to places with rapidly developing economies like the Pearl River Delta, the Yangtze River Delta, Beijing, Tianjin, Tanggu, Hainan and Fujian. The trans-regional relocation of these rural workers, on the one hand, indicates that there are no jobs available locally. The pattern whereby peasants leave the soil but not their native place, going to the factory without going to the city does not seem to be holding, as many peasants leave their homes for factory work in the city. On the other, the trans-regional flow of surplus agricultural workers is the inevitable result of the exchange of key comparative production elements. Therefore, from a long-term point of view, inevitably during the course of economic growth labor power flows from various regions into the cities; this trans-regional flow will continue to increase with the passage of time. Such a large-scale population flow will not only increase burdens on transportation and disturb normal urban order; it will also affect social stability. Therefore, China is currently studying how to better the residency registration control system and use the role of the market economy to position elements to guide and control the trans-regional flow of workforce.

Section Five   Policy Choices

The formation of a new growth mechanism for the rural economy and changing the environment for economic growth calls for the formulation of industrial policies that meet the needs of developing the market economy and conform to national conditions. Principal policy choices will be addressed in two respects.

I. Agricultural Development Policy

Since the 1980s, almost all major fluctuations in the national economy were related to ups and downs in agricultural production. This demonstrates that the agricultural development model in China lacks the capacity for self-correction in a market economy environment. Maintaining sustained, steady agricultural development will require a transformation of the agricultural development model and the establishment of market economy agriculture.

Internationally, the agricultural development model in low income countries has been divided into two completely distinct stages, a taxed stage (also called the industry forced accumulation stage) and a stage during which agriculture is protected. When domestic prices for farm products in one country are lower than prices on the international market, agriculture is in the taxed stage. When domestic prices for farm products are higher than the prices on the international market, agriculture is in the protected stage.

Although the current overall level of protection for agriculture in China retains a negative value, the protection rate has risen from negative 300 percent in the early 1980s to negative 19 percent today. Actual levels of protection vary for different products. The highest actual level of protection calculated in terms of subsidies for agricultural producers is 14 percent for cotton. With the exception of rice, which receives a low level of protection, the protection rates for all grain crops is negative. However, their relative protection rates are high, that for wheat negative 9 percent, for beans negative 6 percent. There is a tendency to change these negative values to positive values, implement protection for agriculture in China. However, if agricultural protection is to be adopted immediately, the biggest obstacle may be the proportion of non-agricultural population and the cost of protection. China's rural population accounts for 71.86 percent of the total population and the urban population accounts for only 28.14 percent. Protection of the majority at the expense of the minority will be expensive and create political hazards. This will not be easy to do. Moreover, in terms of actual results, such a move will increase the burden on consumers and taxpayers, create an inefficient agricultural economy hardly able to stand on its own, hindering transformation of the industrial structure, distorting prices for key production elements, thus misdirecting signals for the allocation of resources. Protection will also increase state expenditure and cause harm to the welfare of the country as a whole.

The theory of comparative trade advantage to guide changes in the agricultural production structure provides one method of curing the contradiction between shortages of farmland and a surplus of agricultural labor power. International trade allows Chinese agricultural products with comparative production advantages on the international market to be exchanged for agricultural products without this comparative advantage, giving prominence to the comparative advantages to be found in Chinese agricultural production, promoting specialization and intensification. This road to agricultural development requires participation in international trade. First of all, the environment for international trade improved, optimized and stabilized. Through international trade an agricultural production structure making use of comparative advantages will promote agricultural development. This path is less costly than choosing protectionism for agriculture.

Agricultural policy should serve agricultural development. (1) The principle of comparative advantage if used to develop international agricultural trade and to promote the export of cash crops in exchange for food grains can increase China's food grain supply. However, as stated before, China is a large country with a huge population. Food grain imports can only be a subsidiary measure in working to bridge the gap between supply and demand in grains. It should not be expected to provide the anchor. Therefore, assuring regular increases in grain production and encouraging the peasantry to grow grain remain very important parts of agricultural policy. (2) Technological inputs into agriculture should be increased. Currently, technological inputs contribute less than a 30 percent proportion to agricultural development, about 40-50 percentage points lower than in the industrialized countries. Increases in technological inputs should focus on technical innovations and the popularization of fine varieties and new techniques. (3) Capital construction in agriculture should be strengthened and agricultural production conditions improved. In recent years, state expenditures on agricultural capital construction increased, but its relative share decreased. This is not beneficial to faster, better quality improvement of the agricultural production environment. Intermediate inputs are crucial to the control of plant diseases and insect pests and the maintenance of stable, high yields. The government must ensure their supply, both in quality and quantity. (4) Organizational innovations encouraging cooperation between rural production, transport and marketing should be promoted. The development of organizations linking companies and peasant households should be encouraged, as should specialized technical associations formed on the basis of technology, so as to solve pre-production, in-production and post-production problems and bring peasants into the market. The government should permit and further encourage peasants to set up national cooperative economic organizations embracing production, transportation, marketing, storage and processing of farm products. These measures are needed to improve the cooperative economic organizations' operating efficiency and strengthen their vitality.

II. Labor Transfer Policies

The Chinese agricultural labor transfer policy must be based on a full labor supply. Future labor transfer policies should effect three combinations.

1. The transfer of agricultural labor power should be combined with the formation of an industrial pattern in which rural industry has a comparative production advantage. Industrial policy should encourage the transfer of agricultural workforce to processors using agricultural and sideline products as raw materials, to the labor-intensive industries; relocation from regions with an oversupply of labor to those undersupplied should be encouraged so as to forestall the tendency toward increasing concentrations of capital as a result of undersupply of labor. The market economy should serve its function in the optimal allocation of resources, establishing a labor market and fine tuning it.

The labor market can then play its role in regulating the flow of labor power, determining the rate of flow and its direction.

2. The transfer of labor power should be combined with increased urbanization. Given China's current urban setup, it will be very difficult for additional extra-large cities or large cities to emerge through the normal operation of the system. In the future urbanization will center on the still not fully developed medium-sized and small cities, because these cities will be the principal support for future economic growth. A corresponding labor transfer policy must be formulated and economic measures used to encourage labor power to go to medium-sized and small cities.

3. Comparative advantage in agricultural production can be used as a motive force to transfer workforce within agriculture. Cash crops, forestry, animal husbandry, sideline occupations and fishery have a higher income elasticity of demand and more pronounced comparative advantage than grain crops. These industries and products, if developed, can absorb a portion of the current surplus agricultural workforce. Available studies indicate that if the land currently used for growing grain was reduced by 3 to 10 percent and used instead for growing cash crops, and the income from these cash crops was to buy food grains, not only would the nation's grain supply not be affected, over 10 billion yuan in additional income would be generated and more than 10 million rural jobs created.

Chapter Five   Industrial Development

In Chapter Two industry was predicted to grow at a rate faster than the national economy between 1991 and 2010. Growth rate during these 20 years will be divided into two stages. During the first stage (1991-2000), industrial net output will increase 11 percent per annum. By 2000, industrial net output will reach 2.1912 trillion yuan RMB, 52.3 percent of GDP. During the second stage (2001-2010), industrial net output will grow 7.6 percent per annum. By 2010, the industrial net output will be 4.5583 trillion yuan RMB, 52.8 percent of GDP.

Analyzing industrial growth and structural change first requires the study of two questions. First, an appraisal must be made of the current level of industry in China in light of general trends in industrialization of the world. In this way, possible future speed and direction of development may be understood. Second, an analysis should be made of which factors are favorable and which unfavorable to China's industrial development. After considering these two questions, we think the continuation of a fairly high growth rate in the future is likely. In addition, distinctive internal changes will take place in the industrial structure.

Section One   Determining of the Current Stage of Industrialization in China

Determining what is the current stage of industrialization in China is of great importance in getting a fix on future industrial growth rates and the directions structural change will take. Analysis in this section will conclude that until 2010 industry will remain in a stage wherein the completion of industrialization and industrial modernization overlap. During the course of this development, with differing stages and levels of industrialization, will present many different kinds of opportunities for growth and many directions for structural change.

The world has been industrializing for more than 200 years. Some countries have already completed the process of industrialization and many other countries are still at different stages of industrialization. China can learn from the experiences of other countries in determining what rate of industrial development can be maintained and what structural changes to expect in the future.

H. Chenery and others understand economic growth as an overall transformation of the economic structure. In the growth pattern they propose based on models in various countries, the process of structural change resulting from growth in per-capita income can be divided into six periods and three stages as shown in Table 5-1.

Table 5-1   Stages of Growth

Income level (per-capita US dollars, 1970)	Period	Stage
140-280	1	1st stage: primary products
280-560 560-1,120 1,120-2,100	2 3 4	2nd stage: industrialization
2,100-3,360 3,360-5,040	5 6	3rd stage: developed economy

Source: H. Chenery: *Industrialization and Growth Comparative Study*, SDX Joint Publishing Co., Shanghai Branch, 1989.

The most radical structural changes will come about during the second stage, industrialization. According to standard model put forward by Chenery, during this stage manufacturing's contribution to

GDP increases from 19 percent to 36 percent and per-capita income rises from US$ 280 to US$ 2,100. However, change in the percentage of total workers working in manufacturing lags behind this increase in contribution to GDP, rising from 10 percent to 20 percent.

This model provides a tool with which to address the question of China's stage of industrialization. The most important variables are per-capita income, GDP structure, employment structure and degree of urbanization.[1]

1. Per-capita income. Per-capita GNP in China in 1993 as calculated by the World Bank was US$ 470, about US$ 150 more than in the early 1980s. This clearly does not represent the actual economic growth in China in recent years. Some studies at home and abroad hold that per-capita income calculated in terms of U.S. dollars underestimates actual income levels in China. We hold that a more fitting appraisal would place contemporary China in the second period of the industrialization stage of industrialization, which would assume per-capita income of US$ 560 to US$ 1,120.

2. GDP structure. To keep data comparable, World Bank statistics will be used. According to the 1993 World Bank's World Development Report, industry supplied 42 percent of the Chinese GDP in 1991, a figure far higher than the 29 percent average for low income countries that same year. It was also higher than the 1970 averages for middle income countries, (37 percent) and high income countries, (39 percent). In comparison, agriculture accounted for 27 percent of GDP in China in 1991, quite close to the average 29 percent for low income countries, but much higher than the 1970 averages for middle income countries, (12 percent) and high income countries, (4 percent). In China, services make a lesser contribution to GDP than in any of three country groups, 34 percent in 1991, as compared to 38 percent in low income countries, 50 percent in middle income countries and 58 percent in high income countries. The high figure for industry and the low figure for services

---

[1] The data used here are taken from *The 1994 Chinese Statistical Yearbook*, *The 1993 World Development Report* and *The 1994 World Development Report* by the World Bank.

were unusual when compared to the averages for any of the three income categories.

3. Employment structure. In 1993, of the total Chinese workforce 56.4 percent was working in primary industry, 22.4 percent in secondary industry, and 21.2 percent in tertiary industry. Comparing these figures with the standard model, the employment structure conforms to the initial period of industrialization. The percentage working in services was clearly on the low side.

4. Degree of urbanization. In 1993 only 27 percent of the population lived in cities or towns, far lower than the average 62 percent in middle income countries, and the average 39 percent in low income countries, as well. This gives further proof that the urbanization process in China is clearly lagging behind the pace of industrialization.

What judgment can be made from the above description as regards the present stage of industrialization in China? Obviously, a contradictory picture is presented. Judging from industry's share of GDP, it would appear that China has completed the stage of industrialization. Judging from the employment structure and degree of urbanization, China would appear to be in the initial stage of industrialization. Clearly, both appraisals deviate greatly from the true level of industrialization in China. We think that a stage of industrialization defined by per-capita income provides a fitting measure of China's current level of industrialization. China is currently in the second period of the industrialization stage wherein per-capita income grows from US$ 560 to US$ 1,120. The Chinese industrialization process' marked deviation from the "standard model" may be explained by the strict and long-standing practices of the administrative resource allocation system and the control over workforce moving from country to city.

These qualities will favorably effect sustained rapid growth of industry in the future. China will continue to complete the process of industrialization over the next 16 years of industrial growth, moving from the third period in the second stage of the standard model to the fifth period of the third stage. Industry's share of GDP will remain more or less constant at the current level of 50 percent or slightly higher. In investment, priority will be given to the chemicals industry, transportation, waterworks, electric power, gas and other primary industries and infrastructure. Their contribution to total output will rise slightly. In contrast, the food, textile and other light industries' share of total output will fall. Home appliances, automobiles, electronics manufacturers and the building industry will experience rapid growth. By the end of the century, technological levels and product quality throughout industry will roughly approximate advanced international levels of the early 1990s. During this same period, agriculture's share of GDP will fall to around 10 percent, and that of tertiary industry will rise to around 40 percent. At the same time this industrialization process is taking place, industrial sectors which have already reached a fairly high level will progress closer toward international advanced levels and the number of industrial sectors working with new and advanced technologies will increase fairly quickly, as more and more high tech products are introduced. Manufacturers of office automation equipment, modern telecommunications equipment and new materials and those working in new energy sources and biological engineering will see their shares grow by substantial margins. New technologies and equipment will transform a wide range of traditional industries. In summation, China will undergo two overlapping stages of industrial development, completing the process of industrialization in some sectors while others undergo industrial modernization, thus providing more capacity for industrial growth for the next 10 years and beyond.

Section Two   Analysis of the Conditions for Industrial Development

I. Favorable Conditions for Industrial Development

Favorable conditions for industrial growth for the next ten years and longer are present.

1. There is exuberant demand for various grades of products at different levels. China is a large country and economic development has not been balanced. Production technology and level of product quality vary widely between different manufacturers'. There is a similar large gap between urban and rural levels of consumption and income levels and available infrastructure in different regions. Such disparities result in market demand for industrial products of varying grades. There will be broad demand capacity for all grades of investment, intermediate products, consumer goods and infrastructure.

2. China has the advantage of being a large country. It is the largest developing country and it has a huge domestic market. Almost every industry can rely on the domestic market which provides the necessary benefits of scale and market competition, conditions unrealistic for many developing countries. Of course, this does not mean rejecting the important role played by foreign trade and economic cooperation. On the contrary, China will actively join in international cooperation and the international market, expanding its participation. A significant advantage of being a large country is that economic development will not be excessively tied down by changes in the international economic environment and there is much room to maneuver in choosing routes for development.

3. Perhaps unexpectedly, there is an advantage in China being a latecomer to industrialization. Latecomers tend to grow more quickly than advanced countries did in the same stage of development. The reasons for this are not the same in every case, but most often the quicker progress may be attributed to the acquisition and use of advanced technologies suited to the conditions in the specific country. In addition, latecomers benefit from cheap labor. Their products are competitive on the international market. This is all the more true when a developing country can combine low labor costs with advanced technology, making it strongly competitive in technology- and labor-intensive industries. Such a combination can play a leading role driving domestic industrial growth and structural upgrading.

4. The reforms that China has been carrying out since 1978 and the

growth these reforms have engendered bode well for further industrial growth in the future.

II. Factors Restricting Industrial Growth

Factors are present which will restrict industrial growth over the next ten years and beyond.

1. There is much urban unemployment, and the unemployment rate is generally rising.

2. A "buyer's market" will become the normal state of affairs. Investors in any project will have to reckon with competition from a large number of other manufacturers producing a variety of similar or identical products, as well as others trying to enter the same market. Investors will find it more and more difficult to find projects sure to make a profit.

3. Some capital will be taken from various industrial sectors for investment in new areas. Production capacity exceeds market demand in most industries. This particularly true for the general processing industries. Newcomers will have to overcome fierce competition if they want to invest in these industries. In addition, in recent years the government has conditionally opened a number of new areas for investment hitherto under state monopoly, including banking, insurance, real estate development and airlines. These opportunities are very attractive to investors, and, as capital flows into these new areas, industrial investment drops.

4. Export growth has sped up in the past but will slow down in the future. Export growth has been an important generator of industrial growth for the past ten years and earlier. However, at present, domestic production costs are on the rise and export products are confronted with trade barriers impeding access to foreign markets. Chinese export's competitiveness in the international market will decrease, as will the growth rate for export of industrial products, sapping the motive force driving industrial growth.

Section Three   Changes in the Internal Structure of Industry

China is industrializing later than other more industrially advanced countries, and as a result has much more choice in selecting industries, products and technologies than those countries had at the same stage. Moreover, as the movement toward global economic integration gains in strength, industrial development will be less affected by a nation's given resource conditions. Therefore, while structural characteristics that typified stages of development for the industrially advanced countries will also appear in China, their impetus will be weaker in comparison. Heavy chemical industry will develop quickly, but the attendant growth rate and increase in output share will probably be significantly lower than the "standard" or "average" suggested by the experiences of advanced industrial countries. Some industries and products will contribute relatively more to the growth, and therefore the role of "leading industries" will be much weaker than that played in the advanced industrial countries during the same stage of development. Large enterprises have the advantage of scale economy. They will play the leading role in industries characterized by fierce competition and pronounced economy of scale. Still, small and medium-sized enterprises will have adequate opportunity for faster growth.

Industry can be expected to undergo the following important internal structural changes over the next ten years and subsequently.

I. Structural Coordination and Structural Upgrading Will Proceed in Combination

Shortages of a few primary industries and products will not be completely corrected by the end of the century. Accordingly, faster growth in these industries is still an important goal to be pursued in structural change. However, the presence of these shortages will not affect the tendency toward structural upgrading in industry. The processing industries will continue to maintain faster growth on the basis of the new technologies and new products. Therefore, structural change in industry will witness dual tendencies of structural coordination and structural upgrading.

Certain industries inadequate in number or production affect the entire economy. These include the power industry, petroleum industry and railways. While these are limited in number, they exercise a widespread influence on economic growth. Any one project may require a huge investment. For example, most oil reserves are located in the environmentally poor western regions, inaccessible to modern transportation, presenting substantial obstacles to increased production. The Three Gorges Hydraulic Power Station is requiring a staggering investment and will take a long time to complete. The project will obviously promote the manufacture of power equipment, transformers, transmission equipment and building machinery. The development of these industries will markedly influence structural change.

Structural change related to structural upgrading affects industrial development even more extensively, clearly promoting growth. At present, in most industries production capacity exceeds demand. Continued growth must rely on technological advances and product upgrading, in competitive struggle for a greater market share. Given this, most industries will move toward structural upgrading.

II. Heavy Industry Will Grow Slightly Faster Than Light Industry

For the next ten years and beyond both light industry and heavy industry will maintain a relatively rapid rate of growth. Heavy industry will grow slightly more quickly than light industry, but this difference will not be particularly large. By the end of this century, heavy industry's share of total industrial output will have risen slightly; subsequently, it will remain approximately the same for the next ten years.

Chinese compilers of statistics report that the processing industry, especially light processing industries, grew fairly rapidly during the industrial expansion of the 1980s. This was basically the situation to be expected. There are two reasons for this. (1) The Chinese use different specifications in compiling statistics than what are commonly used internationally. Calculations using this Chinese method significantly underestimate the results achieved in the heavy chemical industry in determining the relative shares of light and heavy industries. (2) As a latecomer to industrialization, China has much greater capacity to choose directions for growth. Changes in the industrial structure can be markedly different from those in the advanced countries.

According to international practice, light and heavy industries' relative contributions to total industrial output are usually limited to manufacturing. Light industry is for the most part defined as processing of agricultural products, including mainly the foodstuffs and textile industries. The heavy chemical industry for the most part refers to metals, the machine-building and chemical industries. Using the Chinese method, light industry also encompasses machinery, metalware and chemicals for use by household consumers, (in contrast to international practice, which includes them in heavy chemical industry). The Chinese include mining in heavy industry, (whereas, in international practice, mining is not included in manufacturing output value). With this in mind, it is misleading to compare the positions of light and heavy industry in China with corresponding figures from other countries or with the Hofman coefficient before making appropriate adjustments.

Adjustments to be made to various data (The left side of the equal sign corresponds to international practice, the right side describes the changes to be made to data compiled according to Chinese practice to make them comparable to that used in international practice.)

Total manufacturing output value = total industrial output value minus total output value of the mining industry

Total output value for the heavy chemical industry = total output value for heavy industry minus the total output value for the mining industry plus that portion of the total output value for light industry supplied by light industry using non-agricultural products as raw materials (i.e., equivalent to the total output value of light industry minus that portion of the total output value of light industry supplied by light industry using non-agricultural products as raw materials).

Table 5-2 Heavy and Light Industries' Contributions to Total Industrial Output Value Calculated According to Chinese Practice

Year	1952	1957	1978	1980	1985	1991
Total industrial output value	100.00	100.00	100.00	100.00	100.00	100.00
Total output value for heavy industry	35.5	45.0	56.9	52.8	52.9	51.1
Total output value for light industry	64.5	55.0	43.1	47.1	47.1	48.9

Source: *The Chinese Statistical Yearbook*, 1984, 1992.

Table 5-3 Heavy and Light Industries' Contributions to Total Industrial Output Value Calculated According to International Practice

Year	1952	1957	1978	1980	1985	1991
Total output value for manufacturing	100.00	100.00	100.00	100.00	100.00	100.00
Total output value for heavy chemical industry	40.4	50.9	68.3	65.6	64.5	64.5
Total output value for light industry	59.6	49.1	31.7	34.4	35.5	35.5

Source: Calculations based on figures taken from *The Chinese Statistical Yearbook* for given years.

Under the Chinese calculation method, mechanical and electrical appliances, chemicals and metalware produced for household consumers are considered light industrial products; according to international practice, they are included with heavy chemical industrial products. This sort of products formed a very important component of the move toward development in light industry in China in the 1980s. (Some would regard the fast growth of this industrial sector as the main manifestation of the move to light industrial products in industrial development.) In fact, this growth should be included in heavy chemical industry. Comparing Table 5-2 with Table 5-3, it can be seen that since 1978 heavy chemical industry's share of total output value is 12 to 14 percentage points higher when calculated according to international practice than when calculated using the Chinese method. The Chinese practice significantly underestimates the advances made by heavy chemical industry in China, overlooking its actual contribution to the industrial growth.

Viewed in light of other countries' experiences and bearing in mind the main factors influencing industrial growth and structural change in China, heavy chemical industry's share of total manufacturing output value can be expected to rise calculated using either of the two methods, but the margin of increase will not be particularly large. The main factors behind heavy chemical industry's increasing share will be rapidly growing demand for consumer goods, such as automobiles, housing and telecommunications equipment, and accelerated infrastructure construction. Moreover, beginning in the 1990s, the processing industry has entered a new round of technological and equipment renovations and replacement which will further promote faster growth in capital goods industries. Using the Chinese method, consumer goods with big growth potential are listed under the light industry rubric. During this same period, within the category of heavy industry, the growth rate for the mining industry will lag behind that of industry as a whole. For this reason, heavy industry's share of total output will perhaps only slightly increase. By the end of this century, calculated according to international practice, heavy chemical industry will probably account for 68 to 70 percent of all manufacturing. Using the Chinese method, heavy industry will account for approximately 54 to 56 percent of total industrial output value.

III. The Importance of Large Enterprises Will Markedly Expand; Medium- and Small-Scale Enterprises Will Continue to Have Great Potential for Growth

The role of large-scale enterprises and enterprise groups in future industrial growth will markedly expand for the following reasons.

1. Competition in areas other than price has become the key competitive factor for most of industrial products. These include reliable quality, a network for timely and complete after-sale service, the capacity to rapidly replace outdated products and advertising and promotion in a variety of media. These cannot be effectively exploited by anyone other than a large-scale enterprise with substantial financial muscle. Given this factor, in recent years large-scale enterprises have seized the leading role in certain industries. A clear tendency toward concentrated production has emerged, best typified by the home appliance industry. Medium- and small-scale enterprises fall short in the struggle for market share with those larger enterprises.

2. Large-scale enterprises have occupied new markets through diversified business operations and are always on the lookout for new investment opportunities, while such opportunities for medium- and small-scale enterprises are comparatively limited.

3. Some large industrial and infrastructure projects have become key areas for investment. These projects by their very nature determined that the scale of investment would give rise to a number of large-scale enterprises. Over a fairly long period of years to come, a number of large projects will be undertaken and older enterprises renovated or expanded to have their capacities greatly increased in the petroleum, electric power, transportation, chemicals, motor vehicle and electronics industries, greatly expanding their scale.

4. The stock system has provided a new channel for the formation and further growth of large-scale enterprises. Large-scale enterprises

will expand their presence, but medium- and small-scale enterprises will still have a broad expanse open for development. First, the medium- and small-scale enterprises will be able to establish some breathing room by establishing cooperative relations with large-scale enterprises. The main problem in China at present is not that there are too many medium- and small-scale enterprises, rather that the relationships between large, medium- and small-scale enterprises are not rational. There are a large number of small enterprises that handle the entire manufacturing process for a product. This runs counter to the necessities of modern production and marketing technology. As large-scale enterprises come to dominate competition, a reorganization of the relationships between large, medium- and small-scale enterprises is imperative. Large numbers of small-scale enterprises currently producing complete machines and vehicles will be transformed into small, specialized enterprises producing parts and accessories, integrating their output with production by large-scale enterprises. Moreover, in some industries the benefits of scale are not evident, market competition is not driven, there is no after-sale service and differences between products are not immediately apparent. In these industries, medium- and small-scale enterprises will retain a clear competitive advantage. In addition, given the poor transportation facilities in a much of China, there are regional markets located far from large-scale enterprises. Here too, large enterprises will lack a significant competitive advantage over medium- and small-scale enterprises.

Section Four   Selection of Leading Industries and the Development of Major Industries

I. Selecting Leading Industries

The term "leading industries" as used here refers to industries with the capacity to make relatively outstanding contributions to the economic growth. In predicting which industries are likely to become the leading industries, consideration should be given to the following three factors: first, the established evolutionary patterns of leading industries as demonstrated during the course of industrialization in other countries; second, the influence of China's particular structural problems on the direction of the structural change; third, the degree of interrelatedness between different industries given current structural conditions and tendencies toward change. Generally speaking, the first factor would lead to expectations of rapid growth in the processing industries, particularly those with high added value or advanced technological content. Consideration of the second factor leads to the expectation that industries in already industrialized countries which grew slowly or even experienced negative growth during the same period of development as they made up for earlier expenditures will grow fairly rapidly in China. Consideration of the third factor helps us recognize the industries that have a high degree of interrelatedness under current structural conditions and possess the interactive and leading force to drive economic growth. On this basis of analysis, by 2010, transportation equipment manufacturers, electronics and telecommunications equipment manufacturers, manufacturers of large-scale, complete industrial installations, the electric power industry and foodstuffs industry all have the capacity to make major contributions to economic growth. For the next ten years and beyond these will be the leaders in industrial development.

II. The Development of Major Industries

1. Energy industry. Given the nation's huge population and that economic development is presently in a rapid growth stage characterized by comprehensive industrialization, an enormous demand for energy coupled with shortfalls in supply will be the norm for the next decade and beyond. Economic development targets anticipate an average annual GNP growth rate of 9 percent between 1995 and 2000. Assuming an energy consumption elasticity coefficient

of 0.48, by 2000 demand for primary energy will total 1.45-1.5 billion tons of standard coal. Raw coal output will need be 1.5 billion tons, requiring an average annual growth of 3.6 percent, crude oil output at 165 million tons, an average annual growth of 2.1 percent, and natural gas output of 25 billion cubic meters, an average annual growth of 6 percent. Looking at the energy industry's current development potential and the state's capacity for investment, these goals will be extremely difficult to reach. However, growth in electric energy production should basically be able to keep pace with national economic development. Power output is expected to reach 1.5 trillion kilowatt hours by 2000, an average annual growth of 8.5 percent.

Alleviating energy shortages will require vigorous adherence to the dual principles of development and economy. First, increased investment is needed. Second, energy consumption must be reduced through repositioning within the industrial structure, accelerating the introduction of new technologies and tightening control over energy resources. Third, exports of energy products should gradually be reduced and imports of crude oil increased as necessary.

The economic growth rate will be slower from 2000 to 2010 than during the previous decade. GNP is expected to grow by approximately 7.2 percent per annum. Moreover, as a result of changes in the industrial structure and increased energy savings, the elasticity coefficient of energy consumption is likely to drop to below 0.4 and output of primary energy increase by approximately 3 percent per annum, easing pressures from the undersupply of power.

2. Raw and processed materials industry. The primary development task for the iron and steel industry is the optimization of product mix while increasing output. Manufacture of products in short supply in China such as oil pipes, silicon sheets, zinc-coated plates, alloy steels and low alloy steels needs be further developed. Investment priority should be given to comprehensive transformation of existing iron and steel companies with the goal of reducing overall energy consumption per ton product to the level attained in the industrially developed countries in the late 1980s. By 2000, China's

steel output is expected to be 120 million tons and rolled steel output 100 million tons. This will result in a shortfall of approximately 10 million tons.

Output of ten nonferrous metals is expected to reach 5.2 million tons by 2000, an average annual growth rate of 5.6 percent.

Production of cement, glass, petrochemicals, sulfuric acid and soda ash is expected to increase by an average of 6 to 10 percent a year.

3. Machine-building and electronics industries. Total output value in the machine-building industry will increase by an average of 15 percent per year between 1995 and 2010. Output value will be 1.5 trillion yuan in 2000 and 3 trillion yuan in 2010. Exports of machinery will generate US$ 25 billion in hard currency in 2000, rising to US$ 100 billion by 2010 as the industry works hard to become the nation's largest generator of foreign exchange.

The mode of development in the machine-building industry will change from quantitative expansion to qualitative improvement. Major products produced in China will begin to catch up with world advanced levels, with the present "technological gap" of approximately 20 years narrowing to 15 years by 2000 and around 10 years by 2010. Leading products of key large-scale enterprises will be upgraded and updated. By 2000, at least 40 percent will be at world advanced levels of the late 1980s and early 1990s, and by 2010, 70 percent will be at world advanced levels of the late 1990s. By 2000, 90 percent of products will meet international standards, rising to 100 percent by 2010.

The electronics industry will stress improvements in key products, notably integrated circuits, new model components, and key materials and equipment. Increased investment, technical transformation and reorganization of enterprises, will be used to construct a number of large enterprise groups and production centers combining scientific research, application, development and production. The output value of the electronics industry will grow by an annual average of approximately 20 percent for the next decade and beyond.

Computers and application software will be at the forefront of the electronics industry. It will be necessary to set up large-scale enterprises integrating scientific research, development and production, developing famous brand products and expanding economic scale. Problems with inefficient scattered production and low level redundant production should be corrected. Everything possible should be done to close the gap between China and the developed countries in the computer industry.

Telecommunications equipment manufacturing is the foundation of the electronic information industry. In the present stage, the key task in telecommunications development is increasing the availability of telephones in both urban and rural areas. It is expected that by 2000, 8 percent of rural households will have telephone lines, up from 2.2 percent in 1994, and 40 percent of urban households will have telephones. If this target is to be reached, telephone capacity will need to increase by an average of more than 40 percent annually during the Ninth Five-Year Plan period (1996-2000). A foundation has been laid for the manufacture of program-controlled switching systems, transmission systems and terminal equipment. Future telecommunications development should aim toward further increasing the Chinese-made telecommunications equipment's market share, closely following international advanced telecommunication technologies, timely upgrading of products and improving competitiveness in the international market.

4. Light industry. Light industry will maintain a high growth rate during the Ninth Five-Year Plan period, ensuring an adequate supply of light industrial goods to meet market demand. The growth rate is likely to slow down after 2000, but production will continue to increase in absolute numbers, satisfying market demand.

The domestic market for light industrial commodities will continue brisk growth for the next ten years and beyond. Supply will slightly exceed demand. Development in light industry will move from quantity to quality and economic returns. Adjustment of the industrial structure, product mix and technological structure will be the central task.

The market for light industrial commodities has gradually been turning to those products characteristic of a more comfortable lifestyle. Air conditioners, interior decoration, modern kitchenware and toilet equipment, instant foods, tourist goods, sports equipment, toys and leisure and entertainment products are selling quite well. There are many levels of consumption, and the Chinese people have begun to move into the middle and high levels. Consumption is ever expanding into new areas and competition is becoming fiercer in the domestic market.

Section Five   Government Industrial Policies and Investment Priorities

Leading industries are not necessarily the industries requiring priority regards government support.

For the most part, leading industries only require the encouragement of appropriate policies; they should not be a priority for government investment. Leading industries already have strong markets and solid profit potential, so they readily attract investors. While some government support is needed in the immediate future given China's less than optimal market for key production elements, most leading industries do not necessarily require substantial, direct government inputs.

Government investment and financial support should prioritize two areas. (1) Some industries without a rapid growth rate and with a share of total output unchanging or likely to decrease, which produce products beneficial to the public as a whole or have a relatively high degree of externality or risk, may have difficulty locating non-government investment. Accordingly, they should receive priority in government investment. Examples would include exceptionally large trans-regional key projects in basic industries and risky high-tech projects requiring huge investment. (2) Support should be given to industries attempting readjustment. Some traditional industries are currently incurring losses across the board, operating under capacity throughout the industry, creating hardships for their workforce. There are four principal causes: (1) Previously, during the period of rapid economic growth, some consumer items became extremely popular. As a result, production capacity for these items was rapidly expanded. However, as consumer incomes greatly increased, consumer preferences quickly changed, leaving the extra production capacity formed during the tide of consumption underutilized. (2) The rise of new industries is often accompanied by the emergence of new industrial areas and the relative decline of the old industrial areas. This structural contradiction has become particularly conspicuous in certain regions. (3) Opening wider to the outside world inevitably brought about certain repercussions as some industries lacking in international competitiveness quickly found themselves in difficult straits. (4) As the domestic economy grows, the relative prices of certain key elements change significantly, influencing relevant products' competitiveness in the international market. The competitiveness of cotton textiles on the international market, for example, is influenced by cotton prices and labor costs. The Chinese economy has been growing rapidly for more than ten years. Radical change in the industrial structure is inevitable. In recent years, difficulties are most apparent in the textile, coal and some traditional machine-building industries. This sequence of industries undergoing structural difficulties approximates the experience of other countries undergoing the same process. These relatively concentrated structural adjustment problems require government support as necessary. Aid policy should be formulated to address the problems inherent in structural adjustment. Leaving the enterprises to manage on their own will slow down the adjustment process, possibly leading to serious social problems.

The experiences of other industrialized countries suggest the following measures to be taken to assist structural adjustment.

1. Industrial adjustment aid funds can be established to help enterprises to discard or change certain practices. The government can

give preferential treatment in funding to enterprises needing to abandon production of goods in excess supply and enter new lines of production. Enterprise making new investment can receive proportionate priority in accessing a loan or preferential terms. They can benefit from a more favorable rate of depreciation or be given some financial compensation for unneeded equipment taken out of service. In some cases governments have "bought" old equipment from enterprises and subsequently scrapped it. These methods are comparatively well suited to industries suffering across the board from the shock of international competition and those industries with a large number of enterprises.

2. Industries especially adversely affected by international competition can be supported through a tariff compensation system. When a country opens wider to the outside world, it often cuts tariff rates. Affected domestic industries may reduce production and lay off employees in response to strong competition from imported goods. Enterprises making use of imported goods, however, will benefit from reduced tariffs. With this situation in mind, a portion of the gains garnered by the latter enterprises as a result of reduced tariffs may be used to fund the readjustment of the former enterprises crippled by international competition, the allotment of aid in proportion to the value ascribed to the unneeded machinery the enterprise has taken out of service. For example, when import duties are cut from 15 percent to 10 percent, benefited enterprises can turn over a portion of their savings to the relevant government organ or a financial institution designated by the government where it will be used to fund low-interest, interest-free or discount loans to enterprises run over by international competition issued in proportion to the assigned value of unneeded equipment these enterprises take out of service. This will help these enterprises to renovate or replace old equipment or move into new lines of production.

3. A special policy can be formulated to deal with the problem of laid-off workers. The government can set up or finance employment agencies and job training organizations. Enterprises can be given government subsidies if they employ laid-off workers from specific

industries or enterprises. Subsidies equal to a certain proportion of the re-employed workers' wages would extend for a given period of time. Enterprises that employ a set proportion of workers laid off from designated enterprises will also receive preferential treatment regards loans and taxation. The duration of unemployment insurance can be extended and subsidies for the unemployed increased. A system encouraging early retirement would also be of use.

4. A complete set of measures in support of readjustment on the regional level can be implemented. In the countries where industry has grown fairly rapidly in recent years, the industries which have lost in importance and have needed to broadly change their line of production have typically been those whose business is closely intertwined with natural resource conditions, concentrated in production areas or otherwise nearby, for example, coal and other mining industries and the textile and metallurgical industries. For this reason, adjustment in these industries is both a question of transfer between industries and adjustment of the regional structure. This necessary coordination increases the difficulty of the adjustment process. Several policies may prove helpful. A special department can be established, funded and given the right to transfer possession of land, enabling the department to manage the development of suitable modern manufacturing industry in the old industrial zone. Preferential policies can be used to attract investment from entrepreneurs from other regions. Investors can be given preferential treatment regards financial administration, taxation and banking. Enterprises employing workers and staff from enterprises now shut down or their children will be given subsidies. If the proportion of workers from such enterprises employed is fairly high, the employers will receive further preferential treatment. If enterprises are willing to re-employ laid-off workers after they receive new training, the government can bear the training expenses. Training and jobs for laid-off workers can be found locally or outside of the area. China can use the above policies adopted in other countries for reference in formulating its own policy in support of industrial readjustment.

Chapter Six   The Development of Rural Enterprises

Township enterprises have developed quickly since the beginning of the reform and the opening. Rural incomes have shot up and great changes have taken place in the countryside, promoting reforms leading to a market economy.

Section One   The Role and Status of Rural Enterprises

I. Changes in the Asset Composition of Rural Enterprises

In 1978, there were 1.524 million rural enterprises in China. By 1995, this number had risen to 22.03 million. Original value of fixed assets rose from 22.96 billion yuan in 1978 to 1.2841 trillion yuan in 1995. The following tables lay out some basic facts concerning rural enterprises.

Table 6-1   Number of Rural Enterprises Under Different Forms of Asset Ownership

Unit: million

Year	Total	Township-owned	Village-owned	Jointly-owned	Individually-owned
1979	1.4804	0.3205	1.1599		
1981	1.3376	0.3352	1.0072		
1985	12.2246	0.4193	1.4304	1.1202	9.2535

1988	18.8819	0.4235	1.1665	1.1999	16.9918
1990	18.5044	0.3878	1.0661	0.9788	16.0707
1992	20.7922	0.3925	1.1275	0.9015	18.3707
1993	23.2100	0.4338	1.2540	1.0384	21.8052
1994	24.9500	0.4200	1.2200	0.7900	22.5200
1995	22.0300	0.4200	1.2000	0.9600	19.4500

Table 6-2   Composition of Rural Enterprises with Different Investors

Unit: %

Year	Total	Township-owned	Village-owned	Jointly-owned	Individually-owned
1979	100	21.65	78.35		
1981	100	25.07	74.93		
1085	100	3.43	11.70		
1988	100	2.24	6.18	6.35	85.22
1990	100	2.10	5.76	5.29	86.85
1992	100	1.89	5.24	4.34	88.35
1993	100	1.77	5.10	4.23	88.90
1944	100	1.68	4.89	3.17	90.26
1995	100	1.91	5.45	4.36	88.29

Table 6-3   Total Output Value of Rural Enterprises

Unit: billion yuan

Year	Total	Agriculture	Industry	Building	Transport	Commerce & Services
1979	55.225	3.960	42.534	4.881	2.323	1.727
1981	73.665	4.012	56.785	7.053	2.523	3.293
1985	275.504	5.969	184.591	41.510	19.190	24.273
1988	701.776	12.382	49.990	84.885	48.451	57.668

1990	958.111	15.126	709.705	93.781	68.583	70.014
1992	1,758.397	24.744	1,319.337	175.098	110.223	128.995
1993	2,902.260	41.346	2,355.868	235.825	200.069	254.594
1994	4,537.849	59.639	3,468.800	417.965	230.192	361.253
1995	6,891.523	101.876	5,125.917	633.597	416.684	618.533

Note: The figures in this table were calculated on the basis of current prices for the given years.

Table 6-4   Composition of Rural Enterprise Total Output Value

Unit: %

Year	Total	Agriculture	Industry	Building	Transport	Animal Husbandry & Services
1979	100	7.17	77.02	8.48	4.21	3.13
1981	100	5.45	77.09	9.57	3.42	4.47
1985	100	2.17	67.00	15.07	6.95	8.87
1988	100	1.76	71.15	12.10	6.90	8.09
1990	100	1.58	74.07	10.16	6.88	7.31
1992	100	1.41	75.03	9.96	6.27	7.33
1993	100	1.30	74.14	10.25	6.30	8.01
1994	100	1.31	76.44	9.21	5.07	7.96
1995	100	1.48	74.38	9.19	6.05	8.98

In 1995, rural enterprises totalled 2,713.2 billion yuan in assets, including 1,449.3 billion yuan of liquid assets, accounting for 53.42 percent of the total and 12.7 billion yuan of intangible assets, 0.3 percent of the total. Total liabilities came to 1,448.5 billion yuan, including liquid liabilities of 1,192.8 billion yuan, 82.84 percent of the total. Bank loans totalled 444.1 billion yuan, accounting for 30.66 percent of all liabilities.

Table 6-5   The Amount of Liquid Funds in Fixed Assets of Rural Enterprises

Year	1978	1980	1990	1991	1993	1994	1995
Original value of fixed assets (bn yuan)	22.96	32.63	285.71	338.52	643.90	886.81	1,284.1
Norm circulating capital (bn yuan)	9.50	17.72	168.40	204.42	809.6	1,056.57	1,449.3*

*The figures for the last three years are for liquid assets.

Table 6-6   Rural Enterprises' Annual Bank Loan Balance

Unit: bn yuan

Year	1978	1980	1990	1991	1992	1993	1994	1995
Bank loan balance	2.12	5.30	116.29	144.38	187.68	220.85	340.2	444.1
Fixed asset loan balance	1.17	2.29	16.22	24.23	34.82			

Economic relations between China's rural enterprises and other countries and regions have been strengthened in recent years. By the end of 1995, 38,743 rural enterprises were jointly operated with investors from Hong Kong, Taiwan, Macao and foreign countries, utilizing US$ 31.8 billion in foreign capital.

II. The Role of Rural Enterprises in Social and Economic Development

The development of the rural enterprises has played a very important role in promoting social and economic progress.

1. Rural enterprises have strengthened the national economy. In

1995 they accounted for 25.3 percent of GDP. Township and village level industrial enterprises alone accounted for 32.8 percent of the national industrial added value. Above all, rural enterprises serve farm production and the peasants' livelihood, providing transportation, storage, preservation and processing of agricultural products and supplying peasants with small machinery, chemical fertilizers and seeds. Coal, electric power, cement, garments and home appliances produced by rural enterprises account for a definite portion of total national production. Nearly all traditional building materials, such as bricks, tiles, sand and gravel, and lime, currently sold are produced by rural enterprises. The manufacture of traditional iron and wooden farm implements, the manufacture and repair of small and medium-sized farm machinery, and the supply of spare parts and accessories for large farm machinery are almost entirely the province of rural enterprises. Output of other products are also significant within total national output. For example, 17 percent of electronics and telecommunications equipment, 26 percent of machinery, 43 percent of foodstuffs, 40 percent of raw coal, 40 percent of cement and 80 percent of garments are produced by rural enterprises.

2. They have raised peasant incomes. Total wages paid by rural enterprises totalled 438.1 billion yuan in 1995, 45.9 percent more than in 1994. Per-capita wages came to 3,553 yuan, 29.6 percent more than in the previous year. Nationwide, peasants received 467 yuan in per-capita net income from rural enterprises, nearly 30 percent of the total rural per-capita net income. This was an increase of 143 yuan over the previous year, representing 39.9 percent of the total increase in per-capital net income. In addition, in some areas where rural enterprises are more developed the enterprises provide peasants with housing, cultivation of farmland, buy them chemical fertilizers, seeds and farm machinery and provide free education for their children.

3. They have increased local revenues. Rural enterprises paid 128 billion yuan in taxes in 1995, an increase of 20.3 percent over 1994. Per-capita taxes paid came to 1,166 yuan, 181 yuan more than the previous year.

Table 6-7   Growth of Tax Payments by Rural Enterprises

Year	1978	1980	1990	1992	1993	1994	1995
Total tax payments (bn yuan)	2.20	2.56	39.14	63.69	105.9	106.7	128.0
Percentage of national tax receipts	4.2	4.5	13.9	20.3	24.9	20.8	21.2

4. They have promoted development in a wide variety of undertakings in rural areas. Rural enterprises have appropriated a portion of their profits for use in education and the construction of small towns and townships and social welfare. Profits from township- and village-level enterprises used for expanded reproduction came to 14.11 billion yuan in 1993, 16.5 percent of the total profits of 83.2 billion yuan; 16.4 billion yuan in profits were used on various projects, 19.76 percent of the total profits. Of this, 3.81 billion yuan was used to subsidize agricultural production, (23.18 percent), 3.15 billion yuan for collective or individual welfare, (19.16 percent), 2.52 billion yuan for rural education, (15.33 percent) and 2.08 billion yuan for the construction of small towns and townships, (12.56 percent).

5. They have increased exports. Total delivery value of export products produced by rural enterprises came to 539.5 billion yuan in 1995, an increase of 40.2 percent over the previous year, exceeding the industrial growth rate by 7 percentage points. More than 40 percent of total national export volume comes from rural enterprises.

6. Jobs have been provided for hitherto surplus rural workforce. Farm acreage has decreased and the degree of agricultural mechanization risen; there are currently about 200 million surplus rural workers. Approximately 50 percent have been absorbed by rural enterprises. By the end of 1995, 129 million workers were employed by rural enterprises, 20.67 percent of the national workforce and 28.67 percent of the rural workforce. Nearly one in ten Chinese work in a rural enterprise.

Section Two   The Development of Rural Enterprises Since 1990

Since the beginning of the 1990s rural enterprises have followed a different development path than in the 1970s and 1980s.

I. Development Has Been Accelerated

Rural enterprises have developed faster this decade. Nationwide, rural enterprises' income from operations rose from 728.4 billion yuan in 1990 to 5,729.9 billion yuan in 1995, an increase of 5,001.5 billion yuan or nearly 800 percent in five short years, an average increase of 51.06 percent per year.

Table 6-8   Growths of Rural Enterprises' Total Output Value (1990-1995)

Year	1990	1991	1992	1993	1994	1995
Rise over previous year, %	13.9	21.3	51.3	65.1	35.0	61.8

II. Rural Enterprises Have Become Larger

In 1995, rural enterprises averaged 41,400 yuan in original value of fixed assets per enterprise and produced an average output value of 313,000 yuan. These figures may be compared with 15,600 yuan in original value of fixed assets and 22,300 yuan in output value averaged in 1978.

In 1995, 4,000 rural enterprises had 100 million yuan or more in their respective original value of fixed assets and 19,196 had 10 million yuan or more in their respective original value of fixed assets. The 500 largest rural enterprises in 1993 on average employed 1,330 persons and had sales income of nearly 200 million yuan. The expansion of rural enterprises has greatly changed the rural economy. In 1995, the output value of rural enterprises in 16 provinces and municipalities exceeded 100 billion yuan. The output value of those in Shandong, Jiangsu and Zhejiang provinces, the largest nationally, came to 918.71 billion yuan, 889 billion yuan and 747.82 billion yuan respectively.

III. The Export-Oriented Economy Has Grown Rapidly

Since the early 1990s, particularly since Deng Xiaoping's significant exhortations during his inspection tour of the south at the beginning of 1992, the export-oriented economy of the rural enterprises has nearly doubled. The total delivery value of the export commodities produced by the rural enterprises rose from 46.2 billion yuan to 539.5 billion yuan between 1990 and 1995. The absolute value increased by 11.7 times. The average annual growth rate was 63.48 percent, 18.41 percentage points higher than in the previous five years. The total delivery value of export commodities produced by rural enterprises in the four years 1986 to 1989 was 89.9 billion yuan, only 16.67 percent of that for 1995.

Exports from rural enterprises have shown the greatest increase in foreign exchange earnings of any sector. Net increases in the delivery value of export commodities produced by rural enterprises accounted for two thirds of the net increase of the country's all export commodities during the Eighth Five-Year Plan period (1991-1995). By the end of 1995, 130,000 rural enterprises were producing export commodities, 396 had the right to import and export goods independently, and 38,700 had established equity joint ventures or contractual joint ventures with overseas investors, making use of US$ 31.8 billion in foreign investment. Another 3,673 enterprises have operations set up abroad.

IV. The Quality of the Rural Enterprises Has Been Further Improved

Most peasant-financed-and-established rural enterprises that mushroomed with the economic reform and opening had the problems of a low quality workforce, obsolete equipment and inadequate product quality in the 1980s. Work was labor-intensive. A general survey taken in 1984 found only 22,000 employees of rural enterprises with specialized professional qualifications, 0.9 per thousand rural enterprise employees. Only 5,000 of these were assistant engineers or more highly qualified, mostly working in management. By the end of 1995, rural enterprises employed 3.17 million specialized technicians; 880,000 were engineers or more highly qualified, more than double the 1992 figure of 307,000.

At the same time the quality of the employees was being improved, rural enterprises have been actively importing new technologies, new equipment and advanced managerial expertise. The contribution made to products by technological advances in 1995 was 10 percentage points higher than in 1990. The organic constitution of technological equipment and capital was greatly increased. Seventy percent of rural enterprises have adopted fairly good management systems, and total quality control was introduced in all major enterprises. Rural enterprises have won 3,342 best quality prizes from the ministries, 69 national gold and silver prizes and 50 international prizes. Many rural enterprises which started as producers of primary products made from agricultural products are now producing high-tech products with high added value.

V. The Industrial Structure Has Become Increasingly Rationalized

Year by year, the shares of agriculture and industry in the rural enterprises' total output value has decreased as that of transportation and commerce have increased. In 1978, the total output value of rural enterprises (then labelled enterprises owned by communes and brigades) was 49.5 billion yuan. Agriculture accounted for 7.5 percent, industry 77.8 percent, construction 7 percent, but transportation and commerce only 3.8 percent. By 1995, agriculture accounted for only 1.48 percent of the total output value of rural enterprises (now labelled enterprises owned by townships and villages), industry 74.38 percent, construction 9.19 percent, transportation 5.97 percent and commerce 8.98 percent.

The share of output value generated by rural light industrial enterprises that save energy, make full use of the local resources and meet market demands has risen and is indeed higher than that for total light industry nationwide. In 1980 light industry created 48.8 percent of the total rural enterprise industrial output value and heavy industry 51.2 percent. Agricultural products were used as raw materials in the production of 48.5 percent of the output value of light industry. Mining produced 18.1 percent of the output value of heavy industry, raw materials 16.1 percent and processing 65.8 percent. In 1994, light industry produced 50.6 percent of rural industrial output value and heavy industry 49.4 percent. Agricultural products were used as raw materials in 57.4 percent of light industry. Mining accounted for 10.8 percent of heavy industry, raw materials 21.4 percent and processing 68.4 percent.

VI. Relations Between the Cities and the Countryside Have Been Increasingly Coordinated

The development of rural enterprises has helped to alter the oppositional positioning of the city and the countryside within the economic structure. Urban enterprises have almost entirely departed from the manufacture of medium and small farm implements, traditional building materials, spare parts and accessories for agricultural machinery, small household items and machinery repair, their place taken by rural enterprises. At the same time, rural enterprises have moved into the manufacture of mineral products, garments, machinery, paper, chemicals and other traditional products, gaining a portion of the market. As production and technological levels continue to rise, many rural enterprises have started manufacturing electronics, new materials, fine chemicals and precision instruments.

Better coordinated urban-rural relations can also be seen in commodity circulation and organization of enterprises. The role of state-owned commerce as the main channel for circulation of goods is manifested not only in the sale of products for state-owned industrial enterprises, but also those of rural enterprises. This has played a great role in accelerating rural enterprises' product turnover and increasing economic returns. Some enterprise groups organized in recent years have broken through the barriers between urban and rural areas and the forms of ownership to include not only state-owned enterprises, urban and rural collective enterprises, but also urban and rural privately-owned enterprises. New forms of organization have strengthened specialized cooperation between enterprises, raising production capacity and providing a still broader arena for the development of rural enterprises.

VII. Progress Has Been Made in Legislation

Before the mid-1980s the Chinese Government had few policies or position papers directly related to rural enterprises. Then, beginning in the late 1980s, increasing importance was attached to such legislation. Following the publication of the Regulations of the People's Republic of China on Rural Collectively-Owned Enterprises in early 1990s, the government formulated laws and regulations concerning overall reform, industrial policy, administration of industry and commerce, credit, taxation, exports, enterprise management, quality control, science and technology, safety, environmental protection, education and training. The Law of the People's Republic of China on Township-Owned Enterprises, which came into force on January 1, 1997, marked the beginning of a new phase of national legislation governing rural enterprises.

VIII. Imbalance in Regional Development

The development of rural enterprises in different regions is not balanced. This is due to differences in history, geography, external environment and understanding. If China is divided into eastern, central and western regions[1], differences in the development of rural enterprises are striking. Development in the eastern region far exceeds that in the other two regions both in quantity or quality.

Uneven regional development is also manifested in great differences in levels of production, technology, management and operations. Currently, automation, mechanization and manual labor are all used in production by rural enterprises. Those in the coastal areas have made more use of foreign capital and acquired more production technology and managerial expertise from overseas. As a result, they possess a higher degree of automation in production and better quality management. Some rural enterprises that began their development earlier have achieved mechanization or semi-mechanization, and a few automation. In areas where rural enterprises were started later, especially in old revolutionary base areas, areas inhabited by ethnic minorities, border areas and impoverished areas, production and technological levels are very low. Manual labor is often the rule due to shortages of electric power, investment and technicians. Some of these enterprises even use human or animal power to drive simple machines. Their managerial level is very poor, with some still using the small peasant household style of management.

The imbalance in the development of rural enterprises can also be seen in differences in foreign trade. In 1995 more than 90 percent of total delivery value of export products was produced in the eastern region. Jiangsu was the leader with a delivery value of more than 140 billion yuan, 26.67 percent of the national total.

---

[1] The department in charge of the rural enterprises has divided the country into three regions on the basis of the degree of development of rural enterprises and location. The eastern region comprises Beijing, Tianjin, Hebei, Liaoning, Shanghai, Jiangsu, Zhejiang, Fujian, Shandong and Guangdong; the central region includes Shanxi, Jilin, Heilongjiang, Anhui, Jiangxi, Henan, Hubei, Hunan, Sichuan and Shaanxi; and the western region includes Inner Mongolia, Guangxi, Hainan, Guizhou, Yunnan, Gansu, Qinghai, Ningxia, Xinjiang and Tibet.

**Table 6-9 Leading Indicators for Rural Collective Enterprises
in Three Regions (1995)**

Indicator	Unit	Total	Eastern region	Western region	Central region
Number of enterprises	1,000	1,618.3	701	128.7	788.6
Proportion	%	100	43.32	7.96	48.73
Employment	million person	60.6043	34.0075	4.1355	22.4613
Proportion	%	100	56.11	6.82	37.06
Original value of fixed assets	bn yuan	912.3	642.2	46.1	224
Proportion	%	100	70.39	5.05	24.55
Value added	bn yuan	935.9	625.2	34.3	276.5
Proportion	%	100	66.80	3.66	29.54
Profits & taxes	bn yuan	177.5	116.5	5.8	55.2
Proportion	%	100	65.63	3.27	31.04

The imbalance in the development of rural enterprises has become an important factor affecting differences in economic and social development in different regions.

Section Three   Major Contradictions Present in Rural Enterprises and Future Development Trends

I. Major Contradictions Present in the Course of Development of Rural Enterprises

Rural enterprises are a key component of China's rural economy. Greatly developing rural enterprises is essential to accelerating modernization in the countryside. However, many contradictions remain in their course of development.

1. The operating mechanisms and management systems of rural enterprises are not well suited. Generally speaking, the operating mechanism is a market mechanism and is fairly flexible, promoting its own development and market reforms in the economic structure.

However, as the reform has been deepened, weak points in the rural enterprise system have gradually become apparent, most notably in the operating mechanisms of collective enterprises at the township and village levels which have weakened and deteriorated. While progress has been made in ownership reforms, many difficult problems have yet to be solved and key relationships defined. Moreover, economic administration organizations at both the township and village levels are overly involved in the production and business activities of enterprises, preventing the enterprises from having the decision making power they should have. Some enterprises have continued with the "iron rice bowl" of permanent employment and the "collective rice bowl" of sharing equally in all gains, practices characteristic of state-owned enterprises and supposedly discouraged by the reforms.

2. There is a contradiction between increased production capacity and limited market capacity. Markets both at home and abroad have indicated their limited capacity for traditional products; there is little justification for increased production of such products. Enterprises must adjust their product mix and promote product upgrading. Unfortunately, rural enterprises have low levels of technological expertise and are frequently unable to develop new products. Therefore they cannot properly respond to market demand.

3. The weakness of rural enterprises seems incompatible with increasing market competitiveness. This is particularly evident in their loose management style. Many enterprises still make management decisions based only on their own experiences and past practices and retain the same management personnel that have been in place for years. Product quality is not high and market competitiveness is enervated.

4. Rapid growth runs in the face of short supply. Shortages of capital needed for technical transformation force more than 80 percent of rural enterprises to rely on outmoded equipment and old production technologies, resulting in low productivity, high expenditure and poor product quality. Shortages of working funds prevent many enterprises

from getting sufficient supplies of raw materials, fuel and electric power, and as a result they operate at substantially less than full capacity. Moreover, they lack a sufficient high-quality workforce, including engineers, technicians, managerial personnel and skilled workers. China has not yet fully established a market for key production elements. There are no channels for the planned supply of production elements and they cannot be bought on a developed market. This greatly restricts further development.

5. A contradiction exists between the intensification of production and the scattered distribution of rural enterprises. This scattered distribution is the primary reason behind the current low degree of intensification of production. Farmland is wasted and pollution worsened. There are no available public infrastructure facilities available, so enterprises themselves must build roads and water and power supply systems, increasing necessary capital construction expenditure. Located in distant, isolated areas with poor transportation facilities and little access to information, they are presented with difficulties in organizing specialized cooperation in production. The only way to rectify this situation is to concentrate production, setting up economic development zones and small industrial zones and accelerating the construction of small towns.

II. Development Trends for Rural Enterprises

The Chinese Government has adopted a series of reform measures in an attempt to cure these contradictions and promote faster and more healthy development of rural enterprises. As a result, new trends have emerged and will continue to emerge.

1. Rural enterprises will more broadly and deeply participate in the market. With the deepening of market oriented reform, all markets will be gradually optimized, the role of government further alter, and rural reform made more thoroughgoing. These changes will provide the objective environment for rural enterprises to delve still further into the market. As outlined previously, the rural enterprises' operating

mechanism is a market mechanism. The market is in fact a primary market: the market regulates the purchase of capital goods and the sale of products. Regards other key production elements, a natural economy of self-sufficiency remains. For example, the land an enterprise occupies is not assigned a market price and is used almost without compensation. The workforce is drawn from the local community, as, for the most part, is capital. Property rights are not transferable. These will be fully regulated by the market in the future.

2. Rural enterprises, currently scattered in distribution, will become increasingly concentrated. In 1992, 92 percent of the 20.79 million rural enterprises were located in natural villages, 7 percent in small towns and 1 percent in county towns. This situation inspired the Resolution of the Central Committee of the Communist Party of China on Certain Questions Concerning the Establishment of the Socialist Market Economic System to state the necessity of "strengthening planning, directing the proper concentration of rural enterprises, remolding and making full use of existing small towns and building new small towns in order to effect a more reasonable distribution of enterprises." In accordance with the principles outlined, the state will encourage planning at the county level and provide effective plane layouts for small town construction. All new projects with a given economic scale must establish fixed production sites for enterprises and be built at planned locations as prescribed in the plane layouts. Those built within these requirements will receive preferential treatment in enterprise registration and obtaining a site. Older enterprises will be relocated at the time they undergo technical transformation. Needless to say, household crafts which would not benefit from such concentration of operations would not be subject to these mandatory measures.

3. Employees will be further removed from agriculture. The development of small towns, gradual changes in the residency controls for small towns, peasants' new permission to work or do business in small towns, and the lawful sale of land use rights will further promote

the separation of rural enterprise employees from their former life in agriculture.

This separation is a product of the division of labor and an expression of social progress, beneficial to both industry and agriculture, and will bring about a profound change in the nature of rural enterprises.

4. A new pattern will emerge in the property rights structure. Currently, rural enterprises are owned by townships, villages, jointly by households or by individuals. The principal investors in collective enterprises at the township and village levels are the townships and villages and their management is controlled by the township governments and villagers' committees. This circumstance is not conducive to effecting a separation of government administration and enterprise management. The enterprises owned jointly by several households use a cooperative shares system. This system does not benefit accelerated development of production as enterprises expand in scale and technologies and products are upgraded. Businesses run by individuals are typically weak financially and easily fall prey to fierce market competition. These shortcomings point out the need for change in the current property rights system.

5. Development will be accelerated in the central and western regions for the following reasons. First, the central government has attached great importance to the development in the central and western regions. After issuing the Decision of the State Council on Accelerating the Development of Township-Owned Enterprises in the Central and Western Regions, the State Council formulated the Project to Support the Poor. The Ministry of Agriculture has also formulated and published the Project for East-West Cooperation of Township Enterprises. These documents all contain forceful measures and preferential policies for encouraging development of rural enterprises in the central and western regions. Second, governments at all levels and the masses of peasants in the central and western regions have learned that the development of rural enterprises offers the only way for them to end poverty and gain prosperity and are now very

enthusiastic about achieving this goal. Third, the western region has abundant mineral, agricultural and animal husbandry resources. Fourth, the industrial structure of the rural enterprises in the coastal areas is currently undergoing readjustment thus opening a window of opportunity for development in the other regions. Fifth, international cooperation is being to spread from the coast to the inland. Sixth, the State Council has decided to appropriate an additional 10 billion yuan annually for use as special loans for the development of rural enterprises in the central and western regions.

These measures accelerated and will continue to accelerate the development of rural enterprises in the central and western regions. Significant success has already been won in the project encouraging cooperation between the east and west, drawing much notice. Many provinces and municipalities in the east have made plans for moves in the west. Their counterparts in the central and western regions are actively selecting projects and building small industrial districts. A national model district for east-west cooperation in the development of rural enterprises is now being built. These measures are achieving their goal. In 1993, 6.63 percent of the nation's rural enterprises were in the west, by 1995, 7.96 percent; share of employment in such enterprises increased from 5.77 percent to 6.82 percent, share of gross output value from 2.89 percent to 3.66 percent and share of total profits and taxes from 3.58 percent to 3.79 percent.

III. Rural Enterprises' Prospects for Growth

Rural enterprises will develop quickly. By 2010, rural industry will account for approximately half of national industrial output value, becoming the most potent force in industrialization. Growth in other sectors, particularly tertiary industry, will be spurred on by the expansion of rural enterprises. By 2010, tertiary industry's share of the total output value of rural enterprises, currently approximately 15 percent, is expected to double to account for nearly one third of the total output value.

Rural enterprise total output value grew at an average annual rate of over 30 percent in the 15 years following the initiation of economic reform. An annual growth rate of 33.6 percent was achieved from 1981 to 1991 and 35 percent in 1994 over the previous year. This growth came at a speed three times that of increase in output value nationally over the same period. (From 1981 to 1991 the national average annual growth rate was 10.8 percent). Such expansion increased rural enterprises' share of the national economy. Rural enterprises' contribution to national total output value rose from 7.2 percent in 1978 to 32.1 percent in 1992, an average increase of 1.8 percentage points per year. If this rate of increase continues, rural enterprises would supply approximately 46 percent of national total output value by 2000 and 60 percent by 2010. Given the influence of rerouting the rural enterprise system and increasing basic values, growth will presumably slow down between 1995 and 2010, with the annual growth rate in total output value dropping from 30 percent to around 20 percent. However, this will still serve to more than double the national growth rate for total output value. If rural enterprises' share of the nation's total output value continues to grow by only one percentage point a year, rural enterprises will supply 45 percent of the nation's total output value by 2000 and nearly 60 percent by 2010.

Rural industry accounts for the bulk of rural enterprises, with output value constituting three quarters of the total for such enterprises. The rapid growth of rural industry has certainly engendered the great rise in the output value of rural enterprises. Moreover, the development of rural industry has greatly changed the nation's industrial structure. The output value of rural industry was only 38.5 billion yuan in 1978, accounting for only 11.6 percent of the output value of state-owned industry and 9 percent of the national total for that year. An annual growth rate of over 30 percent, (33.4 percent in the years of 1981-93), enabled rural industries quick rise in importance and share of the nation's total industrial output value, (which experienced an average annual growth rate of around 13 percent between 1979 and 1994). By the end of 1993, the total output value of

126

the rural industry was 2.21 trillion yuan, about 44 percent of the national total industrial output value, almost equal to the output value of state-owned industry (2.27 trillion yuan in 1993). In 1994, the growth rate in value added by rural industry at the township level, (27.3 percent), was four times that of the state-owned enterprises, (6.8 percent). Of course, as discussed above, with base values increasing, the growth rate of rural industry will gradually slow down from around 30 percent to below 20 percent, still about twice the growth rate for all of industry. Even at this slower rate, rural industry's share of all industry nationally will continue to grow by 1.5 percentage points annually. By 2010 rural industrial output value will account for approximately 60 percent of the national total industrial output value.

Beginning in 1992, the State Statistical Bureau has used value added as an indicator of economic development. By deducting transferred value consumed, the value added indicator provides a more objective reflection of economic development than total output value indicator. Generally speaking, because the organic composition of rural enterprises is low and most products are labor intensive, the growth rate of value added by rural enterprises lags behind the growth rate of total output value. Nonetheless, the growth rate of the former is still higher than that of state-owned enterprises, enabling rural enterprises to gain in importance and share of GNP. In industry, for example, rural enterprises added 700 billion yuan in value, (38 percent of industrial value added nationally), 30 percent more than the previous year. Value added created by township-owned industry grew by 27.3 percent. This growth rate was about 1.5 times the industrial growth rate nationally. If this rate continues, the value added by rural industry will account for 50 percent of the national industrial value added by 2010.

Rural enterprise tertiary industry will also maintain rapid growth rate for the next ten years and beyond, contributing to the enterprises' increasing importance and share of the national economy. The annual growth rate for rural enterprise tertiary industry will be maintained at approximately 25 percent, slightly higher than the anticipated growth rate for rural industry for the years from 1996 to 2010. By 2010, rural enterprise tertiary industry will account for one third of the total value added created by rural enterprises.

Chapter Seven　Development of
the Construction Industry

The construction industry will be a pillar industry of economic development for the next ten years and beyond. This chapter will deal with the development of this industry, its future and attendant policy choices.

Section One　A Review of the Development of the Construction Industry

I. Achievements in the Development of the Construction Industry Since the Initiation of Reform and Opening

The construction industry has grown rapidly since the reform and opening era began. Value added by the construction industry increased by 531 percent during the years from 1979 to 1994, an average annual growth rate of 11.4 percent, higher than that for the GDP.

During this time, considerable changes have taken place in the construction industry, which may be viewed from three perspectives.

1. The scale of the workforce continuously expanded. In 1994 31.88 million persons worked in construction, 5.18 percent of the nation's total workforce. This was 2.64 times as many as in 1980, representing an average annual increase of 8.4 percent. The same year, there were 94,942 construction companies, 65 percent more than in 1980.

2. The technical and equipment levels have continually improved. By the end of 1994, construction companies owned 2.9526 million

machines with a net worth of 50.584 billion yuan, providing 60.3494 million kilowatts of power.

3. Production capacity continually expanded. In 1994 total output value for the construction industry was 768.436 billion yuan, and per-capita labor productivity was 14,458.5 yuan. The same year 323.833 million square meters of floor space was built, including 141.4297 million square meters by state-owned companies and 176.74 million square meters by collective enterprises.

II. Reforms in the Construction Industry's Management System

Reforms may be divided into eight areas.

1. The system whereby contracts are awarded has been reformed. Administrative allocation has been replaced by competitive bidding. This has opened the construction business, bringing in a market mechanism.

2. The business operations and management system of state-owned construction companies have been changed with the introduction of a number of variants of the economic responsibility system, primarily in the form of contracts. In the future, state-owned companies will have responsibility for managing a contracted project ensuring a set profit for the state; profits in excess of this amount will be divided. Profits for the company will increase progressively and assets increase in value. Construction companies will contract for a budgeted cost plus an additional coefficient, with building costs being determined per square meter, per unit production capacity and so on. Within the company itself, projects will be on a contract basis with personal financial responsibility for the risk involved. The reform is gradually doing away with the old "big rice pot" system wherein all employees shared equally in profits regardless of their contributions. Responsibility, decision-making power and potential for profits have been combined. This has aroused great enthusiasm from both the companies and their workers.

3. The old system whereby a company only use its permanent workforce has been made more flexible, allowing the use of contracted and temporary workers. At the same time, the supply of workers is increasingly being handled through personnel centers, and work in these centers is being strengthened.

4. The wage system has been changed. State-owned companies have adopted a system wherein the worker is paid a contracted amount for every 100 yuan in output value. The old system wherein a company's total wages were approved by the state has been replaced by a new system under which the state fixes a scale factor for wages and output value. The company relies on the finished output value to determine the corresponding total wages. The new wage system embodies the distribution principle of more pay for more work, while giving a company the power to allocate wages.

5. The organization and style of work has lost its former rigidity, now being determined by the individual project. The goal of the project becomes the target and this determines the organization of project management groups and a dynamic, flexible, optimized integration of key production elements. This new approach supercedes the old practice wherein a company's internal administrative system organized work inflexibly in line with a set hierarchy, thus failing to take advantage of economy of scale.

6. The boundaries between the systems of enterprise ownership have been broken through. A systematic reform has been brought about. A general engineering contract is made for the entire project. The body of work is accomplished through contracts for construction, supplemented by specialized and labor subcontracts. This serves to develop the specialization of work and encourages the taking advantage of the respective strengths of different systems of ownership. Step by step, the current situation wherein state-owned enterprises, big or small, do the complete range of construction work, is being changed.

7. The enterprise operational structure has been adjusted and operations diversified. Construction companies no longer work strictly

in construction. They operate in other areas, increasing returns, reducing the risk of a single line of work and provide jobs for their surplus workers.

8. Market control has been strengthened and the macro regulation mechanism improved. First, a quality control system has been adopted for construction companies and strict controls exercised over the quality of the workforce. Second, a supervisory system for construction projects works to ensure quality. This new management system meets the needs of developing the market economy and promotes the optimization of the market.

Section Two   Assessment of the Status of the Construction Industry

The construction industry occupies a very important place in the national economy. As a result of its fast growth since the initiation of the reform and opening policy, its value added rose from 3.8 percent of the GDP in 1978 to 6.5 percent in 1994. Despite significant ups and downs resulting from fluctuations in fixed asset investment, development has been unusually fast, advancing along with overall economic development and the reform of the economic system in a market environment of growing investment.

I. The Relationship Between Growth in the Construction Industry and the Changes in the National Economy

The extent of change in construction output value exceeded that of total output value most of years since 1949. During the First Five-Year Plan period (1953-57), for example, total output value grew at an average of 11.3 percent while that of the construction industry averaged 18.8 percent, a rate greater than in other sectors. Total output value decreased 0.4 percent during the Second Five-Year Plan period

(1958-65), but that of the construction industry plummeted 10.2 percent, a drop several times that in any other industry.

One can by and large find the same pattern comparing the annual GNP growth rate with growth rates for different industries. During the years from 1978 to 1992, GNP averaged 8.98 percent in growth annually; value added by industry averaged an annual increase of 10.75 percent, construction industry 10.51 percent, transportation, posts and telecommunications 9.40 percent and commerce 6.36 percent.

The above compares average annual change over different periods. Comparisons on a year by year basis would show even more pronounced ups and downs. These major fluctuations were primarily the result of changes in fixed asset investment. Accordingly, changes in investment are reflected in the construction industry's output value.

II. Several Development Characteristics of the Construction Industry

Some Western economists consider rises and falls in the construction industry to be a barometer of economic changes. The Chinese economy is currently in the industrialization stage. Given this, a rapid rate of economic growth will be maintained and the construction industry will have increasing opportunity for development and expanding market potential in the years to come. It will become a leading, pillar industry in the national economy.

In addition to priority growth, the construction industry has the characteristic of relative independence within the nation's industrial structure. This can be demonstrated by its relationship with other industries. The 1981 national economic input-output sheet gives an intermediate demand rate of 0 and an intermediate input rate of 0.726. As shown in Table 7-1, the construction is clearly a final demand type industry. It directly provides material conditions for production and for the people's daily life. Consuming 70 percent of the products manufactured by other industries, it has a major influence on their production. In the 1981 input-output sheet, 26 industrial sectors produce 100 final products. Of these, the construction industry produces 17, second only to agriculture. However, the intermediate input rate of agriculture is only 0.26. The inducement to production is far greater in the construction industry than in agriculture.

Table 7-1

	Small intermediate demand	Large intermediate demand
Large intermediate input product	Final demand type industry	Intermediate type industry
Small intermediate input product	Final demand type primary industry	Intermediate product type primary industry

The associated movement of the construction industry and other industries, the influence of the former on the latter, can further be illustrated by calculating the relevant ratios of the results involved.

The degree of impact of one industry on others is referred to as the force of impact; the reciprocal degree of receiving this influence is called the degree of induction. If either of these two ratios for a given industry is greater or lesser than one it indicates that the force of impact or degree of induction for that industry is greater or lesser than the average for all industries. The force of impact for the construction industry was 1.165 according to figures in the 1981 input-output sheet and 1.192 in 1987, both above average; the degree of induction was 0.670 in 1981, the lowest of 26 industrial sectors, and 0.445 in 1987, the lowest among 33 industrial sectors. Construction's force of impact was the fifth among the 26 sectors in 1981 and the sixth among the 33 sectors in 1987. These ratios confirm the above analysis: changes in the industrial structure have little effect on the construction industry, while the construction industry's influence on other industries is substantial.

Although the construction industry's force of impact ratio is not the highest, its production inducement ratio as determined by the characteristics of its product is very high. Figures provided in the 1981 input-output sheet provide a production inducement ratio of 0.733 for the construction industry. That is to say, if total demand for final products increases by one quantitative unit, the construction industry will induce production of 0.733 quantitative units.

Finally, the status and function of the construction industry can be inferred by calculating an income elasticity ratio. Table 7-2 compares the income elasticity ratios for five industrial sectors.

Table 7-2   Income Elasticity Ratios for Five Major Industrial Sectors

	Agriculture	Industry	Construction	Transportation	Commerce
1953-92	0.97	1.05	1.02	1.01	0.99
1979-92	0.97	1.04	1.01	1.01	0.99

For convenience in making comparisons, the income elasticity ratios were calculated using average increase in output value as an approximation of average increase in product demand. During the 40 years between 1953 and 1992 and the 1979-92 reform period, the construction industry has consistently shown strong income elasticity of demand. Although the growth rate for fixed asset investment slowed with the introduction of government controls after 1989, affecting growth in construction, the income elasticity of demand for the construction industry has remained quite large. It has a broad market demand potential and has the potential and objective conditions for future economic development.

Four characteristics of the construction industry have been described.

1. The building industry has relatively independence within the evolution of the industrial structure and a small degree of induction in its relations with other industries. The rise or fall of other industries

does not directly affect growth in the construction industry. As long as investment demand expands within overall economic growth, it has opportunity for development.

2. The construction industry tends to accelerated growth following growth in the national economy. Given the present stage of the economic development in China, the future economic growth rate will remain high; there will be considerable growth in the construction industry.

3. As a final product type industry, construction consumes large quantities of products of other industries, has a large force of impact and provides a strong production inducement for growth in demand for final products. It can promote the development of other industries and has the characteristics of a leading industry.

4. This allows the prognosis that the construction industry can expect a broad market during the course of future economic development. For this reason, development of the construction industry must be stressed so as to meet the requirements of the nation's economic development, making construction a pillar industry of the national economy.

Section Three   Prospects for Development in the Construction Industry over the Next Ten Years and Beyond

I. Factors Determining Future Development of the Construction Industry

Many factors will determine future development of the construction industry. Foremost of these will be the selection of an economic development strategy, the orientation and degree of adjustment to the industrial structure, and the state industrial policy. China's economy will continue to maintain a high growth momentum for the next ten years and longer. A high growth rate will inevitably give rise to a large demand for investment. This will provide opportunity and a market for the construction industry. Still, the scale of investment will be limited to a certain extent in order to rein in the tendency toward blindly pursuing rapid growth in production and the development of the extensive enlarged reproduction. It will be in this environment presenting both opportunities and limits that the construction industry will seek development.

II. Analysis of Prospects for Development

As stated above, growth in the construction industry has consistently been related to a given scale of investment. Given market demand for investment and objective conditions limiting the scale of investment, how will China's construction industry fare in the future?

First, adjustment of the structure of the amount of stock does not imply a reduction of incremental investment. On the contrary, stock adjustment often requires coordination with and guidance from incremental investment. Looking at the relationship between ratios of accumulation and consumption formed over many years, the investment rate has more or less hovered around 33 percent, while showing a tendency to gradually rise. This rate of investment provides good market conditions for development in the construction industry. With the growth in the national income, the scale of investment will grow year by year.

Second, with the further deepening of reform and opening, more foreign capital will be used and more overseas projects will be undertaken and labor employed abroad. The market for real estate development will become ever more active and housing will be increasingly commercialized. All this will further increase demand for construction.

1. Housing construction will be a continually ongoing undertaking. Housing construction in urban and rural areas averaged 860 million square meters a year between 1985 and 1992. The peak year of 1988 saw more than 1 billion square meters of housing completed. In 1994

approximately 800 million square meters of housing was completed. This included 172.03 million square meters constructed by state-owned companies with an investment of 159.72 billion yuan. At least 180 million square meters of urban housing construction annually is projected by 2000. Reforms in the urban housing system and changes in the consumption structure will inspire individuals to buy houses fueling further increases in spending on housing. This presents the greatest latent market for construction.

2. With the rise of the real estate industry, particularly with the liberalization of the real estate market, market demand for housing will grow. More development capital will be brought into play in close coordination with housing development, housing system reform and paid land use, spurring further growth in the construction industry. Construction companies themselves can take advantage of conditions to build housing for sale, advancing their own growth.

3. The Chinese construction industry remains a labor-intensive industry. This can be an advantage in providing labor for overseas employment and in undertaking projects overseas, given the industry's abundance of comparatively cheap labor. Much can be done in the evolving international economy, especially in Asia. Chinese construction companies can find markets overseas, opportunities for further growth.

4. With technological development and the deepening of structural reform, a number of high-tech industries will come into being. The rise of such industries and the development of cultural endeavors will provide a certain demand for construction.

5. China has great potential demand for building products. The economy is growing rapidly and urbanization is becoming an increasingly salient trend. Infrastructure construction will continue to increase, as transportation and telecommunications are further improved, and the daunting task of refurbishing old cities and building new towns is undertaken. Potential market demand will snowball through multiplied investments with a slight upturn from economic deficits or from the stimulus of infusions of foreign capital. The scale

of investment has repeatedly expanded and contracted over the years, reflecting tides in the latent demand and investment cycles. This demonstrates that there is permanent market demand for construction and opportunities for rapid growth in China's present stage of development. For this reason, Japanese economists have called construction a "perpetually booming" business.

III. Projected Development of the Construction Industry

On the basis of overall targets for national economic development predicted in Chapter Two, growth rates and changes in the internal structure of the construction industry by 2010 have been forecast using both quantitative analysis and qualitative analysis. These forecasts show that the value added and total output value of the construction industry will continue to grow rapidly, with average annual growth rates of 8.5 percent and 9.8 percent respectively, higher than the overall national economic growth rate. Growth in total output value for state-owned construction companies is projected at 7.7 percent, slightly lower than the growth rate for the entire construction industry. However, growth in the total output value for collective construction companies and rural construction brigades are projected at 8.9 percent and 10.5 percent respectively, higher than the projected growth rates of the industry.

The forecasts anticipate the following regular patterns of relationship.

1. Development in the construction industry will be primarily manifested in the growth of rural construction brigades. The faster the rate of growth, the greater will be rural construction brigades' share of total construction output value. This complies with national conditions. Rapid growth in construction explains the abundance of fixed asset investment. This expands the capacity of the building market providing opportunities for rural workforce to find work in the cities and towns, in turn promoting the development of rural construction brigades.

139

2. Growth in the total construction output value helps drive growth in the output of state-owned and collective construction companies and others. The faster the total output value growth rate, the smaller will be building's share of total output value. This demonstrates that the income construction companies derive from sources other than building revolves around building. As building jobs increase the levels of commercialization and creation of product rise. This also indicates that only when basic construction is increasing relatively quickly can technological level and industrialization be raised.

3. Examination of structural changes reveals that the total output value of collectively-owned construction companies' share of the total output value of all construction companies does not increase with growth in the total output value of the construction industry. If the annual average growth rate for the construction industry exceeds 10 percent, the collective construction companies' share of total output value will probably decrease. This is because as the demand for construction grows, more rural construction brigades are formed taking a greater share of total output value. While collective construction companies have more flexibility than state-owned companies, conditions for the development of collective construction companies are still not as good as that for rural construction brigades.

4. The above analysis suggests the conclusion that over rapid growth in fixed asset investment in urban areas will necessarily create a rush of rural workforce into urban construction companies. In this way, excessive growth in investment can adversely affect future development of the construction industry and the establishment of an orderly construction market.

Section Four   Policy Selection

I. Problems Confronting the Construction Industry

While the construction industry is growing very quickly and its future looks bright, there remain many problems, some quite serious.

These problems should be taken into consideration in determining policy so that they may step by step be solved.

1. The investment market is not stable. As a result, development in the construction industry has consistently retained a passive status. Since the initiation of the reform and opening policy, the absence of experience and measures to exercise macro control over the market have resulted in policies that often failed to keep abreast with changes in the market, thus losing the desired macro control. The most conspicuous failure was the loss of control over investment. Subsequently, administrative means were used to reduce the scale of investment, seriously affecting growth in the construction industry.

2. Construction workers are mainly concentrated in the cities and coastal areas. While the rural market accounts for more than a half of the total output value of the construction industry, it remains comparatively backward and undeveloped, operating on a small scale. As a result, the rural workforce have flowed into the cities, creating an imbalance between supply and demand in the urban construction market and a certain portion of market disorder.

3. Growth in the construction industry has been accompanied by a downward slide in economic returns for the construction companies year after year. This has been most apparent in the large and medium-sized state-owned enterprises. Profits for the collective enterprises have steadily risen, but, when adjusted for price factors, these too have dropped. Moreover, changes in the output value to profit rate and capital to profit rate can also reflect the current drop in returns.

There are a variety of reasons for this drop, including market competition and enterprise management. But, more important reasons remain the construction companies' production organizational structures and the prices of construction products.

4. Low prices of construction products have resulted in a low rate of accumulation by construction companies, weakening their capacity to improve themselves. Low per-capita profits leave these companies vulnerable to market fluctuations and the risks of competition. Large and medium-sized state-owned companies are particularly hampered

when threatened by competition because of the problems present in their current setups. State-owned companies were rocked as their returns started to slide following the opening of the building market in 1985. Reduced fixed asset investment after 1989 caused losses for construction companies in general.

5. Technological and management levels are low in the construction industry compared with other sectors. Most construction companies continue the practice of only contracting for labor. Accordingly, many regard construction as a service or tertiary industry. These companies, including key, large-scale state-owned companies, have low levels of specialization and industrialization compared with the large international construction companies, sapping their ability to compete in the international market.

A solution to these problems will rely on deepening reform in the construction companies and improving the technological quality, transforming the organization of the production structure and upgrading the whole industry. Thus, transforming the industry will require the combination of reform and upgrading. This will remain the issue at the core of future development in the construction industry.

II. Policy Selection for Reform and Development of the Construction Industry

According to many economic indicators contained in forecasts, collective enterprises and the rural construction brigades have the advantage over the state-owned enterprises in terms of future growth. However, an examination of all economic indicators leads to the conclusion that state-owned enterprises will continue their dominance for the next ten years and longer. The important question of how to give full play to the leading role of large and medium-sized state-owned construction companies and substantially raise their profits remains to be answered.

In the future reform must continue to guide every aspect of the construction industry. Targets should include improved labor productivity and economic returns and better quality technology and management. The following major policies are suggested.

1. Stable and sustained growth in fixed asset investment is to be desired. Analysis of past figures regarding the Chinese economy provides the equation that an increase of one unit of fixed asset investment creates an increase of 1.165 units of total output value in the construction industry and 2.65 units output value of capital goods. Growth in investment is needed for national economic development and is indispensable for growth in the construction industry. Therefore, major fluctuations in investment, both rises and falls, must be avoided.

2. Technological advances can be relied on to promote development. The construction industry is unlike some new industries in that it must remain labor intensive. However, it must transform itself by organizing a number of intellect-intensive and technology-intensive companies. Accordingly, a suitable program must be designed to promote technological progress in construction. (1) Management over the industry should be further strengthened. This management should be based on the market and supported by legislation and take profit as the guiding motivation. Management should operate more or less on three levels, all coordinated: {1} A policy-making level of government legislation and macro control, {2} a coordination level of trade associations and all kinds of specialized associations, {3} a supervisory level of a variety of advisory organizations. With this in mind, legislation should be strengthened and importance attached to the establishment of trade associations and giving the full play to fulfilling their role. Given China's imbalanced regional economic development, management over the industry and plans for its development should for the most part rely on the cities. (2) Loans for technological transformation of construction companies should be suitably increased. Loans should be based on cities so as to achieve important targets for local technological progress and technological development projects. Responsibility for repayment of project loans should be clearly defined in order to ensure efficient use of funds. Companies should be directed toward specialization. Step by

step a number of high-tech stock companies should be established. (3) Pilot BOT (build, operate, transfer) projects should be encouraged so as to raise the companies' power of initiative in managing operations. (4) Full use should be made of existing technologies and equipment. The utilization rate for construction equipment should be raised.

3. Orderly adjustment should be made to the organizational structure of the construction industry. (1) This adjustment should be combined with the establishment of a modern enterprise system to create a number of stock company groups with certain specialized technological strengths. These companies must not only break away from their original position of administration subordination, but also break down the barriers of systems of ownership. The government should provide support through technological transformation loans and the use of foreign capital. (2) Adjustment of the organizational structure should be integrated with technological progress so that the adjustment brings about the greatest possible economic benefits of scale. (3) Subcontracts can be used to link up companies from different regions, with different forms of ownership or varying levels of subordination, promoting horizontal integration. Subcontracts enable specialization and commercialization in restructuring the construction industry. A loose integration through subcontracts based on the local conditions of the particular project should be encouraged. The government should strengthen examination and supervision over the quality of companies in order to maintain oversight of subcontracts. Rural construction brigades and small collective renovation teams, apart from occasional repair projects, should only contract as labor services companies. As a rule, they should not be allowed to independently take on construction projects. Likewise, specialized engineering companies should only take subcontracts within their specialty. (4) Project management should be promoted and the management and labor levels within individual companies gradually differentiated.

4. Great efforts should be made to develop the township construction market. The level of urbanization will rise quickly with

economic development. Therefore, it will be necessary to open a secondary construction market in the townships. This will contribute toward limiting the influx of rural workforce into large cities and controlling urban population growth. (1) Planning work for the construction of townships should be strengthened and rural urbanization promoted. For this reason, the government should make policies guiding rational land use for the construction of townships, strengthening the standardized construction of rural housing and other buildings and strictly guaranteeing their quality. (2) Great efforts should be made to develop small and medium-sized structural components suitable for rural housing construction and set up systems for the supply of building products to rural areas. Quality checks for building products should be strengthened to strictly guarantee the quality of products used in the rural areas. Such a guarantee is essential if peasants are to actually benefit from market supply and be moved toward a marketization of construction. (3) As rural construction is upgraded, a contract system for house building and other projects should be gradually introduced. With this goal in mind, pilot projects may be initiated in economically developed areas.

The development of the construction industry in China will be inevitably closely linked with reform of the economic system. The problems confronting the construction industry cannot be overcome if progress is attempted in its present form separate from the reform of the system. Although most state-owned construction companies require the protection of government policies, the industry as a whole can only achieve true industrialization and rapid growth by throwing off the yoke of its present system and operating according to the dictates of the unavoidable laws of the market in economic development and the particular characteristics of the construction industry itself.

Chapter Eight   The Development of Tertiary Industry

Tertiary industry will sustain rapid growth for the next ten years and beyond. First, this will be necessary for domestic industrial and agricultural production. Growth in these two sectors both creates the material foundation for tertiary industry and opens it a wide ranging market. Second, technological progress will drive an expansion in the range of services provided by tertiary industry and optimize the industrial structure, improving labor efficiency. Third, trade in service is providing an increasing proportion of foreign trade as the modernization and internationalization of tertiary industry accelerates. The rapid development of tertiary industry will further improve the Chinese economic structure.

Section One   Historical Review of the Development of Tertiary Industry

I. Achievements in the Development of Tertiary Industry

In the 17 years between 1979 and 1995 primary industry grew by 130 percent, secondary industry by 580 percent and tertiary industry 480 percent. A nationwide survey made in 1993 attributed 34.3 percent of the 1992 GDP to tertiary industry.

Changes in the composition of primary, secondary and tertiary industries between 1978 and 1995 are shown in Table 8-1 demonstrating the great advances made in tertiary industry during those years.

Table 8-1

Year	GDP (bn yuan)	Primary Industry (bn yuan) %		Secondary Industry (bn yuan) %		Tertiary Industry (bn yuan) %	
1978	362.41	101.84	28.1	174.52	48.2	86.05	23.7
1980	451.78	135.94	30.1	219.20	48.5	96.64	21.4
1985	896.44	254.16	28.4	386.66	43.1	255.62	28.5
1990	1,854.79	501.70	27.1	771.74	41.6	581.35	31.3
1991	2,161.78	528.86	24.5	910.22	42.1	722.70	33.4
1992	2,663.81	580.00	21.8	1,169.95	43.9	913.86	34.3
1993	3,463.44	688.21	19.9	1,642.85	47.4	1,132.38	32.7
1994	4,662.73	945.72	20.3	2,237.22	48.0	1,479.29	31.7
1995	5,773.37	1,136.52	19.6	2,827.43	49.1	1,809.42	31.3

Source: *The 1996 Summary of Chinese Statistics*, pp. 6-9.

1. Original service capacity was restored. Services in large and medium-sized cities were fairly developed in the early years after the founding of the People's Republic in 1949. Under the planned economy, however, the development of tertiary industry was restricted by ideas and attendant policies attaching paramount importance to production and slighting circulation and services. This was particularly true during the Great Leap Forward in 1958. All economic sectors were put in support of industry and a great portion of the capital and personnel hitherto devoted to commerce and services was transferred to industry. During the "Cultural Revolution" beginning eight years later services sank still deeper into repudiation and self reliance for services was encouraged. By way of illustration, there were 15,000 restaurants in Beijing in the early years after 1949, but few more than 600 by the late years of the "Cultural Revolution." In the early eighties people all over the country could complain of difficulties in finding a restaurant, hotel, barber shop, tailor or transportation. More than ten years of progress have for the most part solved these problems.

2. Old accounts were settled. The sole focus on industrial development for more than 20 years from the fifties to the seventies created an imbalance in the economic structure, a weak agricultural foundation and underdeveloped services. The industrial structure was adjusted and major efforts were made to develop transportation, telecommunications and the various service industries providing the impetus for tertiary industry's rapid rise during the eighties.

3. The market was invigorated. Commerce, foreign trade, transportation, postal services, telecommunications, banking, insurance, science, technology and information related consultancy and services, advertising, employment agencies, job training and real estate have all grown at annual rates of over 10 percent. The tourist industry has expanded at an astounding rate. Foreign exchange income from tourism which totalled US$ 617 million in 1980, rose to US$ 8.73 billion by 1995, an average annual increase of 19.3 percent.

4. New jobs were created. Tertiary industry has a huge capacity to absorb workers. The continuous transfer of labor power from primary and secondary industries to tertiary industry is an objective law which has led to a huge influx of workers into the latter. Employment in tertiary industry was 48.69 million in 1978, accounting for 12.1 percent of the total employment. This rose to 170.9 million in 1995, or 24.8 percent of all the employment.

5. The material and cultural life of the people was improved. Significantly, in addition to material needs, tertiary industry can provide the services to man's needs for conveniences, entertainment and cultural activities (see Table 8-2).

Table 8-2   Annual Per-Capita Rural Living Expenses (yuan)

Item	1985	1990	1993	1994	1995
Living expenses	317.42	584.63	769.65	1,016.81	1,310.36
Food	183.43	343.76	446.83	598.47	768.19
Clothing	30.86	45.44	55.33	70.32	89.79

Housing	57.90	101.37	106.79	142.34	182.21
Home fixtures & services	16.25	30.90	44.67	55.46	68.48
Health	7.65	19.02	27.17	32.07	42.48
Transportation	5.48	8.42	17.41	24.02	33.76
Culture, education & entertainment	12.45	31.38	58.38	75.11	102.39
Other	3.40	4.34	13.07	19.02	23.06

Source: *The 1996 Summary of Chinese Statistics*, p.58.

People's living expenses can be divided into two parts, those for material commodities and those for service commodities. Expenses for food, clothing, housing, home fixtures and services include both materials and services, but primarily represent material consumption and here will be treated as such. Medical services and preventative care, transportation, culture, education, entertainment and so on primarily represent service consumption and here will be treated as such. So viewed, in 1985 per-capita rural expenditure was 317.42 yuan, 288.44 yuan in material consumption, accounting for 90.9 percent, and 28.98 yuan in service consumption, 9.1 percent. In 1995 rural living expenses totalled 1,310.36 yuan, 1,108.67 yuan in material consumption, accounting for 84.6 percent, and 201.69 yuan in service consumption, 15.4 percent. It can be seen that service consumption has been steadily rising.

II. Problems Currently Impairing the Development of Tertiary Industry

1. Tertiary industry remains fundamentally backward. An examination of the world production structure indicates that the international community has already entered a stage of development of the service economy (see Table 8-3).

Table 8-3

	GDP (US$ million)		Agriculture (%)		Industry (%)		Services (%)	
Year	1965	1993	1965	1993	1965	1993	1965	1993
Low income	163040	990262	44	27	28	35	28	38
Middle income	206000	3884168	20	12	35	37	45	51
Upper income	1413280	18247536	5	2	41	33	54	65
Total	1782320	23121966	11	5	39	34	51	61

Note: Data taken from World Bank's *The 1991 World Development Report*, pp. 208-209, and *The 1995 World Development Report*, pp. 166-167.

Total world GDP was US$ 23.121966 trillion in 1993, 5 percent of which was generated by primary industry (agriculture), 34 percent by secondary industry (industry), and 61 percent by tertiary industry (services). As is evident, tertiary industry has become an important part of the world economy. In modern society, the state of tertiary industry is an important indicator of a country's degree of economic and social development.

2. While tertiary industry in China has expanded in terms of quantity, the quality of the services has worsened, presenting a hidden obstacle to development of the industry in some localities. This sag in quality is manifested in several ways. First, service equipment is obsolete and the replacement process is too slow to meet the needs of the modern production and modern life. Second, the educational and technical levels of workers have dropped. Large numbers of workers have rushed into the tertiary industry, but only a limited number have received formal education or technical training. Third, the ethical element essential to quality service has been adversely affected by unhealthy trends and practices, causing perhaps the greatest injury to quality.

3. Prices have gone up too fast. The low prices for services in the early eighties were an important factor affecting the development of tertiary industry. Removing restrictions on the prices of services and allowing price levers to play their natural role will be an important policy for the industry's development. However, in recent years prices for services have risen too much in almost all service trades. This is particularly true with services which function almost as monopolies where prices have climbed to the highest international levels.

4. The internal structure of tertiary industry is insufficiently rational. (1) Services directed toward individual consumers have grown rapidly while those serving production have lagged behind. An example may be found in the agricultural service system. Although many places have set up service organizations at the county, township and village levels supported by supply and marketing cooperatives and have to a certain extent improved services for agricultural production, demand for various services are still far from being met. The service system for industrial production is similarly underdeveloped. Many industrial enterprises have set up a complete range of facilities simply because the services they require are not available. In short, production-oriented services remain quite inadequate and require substantial development. (2) Traditional services have developed rapidly, but new services remain underdeveloped. Generally speaking, new services include the tourist industry, advertising, the information industry, and scientific and technical services and consultancy. While tourist services and advertising have developed rapidly, they still require consolidation and improvement. The scientific and technical and information services and consultancy are only beginning to establish themselves.

Legislation regarding tertiary industry has lagged behind that needed. An important factor contributing to poor quality service can be found in the lack of standardization and law governing businesses providing services.

Section Two   Development Targets for Tertiary Industry

I. Factors and Trends in Development

Tertiary industry is comprised of business activities providing services for the production and circulation of material products and the material and cultural life of the people. Its development is restricted by the level of development of the productive forces, social demand and the mode of economic operation. Future development of China's tertiary industry will be mainly decided by the following three factors.

1. The level of development in primary and secondary industries will directly influence that of tertiary industry. The scale and efficiency of development of the former two is the foundation for development of the latter. Only when labor productivity in primary and secondary industries continually increases and the quantity of surplus products is constantly increased is it possible for the state to increase public expenditure for various public services and facilities and can the people consistently increase their expenditure on living expenses and increase their capacity to pay for the services provided by tertiary industry. China's experience since 1978 has shown that in years when secondary industry grew quickly, tertiary industry grew in step, and when growth of secondary industry slowed down, the brakes were applied to tertiary industry.

2. The degree of the urbanization also affects tertiary industry. Tertiary industry's share of the nation's economy will only increase by a substantial margin when the majority of the population has moved from the countryside to the city, providing the necessary concentration of humanity for the creation of a larger market. So long as the majority of the population is still scattered about the rural areas and few of the goods these rural dwellers need for production and daily life are commodities it will be difficult for tertiary industry to achieve rapid growth. The market demand for its services is too small to achieve the benefits of the scale. The growth of urban population and the growth

of tertiary industry in China between 1980 and 1992 demonstrates a fundamental synchroneity. When urbanites accounted for 19.39 percent of the total population in 1980, tertiary industry provided 20.15 percent of the total output value. The urban population increased to 27.63 percent by 1992, while tertiary industry rose to 27.8 percent. During these 12 years, each 1 percent increase in urbanites as a portion of the total population was matched by a 0.886 percentage increase in tertiary industry's share of the total output value. Examination of past experience shows tertiary industry's growth rate to be slightly slower than the urbanization rate. The nation is expected to be 42 percent urban by 2010, an increase of 14.4 percentage points over 1992 and tertiary industry's share of GNP is expected to rise by 12.7 percentage points to around 40 percent. If the fact that tertiary industry is probably underestimated in current statistics is taken into consideration, services may quite possibly be expected to account for approximately 45 percent of GNP by that time.

3. The degree of socialization and commercialization of production and consumption will also have a deciding effect on the development of tertiary industry. The influence of natural economic notions and production modes centered on self-sufficiency and restrictions imposed by the traditional planned economy system have resulted in a fairly low degree of socialization of production and consumption modes. Enterprises, big and small, have set up a complete range of production services, including storage and transportation service systems. Most government organs, social organizations, enterprises and institutions have established their own systems for supplying services used in daily life. These service systems providing to the needs of production and daily life are in fact the province of tertiary industry. As they provide service to but one enterprise or organization their utilization ratio is low, resulting in serious waste in the allocation of resources.

An important factor hindering the development of tertiary industry is the extent of welfare and high level of consumption subsidies supplied for urban residents, most conspicuously represented in the uncompensated housing distribution and low rent housing system. Currently, housing rent expenses account for only around 3 percent of family income. Progress in the commercialization and marketization of housing will play an important role in promoting the future development of tertiary industry. If urban residents spend 12 percent of family income on housing, the value added by the circulation and consumption of housing will account for more than 10 percent of value added by tertiary industry, resulting in an increase of 4.5 percentage points in tertiary industry's share of GNP.

II. Growth Targets for Tertiary Industry

Tertiary industry grew at an annual average rate of 10.6 percent in the eighties, a rate 1.6 percentage points higher than that of the GNP. However, fluctuations in the national economy dropped the growth rate for tertiary industry to 2.1 percent in 1990 and 5.6 percent in 1991. Following a big increase in the economic growth rate in 1992, the growth rate for tertiary industry rose again, to 9.6 percent. Calculated in 1990 constant prices, the share of value added contributed to GDP by tertiary industry is expected to exceed 30 percent by 2000, increasing from 494.69 billion yuan in 1990 to 1,252 billion yuan, an annual average increase of 9.7 percent. By 2010, the added value created by tertiary industry is expected to come to 3.102 trillion yuan, 2.4 times that of 2000, an average annual increase of 9.5 percent. By this time it should account for 36 percent of GDP. The average annual growth rate for tertiary industry in the 20 years between 1990 and 2010 will be 9.6 percent, 1 percentage point lower than in the eighties.

III. Development of Major Sectors Within Tertiary Industry

Tertiary industry comprises many types of business with different modes of production. These include both highly socialized, modern, capital-intensive and technology-intensive industries and scattered labor-intensive service trades mainly reliant on manual labor. Given the different levels of productive forces, the government has adopted the principle of providing varying guidance for different tertiary industry sectors, giving prominence to key areas of concern.

1. The growth rate in commerce should exceed the average growth rate for tertiary industry. Commerce provides the carrier for the exchange of commodities. Therefore, it is the connector and, in a certain sense, the organizer of all sectors of the national economy and of economic activities in all regions. Commerce's degree of development is often an indication of local economic and social development.

Commerce as a proportion of all tertiary industry is shown in Table 8-4.

Table 8-4   Output value unit: bn yuan

Year	1978	1980	19985	1990	1995
Total value	86.05	96.64	255.62	581.35	1,809.42
Commerce	26.55	21.36	87.84	141.97	509.44
%	30.8	22.1	34.4	24.4	28.2

Source: *The 1996 Chinese Statistical Yearbook*, p.42.

Commerce's high tide was in 1985 when it supplied 34.4 percent of total value added in tertiary industry. Its low point was in 1980 when it supplied 22.1 percent. Most recently, it supplied 28.2 percent in 1995. It is expected to reach 30 percent by 2000 and approximately 32 percent by 2010.

2. The position of the basic services of transportation, postal services and telecommunications should be strengthened. Transportation, postal services and telecommunications serve production, circulation of goods and directly affect people's daily life. These sectors are intimately bound up with the circulation of material

objects used in production and the result of production and are basic services essential to the smooth operation of the economy and society.

Table 8-5   Unit: bn yuan

Year	1978	1980	1985	1990	1995
Total value	86.05	96.64	255.62	581.35	1,809.42
Transportation & telecommunications	17.28	20.50	40.69	114.75	323.65
%	20.1	21.2	15.9	19.7	17.9

Source: *The 1996 Chinese Statistical Yearbook*, p.42.

Table 8-5 shows that transportation and telecommunications generally account for approximately 20 percent of the output value of tertiary industry. On the basis of this data, the annual average growth rate between 1991 and 2000 is expected to be 9.7 percent or 10.9 percent for transportation and telecommunications, and 8.2 percent or 9.4 percent by 2010. China covers a vast territory with greatly variegated landforms, but transportation facilities are poor. This has become a major obstacle to economic and social development, the principal obstacle in some regions. The average growth rate in these sectors should be raised. The targets for the development should be fixed at 13-14 percent and 10-11 percent for transportation and telecommunications.

3. Banking and insurance should be actively developed. As China establishes its socialist market economic system, the nation's economy's dependence on monetary credit and therefore on banks and the banking industry will steadily increase. Major development in the banking industry is inevitable.

Selected Data from the First Survey of Tertiary Industry in China reports that the banking industry created 152.72 billion yuan in added value in 1992, 16.7 percent of tertiary industry's 913.93 billion yuan in total output value. The banking industry should aim at average growth rates of 9.7 percent and 8.2 percent between 1990 and 2000 or 11 percent and 8.4 percent between 2001 and 2010. The establishment of a socialist market economic system requires that the state ensure the effective operation of the main body of the banking industry, the state-owned banks, more precisely the state-owned commercial banks under the leadership of the central bank (the People's Bank of China). If the state-owned banks are sound, consummate and highly efficient, they can effectively serve production and the people in their daily life and, moreover, effectively regulate the financial markets, give full play to banking's positive role in the economy.

The insurance industry provides insurance services both for production and for individuals. It is one part of the social security system. Insurance companies sell policies in exchange for premiums paid by consumers. A portion of the money paid to the insurance companies in premiums is invested by the companies in the financial market. For this reason, the insurance industry is closely linked with the banking industry. Banks open insurance companies and insurance companies open banks.

The development of the insurance industry in China is shown in Table 8-6.

Table 8-6   Output value: million yuan
Rate: chain index

Year	1978	1980	1983	1985	1988	1990	1991	1992
Total value	885.75	1,325.41	1,705.95	2,231.54	3,254.29	3,857.59	3,676.2	3,300.17
Rate	100.0	149.64	128.71	130.81	145.84	118.54	95.30	89.77

Source: *The Chinese Statistical Yearbook,* pre-1993.

After being abolished during the sixties and seventies, insurance services were restored after the initiation of the reform and opening policy. Accordingly, development came quickly during these first few years, before slowing down again during the nineties. As the chart makes clear, growth has not been steady. Insurance companies do more than provide compensation when an injury or accident is suffered. More importantly, they provide the insured with help preventing accident or injury. Some Chinese insurance companies, while quite active in collecting premiums, are less so in providing services, relying on administrative measures requiring insurance. This can only lead to the decline of the insurance industry. Poor quality service results from the state-owned enterprises monopoly over the insurance business. Developing insurance services and steadily optimizing the social security system will require an end to this exclusive control over the business. Allowing a variety of operations to compete will up quality and invigorate the market.

4. Education and culture should be promoted to improve the quality of the people. The achievement of socialist modernization will be impossible without advances in educational and cultural work.

Enrollment in the schools at all levels is a quantitative indicator of the level of educational development. According to the State Statistical Bureau, total school enrollment in 1995 was 196.773 million, 16.2 percent of China's total population, averaging 24 college students, 511.2 secondary school students and 1,089 primary school students per 10,000 persons. In 1978 total enrollment was 213.468 million, 22.18 percent of the total population, averaging 8.9 college students, 690 secondary school students and 1,519 primary school students per 10,000 persons. In both absolute and relative terms, there were fewer students in 1995 than in 1978, although the figure for college students went up. In the present stage, secondary and primary education forms the foundation of the country's educational work; accordingly they should receive emphasis. By the end of this century nine-year compulsory education will be the rule nationwide and illiteracy will be eliminated. By 2010 China will be working hard to fundamentally satisfy the needs of economic and social development through a wide variety of specialized education.

Cultural services include many kinds of undertakings, such as film, television and radio, theatre, cultural relics organizations, libraries, museums, publishing and distribution, and sports. Cultural services may be delivered in two ways. Society as a whole, (government), may organize activities as social welfare or they may be sold as commodities subject to the law of the market. Under many circumstances, the same cultural service organization may receive government subsidies to provide welfare services to the society and provide these services as commodities responding to market demand. The government must proceed from the basic interests of economic and social development in deciding development targets and the balance between welfare services and commodity services. Cultural services should first target increased quantity and then improved quality. More radio and television stations, stadiums, museums and libraries must be built to give more people more opportunity to study and better themselves.

Medical services and public health work are essential to a civilized society and a key component of the social security system. For this reason they also have the characteristics of both welfare and a commodity. Here the development goal should be to establish a multi-level medical service and health protection system in urban and rural areas to ensure that all citizens can receive health care. There were 180,500 medical and health institutions in China in 1980, including 65,400 hospitals with a medical staff of 3,535,000, including 1,153,000 doctors, 1.17 doctors per thousand persons. By 1990 the number of medical and health institutions had risen to 208,700, including 62,400 hospitals. The average growth rate of medical institutions was 1.5 percent, but the number of hospitals had decreased 0.5 percent each year. Nationwide, medical staff totalled 4,906,000, including 1,763,000 doctors, average growth rates of 3.3 percent and 4.3 percent respectively. There were 1.54 doctors per thousand persons, an increase of only 0.37 doctors per thousand. By 1995 the number of medical and health institutions had fallen to 190,000, but the number of medical staff had risen to 5,373,000. This state of affairs is incompatible with the necessity of establishing a nationwide medical service and health protection system. To better the situation, a growth rate between 2 and 3 percentage points higher than from 1980 to 1990 will be required during the 20 years from 1990 to 2010.

5. Scientific and technical services should be substantially improved. The basic situation with scientific and technical activities in 1991 is outlined in Table 8-7.

Table 8-7   Scientific and Technical Activities Nationwide

	1990	1993	1994	1995
Scientific & technical institutions	18,772	20,735	23,613	24,259
Participants in S & T activities (thousand)		2,449.7	2,655	2,701.3
Total receipts (bn yuan)	40.326	68.584	71.848	87.556
Total expenditures (bn yuan)	36.913	65.27	69.538	80.219
Research & development funding as a percentage of GNP (%)	0.71	0.62	0.5	0.5
Total transactions in national technology markets (bn yuan)	7.51	20.75	22.89	26.83

Source: *The 1996 Chinese Statistical Yearbook*, pp. 661, 671.

This demonstrates the scientific and technical services industry's firm foundation. Between 1990 and 2010 the establishment of a natural sciences and social sciences research system that can track world advanced levels should be completed so as to quickly turn research results into productive forces.

Scientific and technical consultancy service is a new service industry. It provides an important tool for the combination of scientific research with production and the transformation of science and technology into productive forces. In 1995 scientists and technicians providing consultancy services in activities organized by the Chinese Scientific and Technical Association were consulted on 40,372 contracts, generating 147.11 million yuan in income. This was a good beginning, bringing a new vigor into the field of science and technology. China's scientific and technical forces may be limited, but they remain a substantial force to be reckoned with. The crucial point is how best to arouse their enthusiasm. First arises the question of the environment and conditions for scientific research. The experimental means used in natural sciences and the conditions for investigation and study used in the social sciences are the primary factors restricting scientific research. This problem calls for government solutions both regards policy and the system itself. Second, funding for scientific research is inadequate. The portion of GNP spent on research should be gradually raised as the economy develops. The government should make suitable arrangements for the basic sciences to ensure the normal scientific activities. The applied sciences should be commercialized and marketed. The market for trade in science and technology and associated services should be well run. Large enterprises and enterprise groups should be encouraged to set up technological development centers.

6. The real estate industry should be steadily developed. The real estate industry is comprehensive embracing land development and the construction, management and maintenance of the housing. A 1992 survey put the output value of the real estate industry at 52.11 billion yuan. Its total business income came to 173.16 billion yuan in 1995. These figures demonstrate real estate's role as major pillar of tertiary industry and an important sector of the national economy. China now has 570 cities and tens of thousands of small towns. They have housing with a combined building area of billions of square meters. When the nation operated under a planned economy, state-owned land was in most cases allocated by the administration for use without compensation. Public housing was distributed by the government for token rents. Under this system the use value of land and housing could not be or could not completely be transformed into a commodity. This,

of course, hamstrung the development of a real estate economy. The major trend in real estate between 1996 and 2010 will be housing transformation into a commodity as it is placed on the market. The real estate growth rate may be reflected in the increase housing building area (see Table 8-8).

Table 8-8   Unit: million m²

Year	1978	1980	1983	1985	1988	1990	1993	1995
Area under construction	1,022.61	1,291.88	1,488.59	1,689.51	1,371.71	1,528.13	1,823.27	466.9004
Area completed	863.25	1,116.1	1,220.84	1,359.43	1,077.93	1,191.07	1,220.21	148.7385
Houses	694.44	865.4	909.72	1,048.01	862.89	940.02	807.79	

Source: *The Chinese Statistical Yearbook*, 1990, 1993, 1994 and 1996.

If the real estate industry is assumed to account for 10 percent of the total value of tertiary industry, the annual average growth rate for the real estate industry is expected to be 10.3 percent by 2000 and approximately 9.5 percent by 2010.

Chapter Nine Rates of Accumulation and Investment Safeguards

This chapter will first analyze accumulation's important role in China's future economic growth and then explain a strategy that embraces both accumulation and consumption, encouraging their reciprocal promotion. A strategy for safeguarding medium- and long-term investment and a policy for countering the negative effect of "bottleneck" industries will be proposed base on the preceding.

Section One Analysis of the Effect of Accumulation on Economic Growth

A suitable, relatively stable rate of accumulation is a crucial factor affecting medium- and long-term economic growth.

In China's case, the dynamic changes in the rate of accumulation since Liberation in 1949 can be divided into two major historical periods: 1950 to 1970 and the years since 1971. Generally speaking, the rate of accumulation rose and fell precipitously during the first stage, averaging around 25 percent. Accumulation rate was less than 25 percent in 14 years and more in seven years. The lowest rate was 10.4 percent in 1962, and the highest was 43.8 percent in 1959, a difference of over 33 percentage points. This gives a strong indication of the lack of stability in economic development and the constant changes in the economic policies regarding the use and distribution of the national income during this period. During the First Five-Year Plan, the economy advanced on an even keel; the people's living standard rose steadily and the rate of accumulation was maintained around 25 percent. The "Great Leap Forward" caused radical perturbations in the economy. The rate of accumulation reached an absolutely abnormal peak in 1959. Beginning in 1960 economic hardship and an economic adjustment period rapidly forced the rate down to its nadir in 1962. Subsequently, it rose gradually to around 25 percent where it remained before climbing to 32.9 percent in 1970. In the 22 years following until 1992 the rate hovered around 32 percent, falling below this level in eight years and rising above it in 14 years. The high point, 36.5 percent, was reached in 1978 and the low, 28.3 percent, in 1981, a difference of more than 8 percentage points. During this second period the frequency and range of change were relatively small, an expression of gradually increasing stability in economic development.

The dynamic changes in the rate of accumulation during these two periods demonstrate their direct relation to the changes in the economy. Crests and troughs in the rate correspond to ups and downs in economic development. As this makes clear, the selection of an appropriate rate of accumulation, particularly an effective expansion of the scale of accumulation and relative stability in the rate, will have an essential connection with future economic growth, specifically with sustained, stable coordinated development. This direct correlation between the accumulation rate and economic growth has been given proof in the experience of other countries, most notably in the economically developed Asian nations and other newly industrialized nations.

Section Two Establishing Concern for Both Accumulation and Consumption, Encouraging Their Mutual Promotion

In the end, all the nation's income is either consumed or saved as accumulation; generally, if one rate increases, the other, in turn, decreases. Still, this rule may not be so hard and fast when the relation between rate of accumulation and volume of consumption is explored. In the past China held the assumption that an increase in the accumulation rate would necessarily carry the cost of sacrificing consumption. However, experience since the initiation of the reform and opening policy has demonstrated that a suitable reduction in the consumption rate and a corresponding increase in the accumulation rate can encourage greater volume of both accumulation and consumption, each promoting the other. Although the rate of accumulation has been maintained at the fairly high level of approximately 32 percent since 1979 (approximately 34 percent since 1985), the material and cultural life of the Chinese people has rapidly and substantially improved, consumption standards throughout society rising year after year. The increase in the rate of accumulation did not result in a reduction in consumption. This may be demonstrated in the dynamic changes in the amounts involved in the allocation of national income between consumption and accumulation. In 1992, 677 billion yuan was accumulated, 6.2 times the 108.7 billion yuan accumulated in 1978. Volume of consumption in 1992 was nearly 6.9 times the figure in 1978.

While this rapid increase in national income resulted from growth in production, two additional factors also contributed.

1. Net inflow of foreign capital expanded the scale of national income utilized and enlarged the elasticity zone in the proportionality of accumulation and consumption. China actually utilized US$ 133.7 billion in direct foreign investment between 1979 and 1995. Foreign capital skyrocketed from 1.9 percent of China's investment sources in 1982 to 11.2 percent in 1995,[1] becoming an increasingly important factor in the scale of use of national income, scale of accumulation and rate of total accumulation. At the same time, it enabled a corresponding increase in the scale of consumption while maintaining a fairly high rate of accumulation. This state of affairs is quite different from before the initiation of the reform and opening policy.

---

[1] *The 1996 Chinese Statistical Yearbook.*

2. The mode of accumulation changed. China formerly operated under a planned economy and accumulation was the sole province of the government. With the coming of reform both the government and society at large engaged in accumulation. During the course of the economic cycle, various types of enterprises' (collectives') accumulative functions have steadily gained in strength. Moreover, the question of transforming consumption funds into accumulation has increasingly gained in importance and prominence. Of particular significance, the national income is increasingly in the hands of individuals. In both city and countryside, citizens' disposable income has increased year after year, rising from 50.5 percent of GDP in 1978 to 65.4 percent in 1991.[1] Change in the accumulation structure reflects this: the state's share of total accumulation has fallen while that of collectives and in particular individuals has risen quickly. The state's share of total accumulation has dropped from around 80 percent in the years from 1950 to 1970 to around 70 percent today while that of individuals increased from less than 3 percent during the earlier period to around 15 percent now. This change is the result of individuals' increasing share of the national income over the past ten years and is a significant manifestation of that phenomenon.

A further indication of this change, the year-end balance of urban and rural savings deposits rose from 21.06 billion yuan in 1978 to 2.21578 trillion yuan in 1995, (over 80 percent time deposits).[2] At the same time, there has been an increasing diversification of sources of capital. By the end of 1994 the year-end balance of negotiable securities came to 453.799 billion yuan.[3] Total financial assets held by urban individuals came to 1.8547 trillion yuan that same year, an average of 26,600 yuan per household. Various negotiable securities accounted for 19.9 percent of financial assets.[4] These factors undoubtedly intensified the transition from consumption to

---

[1] *Management World*, 1996, Issue 2, p. 66.

[2, 3] *The 1996 Chinese Statistical Yearbook.*

[4] *Management World*, 1996, Issue 2, p. 64.

accumulation and investment. In this way a new pattern fell into place wherein consumption and accumulation both increased, each fueling growth in the other.

Given China's current stage of development, the accumulation rate should be at a minimum maintained at the current level of approximately 34 percent for the next ten years or longer. This is particularly true given the difficulties in strengthening primary industry, building infrastructure and alleviating structural bottlenecks. To this may be added the huge investment demand needed for developing heavy chemical industry, and effecting the structural transition from labor intensive to capital and technology intensive industry. There is an acute shortage of the financial resources needed for the renovation of existing equipment. An intensity of investment is required to sustain rapid economic growth. Considering that consumption has grown too quickly in recent years, that growth in collective consumption and administrative expenditure has been out of proportion and that control over population increases has been less than optimal, there remains potential for a healthy increase in the accumulation rate.

Of course, sustaining a fairly high rate of accumulation will be affected by various factors, two in particular.

1. The net inflow of foreign capital or net outflow of domestic capital influences total accumulation. If the net inflow of foreign capital is deducted, the domestic investment rate in recent years is much lower than actual levels from 1970 to 1980, only around 28 percent in 1992. Outflow of domestic capital is increasing. A proper measure of the inflow and outflow of capital and effective handling of the same will be of great importance, directly affecting attempts to determine or adjust domestic accumulation.

2. Maintenance of a fairly high general rate of accumulation must be intertwined with proper guidance over consumption and necessary and effective control over the consumption demand. Each should support the other. Accumulation should not be placed in opposition to consumption, nor should the two be considered separately. Income

should not be controlled and consumption reduced in order to ensure accumulation and construction. Consumption should be properly guided, over consumption discouraged and hard work encouraged. Two points in particular should be kept in mind. (1) Attention must be paid to the maintenance of the proper relationship between economic growth and growth in the volume of consumption. Generally speaking, the annual growth rate in consumption, including the volumes of both individual consumption and that for society as a whole, should not exceed the actual GNP growth rate for the same year. (2) Given the premise of eliminating the influence of the price factors, growth in wages should not exceed growth in labor productivity. While gradually promoting the marketization of wages, the government should strengthen regulation over the distribution of the income through taxes and other economic levers.

Section Three   The Strategy for Ensuring Medium- and Long-Term Investment

Adjustments in investment strategy will be of great importance in future economic development and restructuring.

I. As Quickly as Possible Replace the Old Practice of Primarily Expanding the Scale of Production and Extended Reproduction with Investment Centered on Heightened Returns; A Normal Relationship Between Economic Growth and Growth in Investment Should Be Established That Is Mutually Adaptable, Interactive and Mutually Promoting

Low investment returns result from the profound influence of the traditional mode of economic development characterized by extensive operations, high input and low output. The serious distortion of the

168

investment system centered on speed has yet to be effectively corrected. This is the basic cause behind the excessive demand for investment, the excessive scale of investment and major imbalance between investment supply and demand that has long existed. The experiences of other countries indicate that under the conditions of modern socialized large-scale production and technological progress, historically, the economic growth rate has approached or exceeded the investment growth rate whether before or after economic takeoff. This enables advances in science and technology and in efficiency to play an ever greater role in economic development and continually increasing intensification. In China, the GNP grew at an average annual rate of 8.8 percent during the ten years from 1981 to 1991 while fixed asset investment grew 19.1 percent per annum, a rate more than 10 percentage points higher. The 1992 GNP was 12.8 percent higher than the previous year, but fixed asset investment increased by 37.6 percent. This was clearly not economical, indeed quite abnormal. In the light of experiences at home and abroad in arranging a suitable relationship between economic growth (GNP or GDP) and contemporary growth in fixed asset investment, growth in fixed asset investment should not exceed economic growth by more than 10 percentage points in the years before 2000. Subsequently, the two figures should be brought still closer to within a difference of 7or 8 percentage points.

II. Change in the Mode of Economic Development and Deepened Reform of the Enterprise System Should Be Supported; As Soon as Possible, an Investment Mechanism Should Be in Place Ensuring That the Body Soliciting Investment Is Solely Responsible for Gains and Losses, Shouldering the Attendant Risks; This Will Serve to Eradicate the Deep Rooted Phenomena of "Investment Hunger" and Lack of Responsibility for Return on Investment

Practice has shown that as investment targets and sources

increasingly diversify it is impossible to address fundamental investment problems merely through government examination and approval, bank checks on loans or even by reexamination of projects every several years, possibly stopping or delaying construction. The problem can only be solved by having the parties involved in the investment assume sole responsibility for risks and benefits, giving full play to the role of the market in allocating resources. Only this, in combination with muscular governmental management over the total balance of investment and macroeconomic policies, can afford a solution to the problems that have perplexed the nation for such an extended period of time.

III. Macro Regulation and Control over Investment Should Focus on Improving the Investment Structure

In a time of rapid, sustained economic growth, investment cuts are not advisable. However, measures can be taken to improve the investment structure. In particular, state planning must address strengthening primary industries, infrastructure construction, and solutions to problems with "bottlenecks" to ensure that investment growth in these areas exceeds the growth rate of the processing industries and elsewhere. Here, the state should give full play to its role in regulation and control. Macro control policies should also increasingly tilt toward the major industries and investment areas, reflecting the goals of state industrial policy regards taxation, pricing and government share of enterprise profits. In this way, primary industries and related enterprises will gain in their capacity for self accelerating development.

Another point crucial for improving the investment structure will be substantial increase in technological standards and utilization efficiency of the huge available stock of assets. Fixed asset investment has grown at an exceptionally high rate in recent years. Of the 2.2 trillion yuan in state-owned assets currently available, about one third, 700 billion yuan, are either idle or have low utilization efficiency.

Available data indicates that the net worth in the Chinese industrial system added by raising asset utilization efficiency accounts for only around 20 percent of total new value added. This may be compared to the 50 percent averaged in Germany and 11 other economically developed countries and the approximately 30 percent averaged in Argentina and 19 other developing countries. Constant expansion and acceleration in fixed asset incremental investment, slow progress toward technological renovation and transformation, low asset utilization rates and serious waste and losses are the direct consequence of the prolonged continuation of the traditional mode of economic development, principally expanded reproduction. Furthermore, it is a reflection of imbalance in the fixed asset investment structure. If this situation continues, not only will it be difficult to increase investment returns and social and economic benefits, it will create an enormous problem in maintaining the investment burden and the ability to raise the funds essential for economic growth. Accordingly, in exercising macro control over the investment structure, given a fixed general scale of investment over a given period, it will be necessary to first search for a use for existing stock before considering additional incremental investment, to consider transformation before thinking of building new projects, to first investigate rational distribution and adjustment of existing productive forces and equipment and then consider new investment.

IV. Two Questions Must Be Fully Addressed in Ensuring the Sources of Investment in Light of the Nation's Actual Conditions

1. Reform of the financial and tax system should be accelerated. The abnormal situation wherein both the ratio of state revenues to national income and of central revenues to total revenues are too low must be corrected. State revenues, particularly central revenues for investment in economic construction, must be increased so as to meet the state's minimum need for investment in exercising macro-

economic control and funding priority projects. Today either in the economically developed countries or in the new emerging countries both ratios have gradually increased to meet the objective amount necessary to exercise macro control and the demand for public facilities. In 1980 in France, Germany, Japan, Britain, the United States and Sweden, government expenditures averaged about 10 percent of GNP; by 1985 it had risen to 47 percent. At the same time, the revenues accounted for around 40 percent of GNP and central revenues accounted for over 60 percent of total revenues. In China, however, misunderstanding resulted in the diffused distribution and use of state financial resources. The inadequacy of central financial power became increasingly acute. Investment dropped substantially, rendering the government extremely limited in its capacity to strengthen broad ranging primary industries and infrastructure construction. By 1995 revenues accounted for only 11 percent of GDP, nearly 30 percentage points lower than the average level in developed countries and 14 percentage points lower than the level (around 25 percent) in Asia's "four small dragons." Central revenues comprised 52 percent of total revenues in China in 1995, again lower than the 60 percent averaged in developed countries. This situation is very abnormal and should be changed as soon as possible.

Moreover, government investment in economic construction in economically developed countries generally accounts for 30 to 40 percent of total investment. In China, state budgeted investment accounted for only 3.1 percent of total fixed asset investment in 1995. This situation not only deprived the country of the financial resources necessary to exercise macroeconomic control; it created an acute shortage of investment capital for primary industry and infrastructure construction normally dependent on state financial support.

In addition, it is necessary to give full play to the role of state credit so as to open more channels for investment and increase restrictions on returns on the use of administrative capital. Addressing this problem, Japan has operated a Fiscal Investment and Loan Program for more than 40 years, a program that may provide a model for China. The Japanese model centers around the Treasury's Capital Utilization Department. Capital is acquired from society at large through postal savings, insurance and annuities. Government related public financial institutions use these funds to engage in financial activities including investments, loans and bond subscriptions in accordance with government formulated economic development programs. This practice played a very important role in Japan's economic takeoff, and in strengthening the role of financial macro control. This was especially true from the postwar years until the mid fifties. Investment poured into the major steel, coal, power and shipping enterprises and primary industries through the program, accounted for 30 percent of the fixed capital raised by the non-governmental businesses. By 1991, the funds raised through the program accounted for 56.5 percent of total state financial resources (that is to say, budgetary funds plus funds raised through the Fiscal Investment and Loan Program), becoming an indispensable "second budget." Accelerating the establishment of a fiscal investment and loan system in China can likewise provide an important tool to help solve the shortfall in investment from revenues.

2. Blind imitation of the low interest policies of some Western countries is not the appropriate means to promote and sustain continuous growth in savings with the intention of stemming inflation, increasing the supply of investment capital and facilitating the effective allocation of capital and resources. These low interest policies rely on abundant capital supply and stable prices. Developing countries have inadequate financial resources and substantial price fluctuations. Artificially compelled reductions in interest rates will not only create difficulties in the capital supply for bank loans; it will encourage the transfer of large quantities of monetary resources into precious metals and foreign exchange and investment in real estate and other non-production businesses. This may engender economic and financial confusion. This is the motivation behind the high interest rate policies followed in many developing countries and regions both before and after their economies take off, (including Asia's "four small

dragons"). In this they are joined by Japan and several other economically developed countries.

V. The Key to Ensuring Medium- and Long-Term Investment Will Be Substantial Increased Returns for Accumulation and Investment; It Will Be Futile to Maintain High Rates of Accumulation and Investment If Anticipated Returns on Investment Are Not Ensured; In China Returns on Accumulation and Investment in Recent Years Are Falling; For Quite Some Time, High Rates of Accumulation and Investment Have Been Accompanied by Low Returns, a Potentially Dangerous Situation; Great Importance Must Be Attached to Increasing the Benefits Gained from Accumulation and Investment

The greatest increase in national income per 100 yuan of additional accumulation, 57.1 yuan, occurred from 1963 to 1965. Although there were major increases and decreases, in general tendency the figure fell during the subsequent five-year plan periods. A big turning point came immediately after the initiation of the reform and opening policy. Nonetheless, the pattern of increases followed by decreases continued (see Table 9-1).

Table 9-1   Increase in National Income Per Additional 100 yuan of Accumulation in China

	Total accumulation (bn yuan)	Increase in national income (bn yuan)	Increase in national income per 100 yuan accumulation (yuan)
1st Five-Year Plan Period (1953-57)	98.8	31.9	32
2nd Five-Year Plan Period (1961-65)	173.2	1.6	0.9

"Adjustment" Period	81.1	46.3	57.1
3rd Five-Year Plan Period (1966-70)	204.7	45.9	22.4
4th Five-Year Plan Period (1971-75)	364.4	57.7	15.8
5th Five-Year Plan Period (1976-80)	499.3	118.5	23.7
6th Five-Year Plan Period (1981-85)	818.7	335.3	41
7th Five-Year Plan Period (1986-90)	1,978.4	736.9	37.3
1956-1985			28.2

Source: *The Chinese Statistical Yearbook*, of relevant years.

Table 9-2 shows that in the 30 years from 1956 to 1985 Japan increased national income 39.8 yen for every additional 100 yen of accumulation. As shown above, China showed an increase in income of only 28.2 yuan per additional 100 yuan in accumulation over the same period, 41.1 percent less than Japan.

Table 9-2   Increase in National Income Per Additional 100 Yen in Accumulation in Japan

	Total Accumulation (bn yen)	Increase in national income (bn yen)	Increase in national income per 100 yen accumulation (yen)
1951-1955	7,047.9	3,337.4	47.4
1956-1960	13,413.8	5,280.8	39.4
1961-1965	28,516.6	14,106.2	49.5
1966-1970	70,279.8	33,131.1	47.1
1971-1975	131,648.5	72,391.2	55.0
1976-1980	196,092.4	76,804.9	39.2

| 1981-1985 | 248,112.0 | 71,840.2 | 28.9 |
| 1956-1985 | | | 39.8 |

Source: "Comparison of Chinese and Japanese Accumulation Rates and Returns," Zhang Shuying, *World Economy*, Issue 3, 1993.

Needless to say, China's poor returns on accumulation and investment and associated fluctuations arise from a variety of causes. Irrational utilization of accumulation and investment structure join the fundamental economic system flaws just discussed.

Section Four   Policies to Alleviate Constraints Imposed by "Bottleneck" Industries

Long-term inadequacies in infrastructure and primary industries have continually impeded economic development, throwing the industrial structure out of balance and creating economic turbulence.

Addressing these inadequacies is essential. Hard work will be necessary to avoid major future economic dislocations and adjustments. For example, China will have a domestic oil shortage of 45 million tons by 2000 if the GNP grows averagely 8 to 9 percent per annum. China has laid out a three stage economic development program. The goal of reaching the level of fairly developed countries in 20 to 30 years calls for one kilowatt of electrical generating capacity per capita or per-capita consumption of 5,000 kilowatt hours. China will require a total power generating capacity of 1.3 to 1.4 billion kilowatts. Including the 14 million kilowatts capacity added in 1992, it will still take at least 80 to 90 years to complete this task. The restrictions on future economic development imposed by inadequate transportation facilities are even more crippling.

The following points should be stressed in efforts to alleviate "bottleneck" constraints.

1. A series of carefully organized and scheduled campaigns to strengthen construction in primary industries and infrastructure facilities should be organized to focus energies on correcting underdevelopment in these sectors.

Asia's "four small dragons" launched several major construction campaigns over the past three decades directed toward solving problems with their underdeveloped infrastructure, especially transportation and telecommunications networks. The first was in the early sixties. Major efforts were made to develop the power industry, harbors, roads and railways. The second, in the seventies, stressed the construction of expressways, electrified railways, subways, modernized harbors, airports and nuclear power stations. The third commenced in the eighties and aimed to upgrade industry and adapt to the situation created by rapidly expanding foreign trade. These experiences can prove valuable to China as it designs policies.

2. The state's capacity to use revenues, particularly central revenues, to ensure public investment and exercise macro control over the build up of primary industries and infrastructure must be recast and strengthened.

(1) The state's capacity to use revenue to ensure investment and exercise macro control over primary industries and infrastructure construction should be steadily strengthened in coordination with the implementation of tax distribution system reform in accordance with the actual requirements of economic growth.

In the future reform of the financial system, revenues should be increased to 25 to 30 percent of GNP and central revenues gradually increased to around 60 percent of total revenues. Synchronous growth of national income (GNP), revenues and disbursements available for investment is as an important dynamic indicator. The growth rate for the latter two should be appropriately higher than the first.

(2) The double entry budget system should be comprehensively implemented. Separate entries and separate accounts should be kept for current and construction revenues and expenditures. This will work to forestall inflation of current revenues and expenditures, lessening

the risk of nibbling away at the supply of funds for investment in construction.

(3) State credit should be actively developed under the premise that the double entry budget will help ensure that income from treasury bonds is not used to make up deficits in current expenditures and investment returns are both guaranteed and improved. This will alleviate pressure from inadequate budgeted investment. At the same time, it will strengthen restraints on the use of compensable investment in basic investment by establishing responsibility for the operations of primary construction projects. Today, special importance should be attached to the issue and effective use of special treasury bonds for major construction projects. Accounting methods need to be specific for particular projects, bonds, entries and accounts so as to strengthen supervision over the use of treasury bonds and investment returns.

3. Guidance over the acquisition and use of foreign capital should be strengthened. Primary or secondary priority should be given to building up primary industries and infrastructure and the renovation or replacement of technical equipment.

4. The state monopoly on raising capital and investing in primary industries and infrastructure needs to be abandoned. Over time, a comprehensive, multi-level investment and operational system integrating the central government, local governments, ministries, enterprises and certain development operations legal entities should be formed.

(1) In implementing the tax division system during the course of reform of the financial system, authority of office and power over financial affairs in primary industry and infrastructure construction must be clearly demarcated between the central and local governments. Budgetary reforms should ensure that the implementation of a double entry budgetary system prevents the financial resources of the central and local governments intended for investment from being used for other purposes.

(2) Conditions should be actively created to strengthen primary industry departments and associated enterprises' capacity to

themselves generate the accumulation necessary to transform and develop themselves. In this way, a new pattern can be formed making full and effective use of available asset stocks, continually improving technological standards. Relying on self-generated accumulation and outside capital, present growth can be used to spur further growth. This goal first necessitates the adoption of special tax policies: low tax rates or, if a unified tax system, particularly a unified income tax rate policy, is adopted, rebates. Second, primary industry and associated enterprises should be given necessary preferential treatment in deciding the portion of their profits they must turn over to the government so as to increase their capacity to accumulate. Third, primary industries and related enterprises should be allowed to utilize special rapid depreciation policies or higher depreciation policies than other sectors and enterprises. Fourth, price relationships should be adjusted with special emphasis placed on correcting irrational external price relationships (for example, between transportation costs and other products) and internal price relationships (for example, between crude oil and oil products). Currently, many primary industries suffer losses or break even. This situation must be corrected to better enable these industries to accumulate the capital necessary for their advancement.

(3) The long-standing practice whereby the state operates without competition as the sole investor under unitary management should be discarded. The acquisition of foreign capital is to be encouraged. At the same time, the establishment of a number of enterprises or enterprise groups that combine project development with operations and have the qualities of a legal entity and are based on market competition should be actively promoted.

Chapter Ten　Personal Consumption

This chapter will begin with a brief description of the improvement of living standards since the initiation of the reform and opening policy, before proceeding to a discussion of the "relatively comfortable" standard of living intended for the coming century. It will close with a forecast of future personal consumption levels and an analysis of coming changes in the consumption structure.

Section One　Improvements in the Living Standards Since the Initiation of the Reform and Opening Policy

Chinese living standards have been transformed as the nation enters a new historical period.

Between 1952 and 1978 the average per-capita annual consumption level rose from 76 yuan to 175 yuan, an increase of 130 percent, 80 percent after adjustment for inflation. This translates into an average annual increase of 2.1 percent. In comparison, the level rose from 184 yuan in 1979 to 2,311 yuan in 1995, increasing by 1,150 percent, 240 percent after adjustment for inflation, an average annual increase of 7.5 percent. Personal consumption increased at a rate of 5.4 percentage points higher after the initiation of reform and opening. This policy benefits to all the nation's people.

Personal consumption may be divided into rural and non-rural personal consumption. (1) The peasant consumption level rose from 62 yuan in 1952 to 132 yuan in 1978, an increase of 110 percent, 57 percent adjusted for inflation, an average annual growth of 1.8 percent.

Between 1979 and 1995, the level rose from 138 yuan to 1,479 yuan, an increase of 970 percent, 220 percent increase adjusted for inflation, an average annual increase of 7.1 percent. The average annual rise in the rural consumption level was 5.3 percentage points higher after the initiation of the reform and opening. (2) The non-rural personal consumption level rose from 149 yuan in 1952 to 383 yuan in 1978, an increase of 160 percent, 110 percent increase adjusted for inflation, an average annual increase of 3 percent. The same level rose from 405 yuan in 1979 to 5,044 yuan in 1995, an increase of 1,150 percent, 200 percent adjusted for inflation, an average annual increase of 6.7 percent, 3.7 percentage points higher than before the reform and opening.

Changes in consumption levels during different periods are shown in Table 10-1.

**Table 10-1   Average Annual Growth Rate of
Personal Consumption (%)**

Time	Total population	Peasants	Non-rural citizens
1st Five-Year Plan Period (1953-57)	4.2	3.2	4.8
2nd Five-Year Plan Period (1961-65)	-3.3	-3.3	-5.2
1963-1965	8.6	8.2	12.3
3rd Five-Year Plan Period (1966-70)	2.2	2.5	2.1
4th Five-Year Plan Period (1971-75)	2.1	1.3	4.2
5th Five-Year Plan Period (1976-80)	4.8	4.1	4.9
6th Five-Year Plan Period (1981-85)	8.6	10.1	4.9
7th Five-Year Plan Period (1986-90)	3.6	2.2	5.4
8th Five-Year Plan Period (1991-95)	9.4	8.1	9.9

The ratio of peasant consumption level to non-rural personal consumption level was 1:2.4 in 1952, broadening to 1:2.9 by 1978. After the introduction of reform and opening, this gap narrowed to 1:2.2 by 1985. Subsequently, the gap again widened reaching 1:3.4 in 1995. This latest tendency is detrimental to the coordinated development of industrial and agricultural production. Measures must be taken to increase peasant incomes and consumption levels.

The rise in personal consumption levels may also be seen in increased consumption of various consumer goods (see Table 10-2).

Table 10-2   Improvement in Chinese People's Material and Cultural Life

Item	1957	1978	1980	1992
1. Foods (kg/per capita)				
Grains	203.1	195.5	213.8	235.9
Cooking oil	2.4	1.6	2.3	6.3
Pork	5.1	7.7	11.2	18.2
Beef & mutton	1.1	0.8	0.8	2.1
Poultry	0.5	0.4	0.8	2.3
Eggs	1.3	2.0	2.3	7.8
Aquatic foods	4.3	3.5	3.4	7.3
Sugar	1.5	3.4	3.8	5.4
2. Clothing (meter/per capita)				
All fabrics	6.8	8.0	10.0	10.7
Woolen	0.01	0.08	0.14	0.25
Silk	0.10	0.28	0.45	0.66
3. Appliances (per 100 persons)				
Sewing machines			4.7	12.8
Bicycles			9.7	38.5
Electric fans			1.4	22.0
Washers			0.03	10.0
Refrigerators			0.02	3.4
TV sets			0.9	19.5
Recorders			0.5	12.2
Radio sets			12.1	18.4
Cameras			0.6	2.3

4. Housing(square meters)			
Rural per capita	8.1	9.4	18.9
Urban per capita	3.6	3.9	6.9
5. Health care (per 10,000 persons)			
Hospital beds	19.3	20.1	23.4
Doctors	10.7	11.7	15.4
6. Education			
School-age children			
Attending school (%)	95.5	93.9	97.2
College students (per 10,000 persons)	8.9	11.6	18.6
7. Culture (per 100 persons)			
Daily newspapers	3.7	3.9	4.4
Books (copies per 100 persons/year)	4.7	5.8	7.5
8. Urban public utilities			
Availability of running water (%)	81.0	81.4	92.5
Availability of LPG or natural gas (%)	13.9	16.8	52.4
Greenspace (ha./10,000 persons)	10.6	9.6	34.5
9. Transportation			
Bicycles (per 100 persons)	7.7	9.7	38.5
Urban public vehicles			
(per 10,000 persons)	3.3	3.5	5.9
10. Retail sales & service outlets			
(per 10,000 persons)			
Sales outlets	13.0	20.5	116.5
Employees (per 10,000 persons)	63.1	93.9	287.4

Section Two   Analysis of the "Relatively Comfortable" Standard of Living

I. The Significance of "Relatively Comfortable" Consumption Standards

The phrase "relatively comfortable" standard of living is intended to describe further progress beyond meeting the basic needs of food and clothing, increased comfort in that necessary for daily life. Both material and cultural life will be enriched. Personal consumption levels will rise and social welfare and working environments will be bettered.

In terms of the economy of consumption, it is intended to describe a stage in the development of the standard of living between the primary stage of sufficient food and clothing and the later stage of genuine wealth. Descriptions of consumption levels during this stage will include public consumption levels as well as individual or personal consumption levels.

China began the process of realizing this goal of a "relatively comfortable" standard of living in 1990. An outline of indicators has been drawn up based on the nation's actual circumstances and with reference to international standards in an effort to measure the consumption standards that will define the "relatively comfortable" standard of living. These may be addressed under three headings.

1. Individual consumption levels. These in turn may be measured using different indicators. (1) Quantitative consumption index. A nationwide per-capita "relatively comfortable" income level may be set at 1,400 yuan in 1990 constant prices, 2,380 yuan in the city and 1,100 yuan in the countryside. In 1990 per-capita housing was 7.1 square meters in the city and 17.8 square meters in the countryside, less than the level defined as "relatively comfortable," 10 square meters in the city and 20 square meters in the countryside. As to the per-capita daily intake of protein, specialists of The World Health Organization and the United Nations Food and Agriculture Organization have stated that a daily intake of 2,385 Calorie, 75 grams of protein and 65 grams of fat is the standard for the maintenance of "an ordinary global citizen's" normal activities. In 1990 the per-capita daily intake of protein in China was 65 grams. The target for a "relatively comfortable" living standard may be designated 75 grams. (2) Consumption structure index. The consumption structure refers to the proportional relationship between the various consumer goods, (including labor and services), consumed by a population under certain economic and social conditions. This provides another prism through which to view a people's level of consumption. The general standard

for food expenditure as a percentage of total income at different development stages as determined by the United Nations Food and Agriculture Organization using Engel's coefficient: more than 60 percent indicates a poor population, 50 to 60 percent adequate food and clothing, 40 to 50 percent "relatively comfortable" and less than 40 percent wealthy. Actual conditions in China suggest a variation from this standard as many factors employed in the calculations using Engel's coefficient are not comparable. In 1990 Chinese spent an average 54.7 percent of their income on food. Expenditure of 45-49 percent may be taken as an indication of a "relatively comfortable" living standard for China. Non-commodity consumption includes labor and services consumed to meet the needs of development or enjoyment. These provide an important part of a heightened quality of life. Chinese spent 10 percent of their income on non-commodity goods in 1990. The standard for a "relatively comfortable" life may be considered 15 percent.

2. Levels of public consumption. The public consumption indicators for a "relatively comfortable" standard of living are systematically combined. In medium income countries tertiary industry's share of GNP averaged 50 percent. This may be compared with 27.2 percent in China in 1990 and a projected 35 percent in current prices for 2000. China had 2.4 hospital beds per thousand people in 1990; 2.9 per thousand can be said to indicate a "relatively comfortable" standard of living. That same year, there were 1.1 telephone lines per hundred people; 2.8 telephone lines can be said to meet the higher standard. Internationally, 47 percent of workers in countries with a population adequately clothed and housed have social security. This figure rises to 75 percent in countries with a "relatively comfortable" standard of living. In China in 1990, however, this figure was 29 percent, although it is expected to rise to 60 percent by the end of the century, approaching the level suggested for a "relatively comfortable" standard of living.

3. Average consumption levels for the comfortably well-off standard. The Gini Coefficient measures equality in the distribution of

income. A general standard for market economy countries considers a coefficient less than 0.2 an indication of a high degree of equality, 0.2 to 0.3 relative equality, 0.3-0.4 a relatively equitable income gap, and over 0.4 a large income gap. Both equality and substantial inequalities in income distribution are found in China. Urban staff and workers have more or less equal incomes. However, major differences in income can be found between the city and the countryside, between the coastal and inland areas and between individuals with different sources of income. In 1990 the Gini Coefficient for China was 0.36 (rural 0.31 and urban 0.23). Given China's circumstances, neither an excessively large nor small difference in income distribution is suitable during the "relatively comfortable" stage. A desirable coefficient would be in the 0.30 to 0.35 range, (urban 0.28 and rural 0.30-0.40). This would help improve economic efficiency and achieve common prosperity.

II. The Transition from a "Relatively Comfortable" Standard of Living to the Consumption Level of Moderately Developed Countries

Transition from a "relatively comfortable" living standard to that of a moderately developed country will be the third step in China's socialist modernization. The realization of the living standards of a moderately developed country will entail a further increase in total volume of consumption, improvements in the consumption structure and the quality of goods consumed, more modern styles of consumption and a greater variety in products. To better understand what is meant by the living standards of a moderately developed country and provide a basis for international comparisons, a brief description of household consumption structures in low, middle and high income countries will follow. This will help illuminate the gap between China and the middle and high income countries and indicate the goals it is to achieve.

The 1993 World Development Report on household consumption

structures in 85 countries (regions) published by the World Bank lays out the substantial differences between countries (regions) with varying incomes. (1) Food. In most low income countries 50 to 59 percent of household income is spent on food; the highest percentage, 64 percent, is in Tanzania and the second highest, 61 percent, is in China. Most middle income countries spend 30 to 39 percent and most high income countries 10 to 19 percent. The lowest percentage, 10 percent, is found in the United States. (2) Clothing including footwear. In low income countries 5 to 8 percent of household income is spent on clothing; households in Benin spend the largest portion of income, 14 percent, followed by China and Ghana, 13 percent. Households in middle income countries spend 9 to 10 percent and 5 to 6 percent in most of the countries with high income. (3) Rent, fuel and power. Households in most low and middle income countries spend 11 to 15 percent of income on rent, fuel and power, the lowest percentage, 6 percent, is in Sri Lanka, followed by 8 percent in China, Pakistan and Mali. Most high income countries spend 16 to 20 percent. (4) Health care. Approximately 3 percent of household income is spent on health care in most low income countries, compared with 1 percent in China and Pakistan. Middle income countries average 5 to 7 percent and high income countries approximate to 10 percent. The highest percentage, 15 percent, can be found in Switzerland. (5) Education. Households in most low income countries spend 3 to 4 percent of income on education, the lowest percentage, 1 percent, is in China, Bangladesh and Nepal. Most middle income countries spend 5 to 7 percent and high income countries 8 to 9 percent. (6) Transportation and telecommunications. There are substantial differences in the percentage of household income spent on transportation and telecommunications in low and lower middle income countries, ranging from 1 percent in China and Nepal to 16 percent in Jamaica. Most households in this group spend 6-10 percent of family income on the two items. In most upper middle and high income countries approximately 13 percent of household income is spent. (7) Other consumer goods, including durable goods. In most low income countries 10 to 19 percent of household income is spent on this final catchall category while 15 percent is found in China, in middle income countries 20 to 29 percent and in high income countries and regions 30 to 39 percent, the highest percentage, 44 percent, in Hong Kong. Other consumption level standards will not be discussed here.

Section Three Future Personal Consumption Levels and Changes in the Consumption Structure

I. Future Personal Consumption Levels

1. Nationwide personal consumption levels. On the basis of increases in consumption levels between 1978 and 1995, an annual GDP growth rate of 8 percent between 1991 and 2010 should result in 7 percent annual growth in the level of personal consumption nationwide, personal consumption reaching 1,603 yuan in 2000 and 3,153 yuan in 2010 in constant prices. Assuming average annual price increases of 5 percent, personal consumption should reach 2,368 yuan in 2000 and 7,588 yuan in 2010. Respectively, these will be 3.3 and 10.5 times 1990's consumption level, 723 yuan.

2. Peasant consumption levels. If peasant consumption levels grow at a sufficiently accelerated rate in the future to roughly keep pace with the 7 percent growth rate in personal consumption levels nationwide, peasant consumption can be expected to reach 1,098 yuan in 2000 and 2,160 yuan in 2010 in constant prices. Factoring in expected 5 percent annual increase in prices, peasant consumption would be 1,622 yuan in 2000 and 5,198 yuan in 2010.

3. Non-rural citizen consumption levels. An annual growth rate in personal consumption of 7 percent in the coming years would produce non-rural citizen consumption levels of 3,452 yuan in 2000 and 6,790 yuan in 2010. Factoring in price increases, the sums would be 5,100 yuan in 2000 and 16,341 yuan in 2010.

The above calculations are tabulated in Table 10-3.

Table 10-3   Future Personal Consumption Levels

Unit: yuan

	Calculation based on constant prices		Calculation base on 5% annual price increases	
	2000	2010	2000	2010
National consumption level	1,603	3,153	2,368	7,588
Peasant	1,098	2,160	1,622	5,198
Non-rural citizen	3,452	6,790	5,100	16,341

4. Various factors hampering growth in consumption. The economic growth rate is the fundamental factor determining the growth rate in consumption levels. Between 1979 and 1995 the GNP grew 9.5 percent per annum and the national income 8.8 percent. Needless to say this was very rapid growth. Rapid growth is expected to continue up to 2010, with annual growth rates in both GNP and national income expected to average around 8 percent.

The rate of accumulation is another major factor affecting consumption levels. Since 1978 the accumulation rate has varied between 28 and 36 percent. It should remain around 34 percent in the coming years.

Personal consumption levels are also determined by the population growth rate. China's population is projected to reach 1.3 billion by 2000 and 1.4 billion by 2010. Insofar as the population growth rate and the accumulation rate are given, increase in the level of personal consumption should roughly match, although slightly lower, the increase in the national income.

Projections regards rural and urban levels of consumption will vary according to how much improvement is expected in their relative shares of total consumption nationwide. The gap between peasant and non-peasant consumption levels widened between 1978 and 1995 as increases in urban consumption outpaced that in the countryside. This tendency should not be allowed to continue if common prosperity is to be ensured.

II. Changes in the Consumption Structure Since the Initiation of the Reform and Opening Policy

Significant changes in the consumption structure have resulted from the rapid economic development and heightened living standards since 1978 (see Table 10-4 and Table 10-5).

Table 10-4   Changes in the Rural Consumption Structure

Unit: %

Item	1978	1992
Living expenses	97.3	91.3
Food	67.7	56.8
Clothing	12.7	8.0
Housing	3.2	10.3
Fuel	7.1	4.4
Appliances etc.	6.6	11.8
Non-commodity expenditure	2.7	8.7
Total	100.0	100.0

Table 10-5 Changes in the Urban Consumption Structure

Unit: %

Item	1981	1992
1. Expenditure on commodity purchases	92.0	87.8
Food	66.7	52.9
Clothing	4.8	14.4
Daily necessities	9.6	9.7
Cultural and recreational commodities	5.7	4.4
Books, newspapers & magazines	0.9	1.0
Medicine & medical goods	0.6	1.8
Building & housing materials	-	1.0

Fuel	1.9	1.7
Other	-	0.8
Non-commodity expenditure	8.0	12.2
Rent	1.4	0.9
Water & electricity	1.0	1.7
Gas	-	0.3
Misc. educational expenditure	0.6	0.3
Child care	0.6	0.5
Transportation	1.3	1.2
Post & telecommunications	0.1	0.2
Entertainment	0.6	0.5
Medical care	-	0.4
Others	-	3.5
Total	100.0	100.0

Changes in the personal consumption structure may be summarized as follows.

1. Food expenditure as a share of total decreased. In 1978, 67.7 percent of peasant expenditure was for food, in 1992 down to 56.8 percent. In the city, food expenditure dropped from 56.7 percent to 52.9 percent between 1981 and 1992.

2. Non-commodity expenditure increased. In 1978, 2.7 percent of peasant expenditure went for things other than commodities, in 1992 up to 8.7 percent. Urban non-commodity expenditure rose from 8 percent in 1981 to 12.2 percent in 1992.

3. Urban rent expenditure was abnormally low, in 1992 only 0.9 percent, still less than 2 percent including purchases of building and housing materials. Rent expenditure was 2.32 percent in 1957 and 2.61 percent in 1964. For forty years it has tended to decrease. Low rents decreasing still further is a peculiarity of urban consumption in China.

4. Expenditure on culture was very low and has fallen still lower. In 1981 city dwellers devoted 7.2 percent of their expenditure to their cultural life, (including cultural commodities, magazines and other publications and entertainment). Ten years later in 1992 that portion of expenditure had decreased by 1.3 percentage points to 5.9 percent. This points to inadequacies in urban cultural life.

III. Future Changes in the Consumption Structure

1. The consumption structure is in the process of change reflecting the transition from adequacy in food and clothing to a "relatively comfortable" standard of living. The most salient characteristic of the former state is the high proportion of total expenditure devoted to food. During the nineties this proportion falls as those for housing, health care, daily necessities and leisure travel rise. This shift does not come suddenly, rather gradually, with many ups and downs. This will be the case because while the problem of adequate food and clothing has been solved for the majority of the population it has not for the small minority. In addition, the diet of all the population as a whole continues to need improvement. Moreover, the Chinese diet includes increasing quantities of processed foods and these foods are being more deeply processed. Food prices are rising quickly, forestalling decreases in the share of expenditure allotted to food and, in turn, preventing any rapid increase in the proportion spent on other living expenses.

The Engel coefficient, food expenditure as a share of total living expenses, demonstrates rises and falls in consumption levels as reflected in change in the consumption structure. A decrease in the coefficient indicates a rise in living standards, and vice versa. However, this rule is not hard and fast. After 1949 living standards improved. People once living in poverty were adequately fed and clothed. In this instance, however, the Engel coefficient rose, despite improving living standards. At that time increased income went first to satisfying basic nutritional needs and only later to clothing and other consumer goods. Since the initiation of the reform and opening policy improvement in living standards has come at an accelerated rate, particularly in the countryside. This can be seen in changes in the consumption structure. However, it was not reflected in any major increase in the Engel coefficient. In fact, in some years the coefficient increased.[1] Much of this certainly reflects increased food prices, but is also an expression of the people's desire to improve their diets. This particularly true in the countryside where many peasants pursue better nutrition. In this way the Engel coefficient may not fall as expected, indeed may rise. Accordingly, appraisal of China's living standard should not rely solely on this measurement tool. In comparisons made to other countries, the data must indeed be functionally comparable. In China, very low cost rent and health care result in a greater proportion of expenditure going to food. In other countries where rent and medical expenses are very expensive a comparatively smaller portion of total expenditure goes to food.

2. The consumption structure is moving from a semi-supply model where the state supplied consumers with some goods to a model wherein consumers provide themselves with the goods they want. Currently, it is unclear what portion of household consumption is covered by subsidies from the government or enterprises and what portion is paid for through income from salaries and bonuses. Answers vary with different methods of calculation. In 1978, it is suggested, members of the urban workforce received an average of 562.7 yuan in various subsidies from the government or enterprises, more than 80 percent of average remaining earnings in salaries and bonuses of 644 yuan. In other words, roughly half of these workers' consumption was provided for by their own out of pocket expenditure and the other "half" supplied to them through a system of egalitarian distribution. Since 1978 average wages have risen considerably and as have

---

[1] In 1981, 59.66 percent of total expenditure of peasant households was for food. The following year, it increased slightly to 60.48 percent. The figures for the urban workforce were 56.66 percent in 1981, 58.65 percent in 1982 and 59.2 percent in 1983, significantly higher in the latter two years.

subsidies. Increases in both have been similar and subsidies continue to account for approximately half of income. In this sense the urban consumption structure continues to adhere to the semi-supply model. Significantly, in this structure some consumption items are very heavily subsidized with the consumer paying very little. For example, in 1990 urban households paid monthly an average of 0.78 yuan in rent per capita, approximately 0.73 percent of total living expenses. Medical expenses averaged only 1.62 yuan per capita per month, 1.52 percent of total living expenses. Such a low portion of total expenditure devoted to rent and health care cannot be found in the developed countries. It is very low even compared with many third world countries. While this is characteristic of the current consumption structure for urban workforce, in the future, with reform of the economic system, particularly reform of the housing and social security systems, subsidies will be gradually reduced, this former income converted into wages or other cash income. In this way, the old model will give way to the new. During this transition, items currently subsidized, such as rent and health care, will take an increasing share of total expenditure, a tendency that will continue until the particular reforms are completed.

3. The consumption structure is moving from self-sufficiency model to a commodity economy model. Before 1949 peasants lived in a natural economy relying on themselves to satisfy their consumption needs. After 1949 until the initiation of the reform and opening policy in 1978 the rural commodity economy suffered several reversals. Growth was slow. Accordingly, peasant expenditure on commodities as a portion of total expenditure remained very low, only 39.7 percent in 1978. Peasants were of necessity almost self-sufficient, a fact reflected in their consumption structure. Since that time, however, the rural commodity economy has developed rapidly, as has the peasants' consumption structure. Commodities as a portion of total peasant living expenses rose to 67.2 percent by 1990, while expenditure on goods supplied by the peasants themselves dropped to 32.8 percent. The rural consumption structure has been fundamentally altered to the

commodity type. Further development of the rural commodity economy will continue these trends.

4. The consumption structure is becoming increasingly diversified. Most Chinese earn about the same income. Leaving aside a comparatively small number of newly rich, per-capita urban living expenses in 1990 averaged about 100 yuan per month, and in the countryside about 45 yuan. In the cities that year 37.55 percent of households had monthly per-capita expenditure between 60 and 100 yuan, 40.21 percent between 100 and 150 yuan and 22.26 percent more than 150 yuan. Only 1.39 percent of peasant households had annual net per-capita income under 150 yuan and only 1.76 percent of peasant households more than 2,000 yuan. Few households were extremely rich or poor. This coherence in income determined the sameness in the consumption structure. The variety of consumer goods purchased by people at different income levels was roughly the same and there was little difference in grades of quality. Given this circumstance, change in the consumption structure can be abrupt. By way of example, when a new product is introduced to the market if one person cannot afford it then his neighbor probably cannot either. There is no market for the product. However, once that person can afford the product, his neighbor most likely will be able to afford it also. Supplies of the product become tight as it rapidly gains in popularity. As the impact of the policy allowing some persons and some regions to become wealthy more quickly than others becomes more fully realized, differences in personal income levels will become increasingly pronounced. The consumption structure will become increasingly diversified and increasingly reflect the differences in economic strata.

Chapter Eleven   The Distribution of Individual Income

This chapter will deal with the current distribution of individual income, analyzing the basic factors that will determine future changes in the income distribution pattern and propose policy choices based on this analysis.

Section One   The Distribution of Individual Income During the Current Stage

I. The Distribution of Individual Income During the Current Stage

The current individual income distribution pattern has been determined by the rapid development of the economy and the profound changes in the economic system produced by the reform and opening. Two points are deserving of first mention.

1. Individual urban and rural incomes rose substantially as a result of the rapid economic growth. Per-capita income in urban households rose from 316 yuan in 1978 to 3,892.9 yuan in 1995, an average annual nominal increase of 15.92 percent or an actual increase of 6.4 percent. Per-capita net income in rural households rose from 133.6 yuan in 1978 to 1,577.7 yuan in 1995, an average annual nominal increase of 15.63 percent or an actual increase of 8.09 percent. Nationwide, average annual wages rose from 615 yuan in 1978 to 5,500 in 1995, an increase of more than 900 percent.

2. The income differential began to widen amidst general across

the board increases in income. There was diversification between urban and rural incomes and within the urban and rural income structures.

First, the situation in the countryside will be examined. Between 1979 and 1995 a stage characterized by economic growth brought an end to the low incomes predominant in rural areas for very many years. In general, a high growth period was followed by a period of stagnation or decline, in turn followed by growth but at a slower rate than during the earlier period.

The years between 1979 and 1984 marked a period of rapid growth in rural income. The introduction of the household contracted responsibility system linking remuneration to output effected a combination of the activation of the most basic "lever," profit, with the most basic material condition for production, land. This quite naturally inspired the peasants to increase production. At the same time, the government greatly raised the purchase prices for agricultural products, with the result that rural incomes increased at an average annual rate of 17.81 percent for this short period of time, 14.4 percent after adjustment for price factors. This enormous income increase was, in essence, a release of latent productive energy.

Peasant incomes stagnated or even decreased between 1985 and 1989. This was because a fundamental change had not yet come over the quality and composition of certain specific productive forces. Growth stalled for the five years after the latent productive energies had been released but before the productive forces had gained definition. Stagnation aggravated by inflation prevented any growth in peasant income, even producing negative growth in actual income in 1988 and 1989.

Beginning in 1990 the agricultural production system was gradually but decisively repositioned. Building on the solidification of the household contracted responsibility system, the dual operating system combining centralized and separated operations was continually improved and more fully integrated, the socialized service system actively developed, operations diversified and commercialization of production increased. Moreover, the development of a commodity-market economy and the activation of the profit motive gave rise to the emergence and development of rural industry. This ushered in a new period of growth in rural incomes. However, while gross incomes increased substantially, net incomes did not. This was because the peasants were increasingly unreasonably burdened by various quotas during these years and rapid inflation. This situation began to improve after 1995.

Changes in rural incomes since the initiation of the reform and opening policy may be summarized as follows.

1. The rural income structure has changed as a result in increases and decreases in agricultural and non-agricultural (principally township enterprise) income. Township enterprises provided 8.8 percent of peasant net income in 1980, 21.7 percent in 1985, 25.2 percent in 1990 and 32.8 percent in 1993, even more than 80 percent in certain developed areas.

2. Growth in peasant incomes was seriously affected by price hikes. In the 17 years since the initiation of the reform and opening peasant incomes have risen by substantial margins, an average annual growth rate was 15.63 percent. However, price increases reduce the actual average annual growth rate to 8.09 percent. In one or two years, there was even negative growth. For example, in 1994 cash income increased by 32 percent over the previous year; adjusted for price factors the increase was only 5 percent. Annual growth rates in 1988 and 1989 were 17.8 percent and 10.4 percent respectively, but double digit inflation (18.5 percent and 17.8 percent) offset any real increase, resulting in negative growth (-0.7 percent and -7.4 percent).

3. Growth in peasant income slowed down. The growth rate of peasant income did not match the growth rate of the rural economy. Since 1985 the gap between increases in urban and rural income growth rate has been excessive.

There has tended to be greater differences in individual peasant incomes. This has been manifested in two different ways. (1) Different regions have different income levels. In 1980 difference in rural net incomes in the eastern, central and western regions expressed as a ratio was 1.39:1.11:1; in 1985, 1.54:1.21:1; in 1990, 1.8:1.26:1. By 1992 the gap had expanded to 2.22:1.25:1. There remain 80 million peasants in the central and western regions who are inadequately fed and clothed. In 1992 per-capita income was less than 376 yuan, about one quarter that in the developed areas. Nationwide, the central government has officially named 325 counties impoverished; another more than 200 counties have been so named at the provincial level. Of these, 85 percent are located in the central and western regions. (2) Difference exist between rural incomes derived from different sources and at different economic strata. Peasants engaged in different lines of work earn different levels of income. Peasants relying on income produced by township enterprises earn two or three times more than those relying on crop agriculture, those working in commerce or services three to six times more and those working privately in transportation or construction six to nine times more. Similarly, employers earn much more than their employees, often very much more is the difference in income between the employers and the employees. Generally speaking, the greater the number of employees, the greater the income gap. According to one survey, the owner of a business employing 10 to 30 employees earns 15 to 40 times as much as his employees, the owner of a business employing 31 to 50 employees 40 to 70 times as much and the owner of business employing 51 to 100 employees 65 to 130 times as much.

Urban income differentials have also widened.

1. Regional variations in income have become more pronounced. In 1983 per-capita urban income was 543 yuan in the eastern region, 493 yuan in the western region and 458 yuan in the central region. By 1992 this income had grown to 2,181 yuan in the eastern region (an increase of 302 percent), 1,671 yuan in the western region (up 238 percent), and 1,510 yuan in the central region (up 230 percent). In the ten years between 1983 and 1992, urban non-wage income increased 530 percent in the East, 490 percent in the West and 390 percent in the central region. The eastern region started off with the highest income and also experienced the greatest increase.

This income gap between the East and the inland regions widened still further in 1994. If income in the western region is assigned a value of one, the income differential between the East and the rest of the country increased from 1.37:0.93 in 1993 to 1.41:0.95 in 1994. The five leaders in per-capita income were Guangdong, Shanghai, Beijing, Zhejiang and Guangxi. The urban Gini Coefficient rose from 0.062 in 1981 to 0.14 in 1995.

2. Income level differentials between different sorts of work have also widened. In 1978 per-capita wage income in state-owned work units owned ranked as follows (1) Geological prospecting, 811 yuan; (2) construction, 756 yuan; (3) transportation, post and telecommunications, 734 yuan; (4) industry, 681 yuan; (5) scientific research, 670 yuan; (6) government organizations, 661 yuan; (7) financial and insurance industry, 650 yuan; (8) housing management and public utilities, 626 yuan; (9) medical services, sports and social welfare services, 605 yuan; (10) commerce and food services, 588 yuan; (11) educational and cultural work, 566 yuan; and (12) agriculture, forestry, stock breeding, fishery and water conservancy, 492 yuan. By 1995, higher income were to be found in the financial, real estate, power and transportation and telecommunications sectors. Incomes in agriculture, forestry, animal husbandry and fishery, as well as mining and manufacturing were comparatively low. Average per-capita income in the financial and insurance sector was 2.38 times that in agriculture, forestry, animal husbandry and fishery, 1.43 times that in mining and 1.48 times that in manufacturing. The income differentials would be still greater if hard to calculate bonuses, allowances, hidden income and actual welfare benefits were included.

3. The income differentials between workers employed by businesses with different forms of ownership continue to widen. According to one survey, in 1986 per-capita wage in foreign-invested enterprises was 1,527 yuan, 14 percent more than the average for all workers nationwide or 200 more yuan a year. By 1992, per-capita wage in foreign-invested enterprises was 4,037 yuan, 1,400 yuan more than in state-owned enterprises and 1,903 yuan more than in urban

collective enterprises. In only a few years, differential had expanded by 600 percent in the first instance and 850 percent in the second.[1] During the first two months of 1994 per-capita incomes in foreign-invested continued to rise substantially over the major increases of 1993. At this time, the average wage growth rate for non-agricultural workers nationwide was 26.3 percent, 25.8 percent in state-owned enterprises and 18 percent in urban collective work units. This may be compared with average growth rate of 92.2 percent in foreign-invested enterprises, 41.7 percentage points higher than the previous year.[2]

4. Income differentials between groups receiving different benefits from businesses have also widened. This instance may be further subdivided into two types: income differentials between employers and employees in privately-owned and foreign-invested enterprises and income differentials between managers and factory directors and the staff and workers in publicly-owned enterprises (including state-owned and collective enterprises and collective township enterprises). Employers and managers earn a great deal more than rank and file employees. The American newspaper *The International Herald Tribune* reported that management personnel with Chinese citizenship in foreign-invested enterprises averaged approximately US$6,600 in annual income, about ten times the annual wage for an ordinary worker. At first glance it would appear that a rational income differential between management and staff and workers in state-owned enterprises has not yet been realized. However, a cursory examination may be misleading. A rational remuneration mechanism is not yet in place. Management receives benefits properly classified as income that may not be recognized as such. For example, in addition to their salaries, managers may receive subsidies and paid expenses, better housing and use of an automobile free of charge, paid domestic and international travel and various expensive paid luxuries.

---

[1] "Widening Income Differentials: a Survey of 10,000 Workers and Staff in 100 Enterprises," *Chinese Business Times*, January 18, 1994.

[2] *China Information News*, March 30, 1994.

II. Addressing Income Differentials

As made clear above, urban and rural income differentials are widening. In 1980 the World Bank estimated China's Gini Coefficient to be 0.33, by 1988 the figure had risen to 0.382. This widening continued in the nineties in both the city and the countryside with the coefficient reaching 0.43 in 1995. Although still below the level of other lower income developing countries in the same stage of development as China, as a Gini Coefficient it rates high. The World Bank states that the average Gini Coefficient for household income in lower middle income countries is 0.4467; in Asia this figure is lower. Drawing upon international experience, China, currently in the lower middle income stage, can anticipate a further widening of income differential. The turning point has not yet been reached.

The urban rural income differential over the last ten or more years may be envisioned as the letter "U" plotted on a graph. Between 1978 and 1984 it narrowed, but then widened between 1984 and 1992. Growth in peasant income was comparatively slow after 1984. Further hampered by a series of burdens imposed on the peasantry, rural incomes in backward sections of the central region and most of the western region did not increase, even decreased, further widening the gap between urban and rural incomes.

In general, current income differentials within the urban population are not particularly substantial. The urban Gini Coefficient was 0.16 in 1978, 0.19 in 1985, 0.23 in 1988, 0.27 in 1993 and 0.28 in 1995. While this indicates an expanding range of income, the change has been less than radical. This demonstrates that the marketization reforms to date have produced relatively slow moving changes in the urban income distribution system. The old "big rice bowl" where everyone eats together sharing rewards equally regardless of the amount of actual work individually done remains in place. However, increased urban income differentials is a fundamental trend of the times and will accelerate with greater marketization. A survey by the State Statistical Bureau reports widening urban income differentials in

1994. In 1993 the top ten percent of households in total per-capita income earned 3.6 times the bottom ten percent; in 1994 they earned 3.9 times. The top ten percent earned 6,838 yuan per capita, up 39.4 percent over the previous year, and the bottom ten percent 1,735 yuan per capita, an increase of 27.6 percent.

Rural income differentials narrowed then widened. The World Bank calculations show a gradual narrowing of income differentials between 1978 and 1982, when the Gini Coefficient dropped from 0.32 to 0.22, and then a gradual widening after 1983, as the coefficient rose to 0.31 in 1986 and 0.34 in 1995. The key factor behind the increased income differential was income from sources other than agriculture, particularly from township enterprises. Imbalanced regional economic development to a great extent exacerbated this income inequality.

Regional difference in income have also expanded. The State Statistical Bureau reports that income differentials between the rural areas in different provinces increased at a constant rate between 1980 and 1995. This was true whether each province's rural net per-capita income was compared or whether the rural net per-capita income of the highest rural income provinces was compared with that of the lowest rural income provinces. The Gini Coefficient was 0.13696 in 1980, rising to 0.15245 in 1985, 0.18774 in 1988, 0.2112 in 1992, and 0.2297 in 1995. Increased income differentials between provinces and within provinces was the result of varying levels of rural industrialization. Peasants in developed areas could receive wage income from non-agricultural sources such as township enterprises, breaking away from the traditional rural income structure and dependence on farmland. Wage income is the basic factor creating variations in income between different provinces and between different peasant households during this new period of development. In contrast, in underdeveloped areas peasants still depend on the soil. The traditional income structure has not yet been transformed by industry and peasant incomes remain low.

Generally speaking, income differentials have widened in step with increases in income nationwide. Most of the factors creating this situation are rational and the effects positive. Still, other factors influencing income distribution can be irrational and erratic. This must be kept in mind during the course of future development.

Section Two   Basic Factors Determining Future Income Distribution

Six factors will be discussed.

I. China's Economy Will Be in a Period of Structural Change and Accelerated Growth

Changes in income distribution are related to specific stages of economic development. In China, the industrialization stage in the standard sense began only in the 1980s following the market-oriented restructuring of the economy. The high productivity created by modern large-scale industry has promoted increased individual incomes. In turn, increased incomes create new demand and greater purchasing power, further fueling rapid economic development.

II. China Has Entered a Stage of Economic Growth Propelled by Urbanization

Since the beginning of the nineties, the development of the market economy has driven the normal mutually promoting relationship of industrialization and urbanization. China was long insufficiently urbanized and this has turned the tide. This will accelerate redistributions and recombinations within the economy, producing new concentrations and combinations of resources. Regions with stronger foundations in urbanization will have an advantage, maintaining high investment and growth rates. The gap between these areas and those less urbanized will continue to widen. Growth in investment will steadily fade moving westward from the seacoast. The income gap between east and west regions will be further aggravated as will differences in consumption levels. Economic sectors directly connected to urbanization, such as real estate, construction and the financial and insurance sector, will clearly benefit and salaries in these fields will be higher than elsewhere. This imbalanced growth will further broaden income differentials between different economic sectors, enriching some currently less remunerative.

III. Higher Accumulation Rates, Economic Growth and Changes in Individual Income

The accumulation rate will remain around 34 percent for the next 20 years. The GDP growth rate has been kept around 9 percent in the nineties and will be around 7.5 percent for the first decade of the next century.

During this period, a basic characteristic of economic development and industrialization will be rapid urbanization. Investment-driven economic growth requires a fairly high rate of accumulation. Weakening consumption demand resulting from the time lag inherent in the course of change of the consumption structure and the lack of the actual conditions necessary for a new round of higher level consumption will result in growing individual incomes being deposited as savings. In this way, high levels of personal savings following high rates of investment, economic growth, accumulation and individual income forms a basic cycle.

IV. Controlling Changing Inflation Rates

The inflation rate and actual individual income levels have a negative relationship. Excessive price rises engender substantial drops in actual urban and rural income levels. This most affects wage earners. In China, however, the sweeping statement that inflation is keyed to the growth rate or that it is in direct response to demand-pull cannot be made. It is possible to control excessive price increases during rapid economic growth. Ideally, the ratio of economic growth to price increase should be kept around $1:0.65$. If this goal is to be met, the average annual GDP growth rate should be 9 percent and the average annual inflation rate approximately 5.85 percent during the nineties, and the average annual GDP growth rate should not be less than 7.5 percent and the inflation rate within 4.86 percent between 2001 and 2010.

V. Controlling Population Growth

Population and individual per-capita income form an inverse ratio. Family planning has become a fundamental, permanent national policy. Population growth will be controlled in the future. Low birth rates, low mortality rates and low natural growth rate will be achieved. The population was 1.2 billion in early 1995. By the end of the century control measures will keep it within 1.3 billion. It is expected to be around 1.4 billion by 2010. China's population is already enormous. Small increases in relative terms are enormous in actual terms. This will significantly affect the growth rate of individual per-capita income.

VI. The Effect of the Distribution System on the Individual Income Pattern

China's economic system is undergoing change. Reform of the income distribution system is geared to replacing an administrative mode of distribution with a market mode. There are three main characteristics of the distribution pattern during this period of the transition. (1) Characteristics of both distribution systems are present. The administrative and market mechanisms are integrated. Negative effects and distortions caused by the market mechanism are often created by contradictions between the two systems. (2) As the old distribution system is rooted out and replaced with the new system, cracks may appear, areas beyond the control of both the government and the market. These confused areas may create opportunities for the funneling of profits from public property into the pockets of individuals. (3) Two choices in income distribution are presented: a multi-form income distribution system revolving around labor or a change to a social distribution system revolving around capital, creating serious social polarization. These choices will have an important impact on the future pattern of income distribution. If the loopholes in the current dual system are not plugged, if capitalization of power is allowed to continue unrestricted and lawless persons in business and government continue to take advantage of the current confusion to reap profits, development will be distorted and imbalanced and society polarized. If the income distribution system increasingly allows the dominance of income derived from property and capital, the property rights system based on the public ownership will crumble and dissolve. Gradually society will be divided into antagonistic interest groups, polarized by conflicting property rights. Only by proceeding from the fundamental interests of the broad masses of the people and upholding returns on labor as the leading factors determining distribution of the income during the course of reform can Chinese society advance healthily.

Section Three   Basic Trends in Individual Income Distribution.

I. The Mechanism Whereby Individual Incomes Are Formed Is Currently Being Optimized

The individual income distribution pattern depends upon the mechanism whereby such incomes are formed. This mechanism may be considered in terms of systemic and growth factors. (1) Systemic factors. Reform has led to the abandonment of the old highly centralized planned economy system. Urban incomes have diversified and are no longer dependent on a single source. Rural incomes are basically decided by the market. Still, the quotas imposed in recent years can only be considered administrative deductions from the income the market would have supplied. The price distortions engendered by the old planned system have to a certain extent been corrected during the course of reform. The economic relationship between the eastern and western regions has been adequately improved but adjusting this relationship will remain a fairly long-term process. The problem of excessive regional income differentials cannot be solved overnight. Reforms geared to urbanization have brought an influx of rural workforce to the cities. However, the tight control imposed by the household registration system is not conducive to rural industrialization or urban economic development. (2) Growth factors. The main question in urban economic growth is the move from a planned economy to a market economy. The key to growth, aside from growth in the non-state-owned economic sector already intimately bound to the market, lies in the reform process in state-owned enterprises. In the countryside the principal question is industrialization. Township enterprises will be the engine leading growth. For the next decade or two, this situation will not change substantially. Whether the township enterprises can drive accelerated growth will be the key factor determining income. The growth factor will increasingly become the most important factor determining the income differentials. Needless to say, its effect is beneficial.

In the years through 2010, the market-oriented reform of the economic system will be further deepened. This will greatly accelerate the circulation of labor power and other production elements. The movement of rural workforce into the city will come very much more quickly. The circulation of production elements between the eastern, central and western regions will be accelerated with the stimulus of correct price signals. This market-determined disposition of income will tend to narrow income differentials. In the nation as a whole, however, income differentials will continue to widen during the present stage of economic development. The formation of a beneficial income distribution system giving equal consideration to efficiency and fairness will be a difficult but essential task for China over the coming years.

II. The Move from an Allotment Mechanism to a Remuneration Mechanism

Market-oriented reform determines that the basic mechanism for income distribution marketized, necessarily moving from the traditional allotment mechanism to a remuneration-based mechanism.

Under the old highly centralized planned economy system, the traditional distribution mechanism was fundamentally an allotment mechanism. This mechanism depended on a graded system of concentrate power. Policy decisions were highly centralized. Thus, in essence, it was an administrative system.

The change from a planned economy system to a market economy system requires the replacement of the allotment distribution system with a remuneration-based distribution system. The commodity-market economy income distribution provides a model remuneration mechanism. Users of elements give remuneration to providers of elements based on their contribution according to the gain assigned to the contribution or its "social" price. In a market economy gains will necessarily be distributed through a remuneration mechanism.

III. Diversification of Income Sources

Income comes from an increasing number of sources.

1. The operating mechanism of a market economy determines that all elements entering the production process require compensation. All production elements used in the formation of a produdct are entitled to a certain recompense. Resources whether material or human, ownership or power of operation, capital or labor, if used must be paid for and are entitled to be included in the distribution of income.

2. Diversification of individual income takes two forms. First, are different sorts of income derived from resources or property rights

owned by an individual, such as personal property or managerial or labor skills. Second, are occupational and non-occupational incomes. This would include income from a second or third job.

The diversification of income sources is a macro characteristic. In the course of actual operations the diversification of income invariably forms a specific structure, the forms of income from multiple sources always form a specific structure. The income distribution system of a specific mode of distribution reflects production conditions with some kind of income dominant.

IV. The Increasing Prominence of Income from Management Functions and Power of Operation

Examining coming trends in income from property rights an important phenomenon becomes apparent. A portion of incomes derived from management skills or management functions, those incomes earned by persons controlling or exercising power of operation, will rise substantially whether openly or covertly.

Establishing a socialist market economy in China, particularly the renovation of the state-owned enterprise system, entails constructing the subjects of the activities of the market economy, enterprises with true property rights and the status of a legal person, and also training the managerial and entrepreneurial layers of the state-owned enterprises. Many entrepreneurs have distinguished themselves in the emerging market economy and more will be produced. The reform has extended enterprise's decision-making power, with the contract system granting considerable power to the managers of state-owned enterprises. Their nominal and real wages are far higher than those of ordinary staff and workers and their actual income will increase in the future. The managerial function is important and compensation should be suitable. However, at present managerial staff have low nominal salaries and insufficient stimulation to better performance. Actual incomes are nonstandardized and unrestricted. Insufficient stimulation is coupled with impotent supervision. The crux for this is how to form the standard mechanism and effective control.

V. The General Tendency to Rising Incomes

Rising individual incomes are determined by multiple factors. These factors have the natural and technological properties of economic development as well as social properties, such as the triggering of profit levers and the strengthening of the market mechanism. Moreover, there are negative growth factors that affect growth in actual income and per-capita growth. The first of these include inflation, while the latter includes the population growth rate and total population in a given year.

By 2010 China's aggregate economy will have substantially expanded. Although in per-capita income it will still rank at the level of a developing country, it is expected to leave the ranks of the low income countries and join that of the middle income countries. Per-capita rural income during the nineties has grown at an average annual rate of 5.5 to 6 percent adjusted for price factors, rising to around 3,000 yuan by 2000. During the first decade of the new century, the actual income is expected to increase more than 5 percent per annum, rising to 7,000 or 8,000 yuan by 2010. Per-capita urban income during the nineties has grown at an average annual rate of 7 percent adjusted for price factors, rising to 6,000 or 7,000 yuan by 2000; then grow at an average annual rate of 5 to 6 percent for the next ten years, exceeding 20,000 yuan by 2010. Rapid economic growth will be accompanied by substantial increase in urban and rural incomes.

VI. The Inverted "U" Course of Income Distribution

The inverted "U" describes the prevailing international trend in income distribution, demonstrating that under market economy conditions income from production elements will gradually become equalized. As China's market economy develops, the income distribution mechanism will become increasingly defined by the market with income from labor providing the main body of income. The gap in individual incomes will first widen then contract as a result of market competition and adequate circulation of production elements.

About two decades of reform have seen continually expanding income differentials between city and countryside, different regions and different economic strata. The turning point is not easily discerned. It is expected that when per-capita rural household income reaches US$1,000 a year, the income differential will began to narrow. Similar turning points may be suggested for other individual income groups.

Regards the circulation of production elements, in the beginning the flow was unidirectional, workers flowing out of underdeveloped areas, from the countryside to the city, from the west to the east. This narrowed the income differential for laborers. Then, responding to comparative advantage, resources and labor-intensive factories moved from the cities to the rural areas, from developed areas to the underdeveloped areas. Circulation of production elements provides increasingly equal opportunities for the people to acquire income, different income strata achieving stability. This constant improvement in the income formation mechanism will result in a clearly better income distribution structure by 2010, a structure relatively stable and fair. Once an income distribution system drawing from multiple sources and revolving around labor is established, serious polarization will be avoided.

Section Four   Risks and Policies to Counter Those Risks During the Course of Income Change over the New Decade

China is currently undergoing a period of change in its economic system and remains at a distance from the establishment of a stable, standardized and comprehensive system of coordinated development. This is particularly true with the income distribution system and the policy-making system. Two points stand out. First, large quantities of illegal incomes can be found at all layers of the system. Second, there still is no standardized, rational income distribution mechanism within the operation of the economy. These problems are even more outstanding in the state-owned enterprises and state-owned organizations. Blind egalitarianism has not yet been rooted out. "Grey income," secret, nonstandard and hidden distribution and transfer of profits can be found almost anywhere. Most typically, this takes the form of deals between "money and power," money given to those with decision-making power. Material distribution, of course, takes many forms. In short, during this period of transformation of the income distribution mechanism when policies are immature and, while practices are nonstandardized and a portion of confusion reigns, the basic facts must be directly addressed. In this way, the task of establishing a rational, standardized, unified income distribution mechanism embodying fairness and effectiveness can be realized.

A strategy attacking both the symptoms and root causes should be established. If income distribution is to be governed and adjusted, the outcome of primary distribution should be regulated through various policies from the perspective of redistribution. Still more important, a rational, standardized income distribution in line with the nation's actual conditions should be established from the perspective of primary distribution. The establishment of a market economy demands that all property rights have a right to attendant income, including ownership rights, operation and management rights, labor rights and intellectual property rights. If these elements are used, their owners are entitled to appropriate compensation, as share of the benefits produced by production. The question remains in establishing a property rights-based income distribution mechanism, should the mechanism revolve around the right to income from ownership of property or labor. This question requires earnest study. The following points should be kept in mind during the establishment of a rational, comprehensive income distribution mechanism adhering to the nation's actual circumstances.

1. The problem of illegal income must be dealt with firmly and directly. Greater efforts need to be made to stop all illegal and corrupt acts by persons seeking instant wealth by exploiting loopholes in the

dual systems, the nonstandardized income distribution system and the temporarily confused situation.

2. Growth in the labor market should be promoted. A market-regulated system whereby income comes completely in the form of money, not subsidies, should be installed. The key links determining income distribution are salary formation and the regulatory mechanism. Wage and salary reform requires the introduction of the law of value and the market mechanism in regulating the system. Efforts should be made to solve two problems. First is how to make compensation corresponding to labor the guiding principle of the system. This important question will decide the future orientation of China's income distribution. Second, how can the labor market be promoted. Without a sound, well-managed labor market, the market mechanism cannot regulate wages and salaries and the competition mechanism will be denied in individual compensation for labor.

3. A property ownership income mechanism and control system attuned to the country's actual circumstances should be established as soon as possible. Income coming to workers from property they own in addition to their principal source of income, capital income providing the principal income of an owner of a private enterprise and the profits coming from state-owned property income are all legitimate forms of income and play a positive role in the current economic stage. While a relatively balanced asset profit ratio in a given period will be formed during the course of market operation, under varying conditions the government should regulate the range of income from ownership of various properties through taxation and other measures, steering income use (for instance into accumulation or investment). At the same time, relevant laws need to be adopted to regulate variant forms of income from ownership of property, such as inheritance and assignment, rationally, in accordance with national circumstances.

4. A social security system should be established as soon as possible. The normal operation of a market economy requires guaranteeing a minimum income for workers in accordance with social and economic development to protect against untoward shifts in the

labor market and income. All provincial level governments are now establishing local minimum wage standards in accordance with the Labor Law and are putting them into practice. It will also be necessary to establish multi-level, multi-category social security systems stressing old-age insurance, unemployment insurance and medical insurance. This will be a foundation project ensuring social stability, sustaining the normal operation of the market economy and promoting the economic development.

5. Inflation should be controlled in order to achieve steady, coordinated economic development and ensure steady increases in urban and rural incomes.

6. An agricultural protection policy ensuring steady increase in peasant income and gradually narrowing the urban-rural income differential should be adopted. Generally speaking, agriculture remains in a position of low comparative advantage during the course of industrialization. Given the enormous peasant population and the low level of agricultural production technology, Chinese agriculture is still at the mercy of the elements. Overall, increases in agricultural labor productivity have consistently lagged behind increases in industrial labor productivity. In addition, there has consistently been a "price scissors" between the industrial and agricultural products, resulting in urban incomes outpacing rural incomes. This income differential will continue to widen in the near future. In view of this, it will be necessary to adopt an agricultural protection policy to ensure a steady rise in peasant incomes. At present, it is first essential to mobilize all sides to support rural economic development in an effort to free all peasants from poverty by the end of the century. At the same time, it is necessary to create conditions whereby a rural social insurance system can step by step be put into place. Second, the rural industrial structure must be adjusted and the development of township enterprises and other non-agricultural industries accelerated while maintaining the premise of steady growth in the production of primary farm products. Furthermore, the agricultural products circulation system requires reform. Risk funds should be established for major farm products and price subsidy system put into practice as necessary.

7. Correct policies for regional development need to be formulated. Following the initiation of the reform and opening policy, China has discarded the old practice used under the planned economy of relying simply on relief to help poor areas, substituting a policy of development, helping poor areas to take advantage of whatever comparative advantage they have locally, relying on the profit mechanism and advances in technology to exploit local resources and develop a market demand guided commodity economy. At an appropriate time, under the guidance of the central government, one coastal province will be given responsibility for aiding economic development in one or two provinces in the hinterland. Regions that have first gained prosperity will pay more in taxes to support development in poorer regions. A more specific strategy for regional development must be formulated. Local governments should be assisted in formulating more realistic, practical strategies for local development.

8. Crucial issues must be grappled with and difficult problems overcome in establishing the new income distribution system. Standardization of the management operations function and management income mechanism, power of operation and control over income from management, is one of these crucial issues. A rational operations and management income mechanism must be established as quickly as possible.

Chapter Twelve The Development of Regional Economies

This chapter will first describe overall regional economic development since the initiation of the reform and opening policy, before proceeding to a discussion of development trend of regional economies coming in the years up to 2010 and policy suggestions for coordinated regional economic development.

Section One Regional Economical Development Since the Initiation of the Reform and Opening Policy

I. Major Adjustments in Regional Economic Development Strategies

The government significantly altered its strategy for regional economic development with the beginning of the reform and opening period. Regional distribution of state investment has gradually shifted in focus from war preparedness and lessening regional income differentials to investment centered on economic returns. Accordingly, it has tended to be directed to regions with greater comparative advantages, particularly the coastal regions. In addition, seeking to meet the needs of opening to the outside world, the central government adopted preferential financial, tax, use of foreign capital, foreign trade and banking policies for coastal special economic zones, open ports and open economic zones.[1] These policies may be compared with earnest efforts in support of "old revolutionary base areas, areas inhabited by ethnic minorities, border areas and impoverished areas," seeking to develop production and invigorate the local economies. This support took the forms of government policies concerning public finance, taxation, loans and supply of qualified personnel. To date, the state has provided a total of nearly 10 billion yuan to these areas in aid to the poor development funds and four billion yuan annually in relief work funding. The central government has also directed large sums to economically underdeveloped areas, especially areas inhabited by ethnic minorities, in fixed subsidies every year. These policies have improved the nationwide distribution of productive forces and vitalized regional economies. In particular, adjustment of the macroeconomic distribution policy and opening the country at multiple levels have greatly accelerated coastal economic development, raising economic growth to a new level. Today, the coastal areas have become the "engine" to driving growth throughout the economy. The state has also obtained good results in supporting the "old revolutionary base areas, the areas inhabited by the ethnic minorities, the border areas and the impoverished areas."

II. Imbalance in Regional Economic Development

Regional economic development has been imbalanced for various reasons.

1. Development in different regions has been unequal. Since 1978 economic growth has come quickly in the eastern region, more slowly in the central region and still more slowly in the western region.

---

[1] The preferential policies are no longer limited to certain coastal areas. Beginning in 1992, the State Council decided to open a number of port cities along the border, cities along the Yangtze River and inland provincial capitals and designate the Three Gorges of the Yangtze River an open economic region. All these enjoy some of the preferential policy treatments enjoyed by the coastal open ports and economic zones.

Between 1979 and 1995, the average annual growth rate was 10.87 percent in the eastern region, 9.42 percent in the central region and 9.26 percent in the western region. Since the initiation of the reform and opening policy the industrial growth rate in the central and western regions continually lagged behind that in the eastern coastal region, the gap widening year after year. During the Sixth Five-Year Plan from 1981 to 1985, the total industrial output value growth rate in the central and western regions was only slightly lower than in the eastern coastal region, the relative difference only 1.8 percent.[1] During the years of the Seventh Five-Year Plan (1986-1990), the relative difference in the industrial growth rate between the central and western regions and the eastern coastal region continued to widen as the economy boomed nationwide, reaching 37.4 percent by 1991. After narrowing somewhat subsequently, it began to widen again in 1994 (see Table 12-1).

Table 12-1   Regional Industrial Output Value Growth Rates at or Above the Township Level

Unit: %

	1981-85	1986-90	1991	1992	1993	1994 (Jan.-July)
Eastern region	11.1	11.3	17.1	25.4	33.8	20.8
Central & western regions	10.9	9.1	10.7	16.3	28.6	14.7
Relative gap	1.8	19.5	37.4	35.8	15.4	29.3

Source: Calculated using data taken from *A General Industrial Survey of the People's Republic of China in 1985 (*Vol. 4), *The Chinese Statistical Yearbook* (1991, 1992 and 1993), *The 1994 Chinese Summary of Statistics* and *China Information News,* August 5, 1994.

---

[1]   The formula for relative difference:

$$\frac{\text{major value} - \text{minor value}}{\text{major value}} \times 100\%$$

Table 12-2   GDP Annual Growth Rates (1979-1995)

Unit: %

	Growth rate		Growth rate		Growth rate
National total	9.79	Guangdong	14.24	Hunan	9.41
Eastern region	10.87	Guangxi	11.67	Western region	9.26
Beijing	8.43	Central region	9.42	Sichuan	9.59
Tianjin	7.54	Shanxi	8.23	Guizhou	8.77
Hebei	9.68	Inner Mon.	9.38	Yunnan	10.43
Liaoning	8.28	Jilin	8.78	Shaanxi	8.17
Shanghai	6.22	Heilongjiang	7.81	Gansu	5.88
Jiangsu	11.53	Anhui	10.53	Qinghai	7.25
Zhejiang	13.71	Jiangxi	8.93	Ningxia	8.84
Fujian	14.54	Henan	10.77	Xinjiang	11.83
Shandong	11.88	Hubei	9.79		

Source: Calculated using data taken from *Collected Historical Statistics of Provinces, Autonomous Regions and Municipalities* (1949-1989), *The Chinese Statistical Yearbook* (1991 to 1995).

It is worth noting that in the eastern coastal regions there is also a clear contrast between the growth rates of the old and the new industrial areas. Between 1979 and 1995, the average annual GDP growth rate was 14.24 percent in Guangdong Province (including Hainan), 13.71 percent in Zhejiang Province, 11.53 percent in Jiangsu Province, 14.54 percent in Fujian Province, 11.88 percent in Shandong Province, the new industrial areas, compared with only 7.54 percent in Tianjin and 6.22 percent in Shanghai, and 8.28 percent in Liaoning, the old industrial areas. The GDP growth rate in the old industrial areas was roughly 28 percent to 57 percent lower than in the new industrial areas. The differences are still greater if the comparison is extended westward. The average annual GDP growth rate in Gansu was only 5.88 percent, 40 percent that of Fujian, 41 percent that of Guangdong (including Hainan) and 43 percent that of Zhejiang (see Table 12-2).

2. The distribution of productive forces was further concentrated in the coastal region. Industry was formerly heavily concentrated in the eastern coastal areas. This irrational situation was changed in the years since 1949, the inland economy, particularly industry, accounting for an ever greater share of the national economy. Beginning in the eighties, however, the nation's productive forces have been increasingly funneled into the eastern coastal areas and the central and western regions' share of GDP had continually declined. Between 1980 and 1995, the eastern region's share of GDP rose from 52.3 percent to 58.3 percent, up 6 percentage points, while that of the central region fell from 31.4 percent to 27.5 percent and that of the western region from 16.3 percent to 14.2 percent, 3.9 and 2.1 percentage points lower respectively (see Table 12-3).

3. Regional development gaps continue to widen. Between 1978 and 1995, the relative difference in per-capita GDP between the central region and the eastern region widened from 33.1 percent to 45.5 percent, 12.4 percentage points in 15 years, and that between the western region and eastern region from 45.9 percent to 56.5 percent, 10.6 percentage points. If this pattern continues to develop, the three regions spoken of will become two, as the gap between the western and central regions closes and that between these two and the eastern coastal region expands (see Table 12-4).

Table 12-3   Regional Shares of GDP

Unit: %

	1978	1980	1986	1988	1989	1990	1991	1992	1993	1994	1995
Eastern	52.6	52.3	53.1	54.2	54.4	53.8	55.1	56.6	57.9	58.4	58.3
Central	31.1	31.4	30.9	29.9	29.8	29.9	28.7	27.7	27.2	27.2	27.5
Western	16.3	16.3	16.0	15.9	15.8	16.3	16.2	15.7	14.9	14.4	14.2

Source: See Table 12-2. Calculations based on current prices of the given year.

Table 12-4   Regional Per-Capita GDP and Relative Differences Between Regions

	Per-capita GDP (yuan)			Relative difference (%)	
	Eastern region	Central region	Western region	Between Central & East	Between West & East
1978	463.7	310.1	250.8	33.1	45.9
1980	569.3	386.2	313.9	32.2	44.9
1986	1,145.6	771.2	616.8	32.7	46.2
1988	1,683.1	1,074.7	881.1	36.1	47.7
1989	1,864.3	1,178.6	967.2	36.7	48.1
1990	1,963.9	1,263.8	1,078.1	35.6	45.1
1991	2,259.1	1,358.2	1,202.9	39.9	46.8
1992	3,032.6	1,712.1	1,518.4	43.5	49.9
1993	4,081.6	2,206.8	1,886.9	45.9	53.8
1994	5,420.8	2,891.4	2,391.6	46.7	55.9
1995	6,777.4	3,690.7	2,945.3	45.5	56.5

Source: See Table 12-2. Calculations based on current prices of the given year.

The widening gap between the east and west regions is not only a phenomenon of recent years, beginning as early as the mid sixties. The relative difference in per-capita national income between the coastal areas and the inland was only 22.5 percent in 1965. It widened to 37.9 percent in 1978 and 40.5 percent in 1988, before narrowing slightly between 1989 and 1991, then widening again, reaching 45.4 percent in 1992, the highest since 1949.

Table 12-5   The Relative Difference in Per-Capita National Income Between the Coastal Areas and the Inland

Year	1952	1957	1965	1970	1975	1978	1985	1988	1990	1991	1992
Per-capita income (yuan)											
Coastal	118	169	213	258	325	404	897	1,429	1,650	1,848	2,322

Inland	85	126	165	187	211	251	552	850	1,016	1,079	1,268
Relative Difference (%)	28.0	25.4	22.5	27.5	35.1	37.9	38.5	40.5	38.4	41.6	45.4

Note: Calculated in current prices of the given year.

Source: *Collected Historical Statistics of Provinces, Autonomous Regions and Municipalities* (1949-1989) and *The Chinese Statistical Yearbook*.

III. The Principal Causes of Imbalanced Regional Economic Development

The development of the regional economies was the joint result of historical, material and socio-economic factors.

1. Geography and location influence development. For a fairly long period after the founding of the People's Republic in 1949, China stressed war preparedness and narrowing regional differences. The coastal areas were exposed on a strategic front and were to a certain extent ignored, making it difficult for them to make full use of their advantageous location. Since 1978 when the reform and opening policy was introduced, the coastal areas have been the vanguard of reform and opening. This has been particularly true of the Pearl and Yangtze river deltas and the crescent encircling the Bohai Sea with their easy access to Hong Kong, Macao, Taiwan, Japan and South Korea and the presence of the metropolises of Shanghai, Guangzhou, Beijing and Tianjin. The economy here developed rapidly. The inland areas which have enjoyed similar rapid growth lie mostly along major transportation lines or have large and medium-sized cities nearby. In comparison, underdeveloped areas receiving major state support typically lack access to modern transportation or are remote from large and medium-sized cities. Clearly, the key to altering this situation is accelerated construction of transportation facilities and the promotion of urbanization in these regions.

2. Investment of capital influences development. Nationwide, the average annual capital investment growth rate for industrial enterprises with independent accounting was 14.2 percent between 1981 and 1990,

15.9 percent in the eastern region, 13.1 percent in the central region and 11.5 percent in the western region, 19 percent lower in the western region than the national average, 27.7 percent lower than in the eastern region. Using the Cobb-Douglas Functions, the difference in industrial growth rates between the eastern and western regions during the 1980s resulting from differences in investment of capital was approximately 1.9 times the differential of the actual industrial growth rate.[1] In recent years investment of capital has grown slowly in the central and western regions and rapidly in the eastern region for the following reasons.

(1) The regions differ in their local capacity to generate accumulation. Between 1978 and 1991 the coastal area's capacity to generate accumulation locally grew continually accompanying the rapid economic development, especially the sudden rise of the rural enterprises. The actual rate of accumulation rose from 36.7 percent to 37.2 percent over this period, while that in the central region fell from 33 percent to 30.9 percent and that in the western region from 34 percent to 29.6 percent.

(2) The government changed its investment priorities. Between 1978 and 1993, the portion of total capital investment by the state invested in state-owned units in the coastal areas rose from 40.1 percent to 53 percent, while that in the inland areas fell from 51 percent to 38 percent (the central region dropping from 30.6 percent to 23.1 percent and the western region from 20.4 percent to 14.9 percent). The ratio of capital investment in the state-owned units in the coastal areas to that in the inland rose from 0.79 to 1.39. The regional distribution of investment for renovation and transformation of equipment in state-owned units followed roughly the same pattern. Most of the enterprises in the central and western regions are state owned and non-state-owned enterprises tend to be less developed. Accordingly, the portion of total investment going to state-owned units is far higher in the inland than in the east. The shift in focus toward the

---

[1] *New Changes in the Development of Regional Economies*, Yunnan People's Publishing House, 1995, pp. 94-102.

east of state investment (including budgetary investment and bank loans) will inevitably exert a significant influence on the regional economies in provinces and autonomous regions, such as Heilongjiang, Guizhou, Gansu, Qinghai and Ningxia, which have long depended on the state for investment.

Table 12-6   Changes in the Regional Shares of Capital Investment in State-Owned Units

Unit: %

Year	Coastal	Inland	Central	Western	Other areas	Coastal/Inland
1953	37.7	36.1	22.9	13.2	26.2	1.04
1957	37.9	50.2	30.4	19.8	11.9	0.75
1962	37.5	52.8	35.3	17.5	9.7	0.71
1965	30.4	63.2	30.2	33.0	6.4	0.48
1970	26.8	65.4	32.2	33.2	7.8	0.41
1975	42.2	48.4	27.9	20.5	9.4	0.87
1978	40.1	51.0	30.6	20.4	8.9	0.79
1979	42.2	50.2	29.5	20.7	7.6	0.84
1980	44.5	49.8	29.5	20.3	5.7	0.89
1981	47.9	47.3	29.2	18.1	4.8	1.01
1982	48.0	46.3	29.1	17.4	5.7	1.04
1983	46.8	47.6	29.8	17.8	5.6	0.98
1984	47.2	47.3	30.5	16.8	5.5	1.00
1985	48.4	45.0	28.2	16.8	6.6	1.08
1986	48.0	41.8	26.0	15.8	10.2	1.15
1987	50.8	40.2	24.6	15.6	9.0	1.26
1988	53.2	38.9	24.0	14.9	7.9	1.37
1989	52.5	38.8	23.1	15.7	8.7	1.35
1990	50.9	40.1	23.3	16.8	9.0	1.27

1991	48.7	41.5	24.4	17.1	9.8	1.17
1992	50.2	41.2	24.7	16.5	8.6	1.22
1993	53.0	38.0	23.1	14.9	9.0	1.39
1995	50.4	39.8	25.1	14.7	9.8	1.27

Source: *Statistical Materials on Fixed Asset Investment in China (1950-1985)*, *The Chinese Statistical Yearbook* (1986-1993) and *The Summary of Chinese Statistics* (1994, 1996).

(3) Extra-regional capital investment. Between 1985 and 1995, China actually used US\$ 149.95 billion in foreign capital; US\$ 130.956 billion, or 87.3 percent of the total, was invested in the eastern coastal region; US\$ 12.706 billion, or 8.5 percent, in the central region and US\$ 6.288 billion, or 4.2 percent, in the western region. In addition, the preferential policies extended to the coastal areas and market forces acted as magnets drawing in capital from the inland. Better rates on bank deposits and loans, the stock market and opportunities for investment, particularly in the special economic zones and open ports, attracted large amounts of capital from Sichuan, Hunan, Hubei, Gansu and other provinces in recent years. Clearly this influx of foreign and extra-regional domestic capital was an important force fueling rapid growth along the coast.

3. The effect of the industrial structure. Generally speaking, given approximately equal inputs, differences in rate of economic growth for the most part correspond to the quality of industrial structure. Regional industrial structures have significantly influenced regional economic growth since the initiation of the reform and opening policy.

(1) After the founding of the People's Republic the government built a large number of large and medium-sized industrial enterprises in the central and western regions. Apart from the military industrial enterprises, the vast majority of these enterprises engaged in mining or energy and raw materials. Processing was done outside of the regions. In consequence, many cities devoted to a single industry, such as

Yumen, Karamay, Baiyin, Jinchang, Qingtongxia and Jiayuguan, grew up. Industry in these areas is limited to a short section of the production chain. The level of processing is shallow. As a result, these major local industries are only loosely linked to the surrounding economy. Production is not integrated with the local economy outside of the industry itself. Accordingly, there is little multiplier effect and the industry cannot easily drive economic development in the vast surrounding areas. Moreover, the regional industrial structure lacks diversity. Dependent on an excessively limited range of industries, it has limited capacity to respond to emergencies and to resist outside interference or effect structural change. This renders the region susceptible to economic instability.

(2) Rapid economic growth in the coastal region in recent years was closely related to rapid growth of the rural economy, particularly the township enterprises. Township enterprises came late to the central and western regions and their level of development is low; they have contributed comparatively little to promoting rural economic development. As can be seen from Table 12-7, rural per-capita total output value of township enterprises in the central region in 1991 was 64.7 percent lower and in the western region 86.5 percent lower than in the eastern region. Township enterprises' share of total output value was 20.9 percent lower in the central region than in the eastern region and 63.5 percent lower in the western regions. Persons employed in township enterprises as a share of the total workforce was 27.7 percent lower in the central region and 57.7 lower in the western region than in the eastern region. Salary income from township enterprises as a share of total rural per-capita net income was 25 percent lower in the central region than in the coastal region and 52.2 percent lower in the western· region. A survey by the Ministry of Agriculture reports approximately 51 percent of the difference in per-capita total output value between the central and eastern regions, and 53 percent of the difference between western and eastern regions were attributable to the differing levels of development of township enterprises. Clearly the backwardness of the inland rural economy, particularly the township

enterprises, is an important factor restricting economic development in the central and western regions.

Table 12-7 Relative Differences in Regional Township Enterprise Development (1991)

Unit: %

	National	Eastern	Central	Western	Relative Difference East/Central	Relative Difference East/west
1. Average annual growth in total township enterprise output value (1978-91) (%)	26.4	27	25.63	23.68	5.1	12.3
2. Average annual growth in total output value of rural industry (1978-91) (%)	25.7	27.06	23.12	20.22	14.6	25.3
3. Township enterprise share of total output value (%)	26.51	30.56	24.17	11.16	20.9	63.5
4. Township enterprise share of rural total output value (%)	61.11	69.62	55.1	28.5	20.9	59.1
5. Rural industry share of total industrial output value (%)	30.8	35.99	24.95	12.14	30.7	66.3
6. Township enterprise workforce share of total workforce (%)	16.47	21.1	15.26	8.92	27.7	57.1
7. Township enterprise workforce share of total rural workforce (%)	22.31	30.01	20.13	11.64	32.9	61.2
8. Township enterprise rural per-capita output value (yuan/person per annum)	1,283	2,333	823	315	64.7	86.5

9. Rural per-capita wage from township enterprises (yuan)	144.2	226.4	109.1	65.7	51.8	71
10. Township enterprise wage income share of rural per-capita net income (%)	20.35	24.41	18.31	11.59	25	52.5

Note: The three regions here are different than as classified in the Seventh Five-Year Plan (1986-1990). Guangxi, Inner Mongolia and Hainan are included in the western region while Sichuan and Shaanxi are included in the central region. Source: The Township Enterprise Department of the Ministry of Agriculture.

(3) In the course of the reform and opening process, the eastern region benefited from its superior location and economic and technological strengths in acquiring imported advanced technology from abroad to transform traditional industries, develop new industries and adjust its economic structure. This led to rapid economic growth. At present, most of the new and quickly rising enterprises producing electronics and telecommunications equipment are found in the coastal areas and a few large inland cities.

Table 12-8   Regional Relative Differences in Labor Productivity and Capital-Output Ratio in Industrial Enterprises with Independent Accounting

	Labor productivity (yuan/person per annum)				Capital-Output ratio (%)				
Year	1980	1985	1990	1992	1980	1985	1990	1992	1995
National	9,337	11,991	17,408	34,338	111.2	121	117.1	93.6	90.2
Eastern region	10,881	13,972	21,117	42,294	144.2	147.9	133.2	105.9	97.3
Central region	7,819	9,796	13,249	24,836	90.3	100.1	101	78.9	83.4
Western region	7,353	9,922	13,677	26,983	68.6	86.5	93.8	74.9	71.1

Eastern/central regional difference	28.1	29.9	37.3	41.3	37.4	32.3	24.2	25.5	14.3
Eastern/western regional difference	32.4	29	25.2	36.2	52.4	41.5	29.6	29.3	26.9

Note: [1] Per-capita labor productivity for 1980, 1985 and 1990 calculated in 1980 constant prices; 1992 per-capita labor productivity calculated in 1990 constant prices. [2] The capital-output ratio is the ratio between total industrial output value and total capital (the year-end net worth of fixed assets plus the average balance of the normed current fund over the course of the year). Source: *The 1985 People's Republic of China General Survey of Industry,* Vol. 4, and *The Chinese Statistical Yearbook* (1991, 1993, 1996).

4. The input-output effect factor. Generally speaking, there is less output for input in the central and western regions than in the eastern region because the inland economic foundation is less developed and technological and business management levels are lower. This effect has been increased by the eastern region's importation of advanced technology and managerial expertise since the initiation of the reform and opening policy. Labor productivity there has been improved considerably. Differences both absolute and relative with the central and western regions have further widened. Between 1980 and 1992, the relative difference between the eastern and central regions in labor productivity in industrial enterprises with independent accounting widened from 28.1 percent to 41.3 percent and that between the eastern and western regions from 32.4 percent to 36.2 percent, widening by 13.2 and 3.8 percentage points respectively in 12 years. The difference in capital-output ratio between the east and the west has begun to close, but still remains substantial. In 1995, the capital-output ratio in the central and western regions were still, respectively, 14.3 percent and 26.9 percent lower than in the eastern region. This gives proof that given approximately the same investment conditions, the economy in the eastern region will grow more quickly than in the inland.

5. The role of government policy. Most of the government reform and opening measures were first introduced in the coastal areas and only later, step by step, in the inland regions. This naturally served to aggravate unequal development. Moreover, government macro policies which did not take into cognizance regional differences placed economically underdeveloped areas with less capacity to rely on themselves for development at a disadvantage. To this may be added the fact that the people in the coastal areas have traditionally been more conscious of the commercial economy and their minds are already more open to new ideas. This psychological factor also helped speed development.

Section Two   Coming Trends in Regional Economic Development

I. Basic Estimates of Future Regional Economic Development

Past and present development trends indicate that for a fairly long period of time to come the regional economies will be out of balance. Absolute differences between the east and the west still cannot be gradually narrowed. Relative differences will widen further in the immediate future.

1. Gradually, narrowing the differences between the east and the west will be an arduous task. The eastern region has superiority in location, convenient transportation facilities, developed production and a good technological foundation. In contrast, the central and western regions have inadequate financial, intellectual and professional resources and relatively backward technology, although, to a small extent, this is compensated for by abundant natural resources. Any effort to diminish the differences between the east and the west will require faster economic growth in the central and western regions.

In the following equations per-capita GDP in the eastern region is represented by A and in the central and western regions by B; their average annual GDP growth rates are a and b respectively. The absolute difference between them is C and the relative difference D. The necessary precondition for diminishing the absolute difference in per-capita GDP year by year follows:

$$A(1+a) - B(1+b) < C$$

$$C = A-B$$

namely $b > \dfrac{A}{B} \cdot a = D \cdot a$

The necessary precondition for diminishing relative difference in per-capita GDP year by year follows:

$$\frac{A(1+a)}{B(1+b)} < D$$

$$D = \frac{A}{B}$$

namely $b > a$

Per-capita GDP in the eastern region in 1995 was 6,777 yuan and that in the central and western regions was 3,399 yuan; the former is 1.99 times the latter. Accordingly, the absolute difference in per-capita GDP between the east and the west can only be reduced when the annual per-capita GDP growth rate in the central and western regions is 1.99 times that in the eastern region. Current development trends make this patently unrealistic in the near future. However, the current base figure for economic development in the central and western regions is fairly small: economic potentials have not yet been fully tapped. With the gradual shift in governmental emphasis in economic development to the inland areas and steady rise in management and operational skills in the central and western regions, it is fully possible that the inland growth rate will eventually catch up and even surpass that of the eastern region.

2. Regional economic development will remain imbalanced. The growth rate in the east will continue to be higher than in the central

and western regions for a fairly long number of years to come. Fundamental change will be difficult to effect in the short term.

(1) Economic growth in the old coastal industrial bases has entered a new phase since the beginning of the nineties with the development of Pudong in Shanghai and the regeneration of Liaoning. The average annual GDP growth rate in Shanghai was 14.5 percent between 1992 and 1995, 2.3 percentage points higher than the national average over the same period. Liaoning's GDP growth rate has lagged behind the national average but is now gaining ground. These figures demonstrate the first returns on the transformation of these areas as the old industrial bases climbing out of the basement of economic growth.

(2) Large-scale construction over more than ten years has steadily improved the investment environment in the new coastal industrial areas. Their capacity to rely on themselves to satisfy their development needs has been gradually raised. They may be expected to maintain their rapid growth momentum. Moreover, with the comprehensive deepening of reform and opening, the areas around the Bohai Bay should be able to take advantage of the fairly strong foundation in the heavy chemical industry. Rapid economic growth can also be expected in the Pearl River and the Yangtze River deltas in the south.

(3) Although there are signs of shifts within some traditional industries, most notably the textile industry, there will not be significant move toward the inland away from the coast. The coastal areas have not yet entered the stage of large-scale movement of industry. Moreover, for a number of years to come, foreign investors will continue to locate foreign invested enterprises in the coastal areas given the facts of infrastructure and the soft environment.

(4) Once China's status within the General Agreement on Tariffs and Trade is restored, the economy in the central and western regions will face competition from the international market in addition to the eastern region. Most inland industries, most notably some fledgling industries, have only recently been established and lack strong foundations. They will be at a disadvanatge.

In order to limit differences between the east and the west and promote the reduction of that difference, a number of vigorous policy measures must be adopted.

II. Forecast of Regional Economical Development Before 2010

The years until 2010 can be divided into two stages. Average annual GDP growth rate during the first stage (1991-2000) should be 9 percent and total population (excluding Taiwan) kept within 1.3 billion by 2000. In the second stage (2001-2010), the average annual GDP growth rate should be 7.5 percent and population grows to around 1.4 billion. Considering that the natural growth of the population in the coastal areas is slow while the mechanical growth is fast and that in the inland areas the natural growth is fast and mechanical growth is slow, there will little change in the proportion of total population living in each area. If 41.3 percent of the population lives in the coastal areas and 58.7 percent in the inland areas as was the case in the eighties, by 2000 the population will be 537 million in the coastal areas and 763 million in the inland areas, and 578 million in the coastal areas and 822 million in the inland areas by 2010. Clearly, if the overall goals for national economic growth are to be met, given varying conditions, the growth patterns in the coastal areas and the inland areas may take different forms.

1. Regional economic development is affected by the spontaneous actions of market forces. Between 1979 and 1990 the GDP in the coastal areas grew at an average annual rate of 9.1 percent while that in the inland areas grew at an average annual rate of 8.6 percent, a ratio of roughly 1.06 : 1. As a result of the gradual growth of the market, this ratio can be expected to expand greatly in the years to come. In fact, the ratio has widened quickly as the market economy has developed since 1991. In that year, GDP growth was 10.7 percent in the coastal areas and 6.2 percent in the inland areas, a ratio of 1.73 : 1. Growth was 20.4 percent in the coastal areas and 12.6 percent in the inland areas in 1992, a ratio of 1.63 : 1. Between 1979 and 1992

the average annual GDP growth rate was 9.96 percent in the coastal areas and 8.69 percent in the inland areas, a ratio of 1.15 :1. Given that the scale of the coastal economy will continually expand and that the special preferential policies will be removed one after another, coastal economic growth will slow down somewhat. Therefore, in the future the growth rate ratio between the two regions can be expected to be lower than in 1991 and 1992, approximately 1.3 : 1. It can be inferred that if the coastal GDP grows at an average annual rate of 10 percent and the inland GDP at an average annual rate of 7.7 percent between 1991 and 2000, the relative difference in the GDP between the coastal and inland areas will widen from 14.1 percent in 1990 to 30.4 percent, and the relative difference in per-capita GDP from 39.3 percent to 51.1 percent, by 16.3 and 11.8 percentage points respectively over ten years. If the coastal GDP grows at an average annual rate of 8.3 percent and the inland GDP at an average annual rate of 6.4 percent between 2001 and 2010, the relative differences in GDP and per-capita GDP between the coastal and inland areas will widen by 11.3 and 7.9 percentage points respectively.

Table 12-9   Forecasts of Changes in Regional Economic Growth and Differences

		Year	Proposal 1		Proposal 2	
			Coastal	Inland	Coastal	Inland
	Growth rate (%)	1991-2000	10.7	7.7	9.2	8.8
		2001-2010	8.8	6.4	7.3	7.7
	Absolute value (bn yuan	1990	923.9	793.8	923.9	793.8
		2000	2,396.3	1,666.7	2,227.7	1,845
		2010	5,318.9	3,099.4	4,506.7	3,873.9
GDP	Relative difference (%)	1990	14.1		14.1	
		2000	30.4		17.2	
		2010	41.7		14	
		Change (1991-2000)	+16.3		+3.1	
		Change (2001-2010)	+11.3		-3.2	

Per-capita GDP	Absolute Value (yuan)	1990	1,971	1,197	1,971	1,197
		2000	4,462	2,184	4,148	2,418
		2010	9,202	3,771	7,797	4,713
	Absolute difference (yuan)	1990	774		774	
		2000	2,278		1,730	
		2010	5,431		3,084	
		Change (1991-2000)	+1,504		+965	
		Change (2001-2010)	+3,153		+1,354	
	Relative difference (%)	1990	39.3		39.3	
		2000	51.1		41.7	
		1010	59		39.6	
		Change (1991-2000)	+11.8		+2.4	
		Change (2001-2010)	+7.9		-2.1	

Note: Based on comparable prices.

2. Regional economic development under moderate government intervention. In 1995 state budgetary investment accounted for only 3.1 percent of all fixed asset investment. Including domestic loans too, the government could control only 24.1 percent of all fixed asset investment. Under this set of circumstances, it is unrealistic to expect that the differences between the east and the west created during the course of so many years could be diminished, let alone eliminated, in the short term. However, if the focus of state budgetary investment is gradually shifted inland and financial support is given to the poor areas and aging industrial basis, any increase in the relative difference between the coastal and inland areas can be kept to a minimum and continuously reduced. With this in mind, suppose that the coastal growth rate will be 5 percent higher than in the inland during the first stage, than 5 percent lower than in the inland during the second stage. More concretely, assuming between 1991 and 2000 GDP grows at an average annual rate of 9.2 percent in the coastal areas and at 8.8 percent in the inland areas, the relative difference in GDP between the

236

coastal and inland areas will widen from 14.1 percent to 17.2 percent and the relative difference in per-capita GDP will widen from 39.3 percent to 41.7 percent, by 3.1 and 2.4 percentage points respectively over 10 years. Then, assuming between 2001 and 2010 GDP grows at an average annual rate of 7.3 percent in the coastal areas and 7.7 percent in the inland areas, the relative difference in GDP will be reduced by 3.2 percentage points and per-capita GDP by 2.1 percentage points. This formula will allow reasonable coordination between the two major policy aims of efficiency and balance. Although implementing this proposal would entail a certain degree of difficulty, it is definitely practicable given sufficient effort.

Section Three   Policy Choices for Promoting Coordinated Regional Economic Development

A large developing country with major regional differences like China requires a variety of different techniques and openness to any suitable measure to achieve coordinated regional economic development.

I. A Comprehensive Plan for the Distribution of National Productive Forces Should Be Decided

As the entire country begins to open up in all directions, its division conceptually into three major economic regions, the east, central and west, has lost its objective basis. It will be necessary to plan the distribution of productive forces on the basis of a new conception of three regions defined by the coast, the land borders and the interior. (1) The areas along the land border are increasingly open and border trade is developing rapidly. A broad strip of "open" land tracing the land border corresponding to the "open" areas tracing the coast is gradually taking shape. (2) The interior, that area surrounded by the coastal areas and border lands has a huge population and abundant energy and mineral resources. It will be the focal point for the development of the energy and raw materials industries. (3) There is consistency within each of these three newly defined regions, in terms of natural resources and socio-economic characteristics. Accordingly, they can serve as the basic regional units for the formulation of a national strategy for regional economic development and the overall planning for the distribution of national productive forces.

1. The coastal areas must focus on developing its export-oriented economy. The coastal areas are advantageously located, have convenient transportation facilities, developed industrial and agricultural production, and a good economic and technical foundation, in short, better conditions for the development of an export-oriented economy. The key issue here will be the handling of the relationship between increasing exports and the structural upgrading of industry. (1) It will be necessary to accelerate the technical transformation of the light and textile industries in the coastal areas, emphasizing the development of light industrial and textile products with greater comparative advantages and international competitiveness so as to produce more easily marketable export products. (2) Priority funding and policy must be given to the machine-building and electronic industries. This is particularly true for the development of machine-electronics integrated equipment and large and medium-sized complete installations if they are to become the coastal areas' second generation of leading export products. (3) The large and medium-sized cities of Shanghai, Beijing, Tianjin, Guangzhou and Dalian must be relied to actively develop new and high-tech industries to gradually replace reliance on imports. On this basis, high-tech products' share of total exports should gradually be increased so that they will become the coastal areas' third generation of leading export products in the 21st century.

2. The interior should focus on a strategy of transforming resources. While continuing to emphasize the development of the energy and raw materials industries essential to the nation's well being,

gradually expand its role in the industrial chain, developing fine and deep processing industries so as to increase the processing depth and added value of its products. (1) The existing foundation in the energy and raw materials industries should be consolidated and strengthened, the quality of products improved, and the variety increased, thereby ensuring an effective supply of energy and major raw materials. (2) Priority should be given to the development of a number of processing industries with currently solid foundations and strengths, in particular fine and deep processing industries and industries that can provide large and medium-sized complete installations for the energy and raw materials industries. These will become the leading industries supporting regional economic growth in the future. (3) Comprehensive exploitation of the region's resources should be strengthened and their economic value increased. The current one dimensional nature of the industrial structure should be modified through diversification.

3. Border trade should be relied upon to promote economic growth in the border lands. In the immediate future, construction of major transportation routes, especially the highway network must be strengthened to open the roads for domestic and foreign trade. Markets in Northeast Asia, Central Asia, Southeast Asia, West Asia and Europe must be actively developed and the export market gradually diversified. A number of stable export commodity production bases aimed at the international market should be established and development of border trade oriented toward integrating trade, industry and agriculture. Domestic and foreign capital, intellectual personnel and technology should be actively pursued. The exploitation of resources, especially the mineral resources urgently needed by the country for energy, should be accelerated.

II. A Strategy of Point and Axial Development Should Be Adopted

China is currently at a stage of comprehensive industrialization. The most effective way to organize space for regional economic development will be formed by points revolving around an axis. The key point will be determining the major axial lines nationwide.

Given the carrying capacity of present transportation routes and the industrial strengths and economic potential of the different regions, the state should concentrate development efforts before 2010 in three major areas: the coast, the Yangtze River and the Yellow River. These three areas can gradually be made the axes around which future economic development revolves.

During the eighties, the government focused its efforts on the development of the coastal region. In the years leading up to 2010, while continuing coastal development, it should concentrate on the lands along the two rivers. In this distribution pattern the coastal area is currently leading economic development. Building on work done in the nineties the Yangtze axis will lead economic growth in the 21st century. These two axes lack energy resources and raw materials. Accordingly, priority must be given to developing the energy and mineral resources rich Yellow River area as a third axis supplementing the other two. After a period of focused development, this third axis may tentatively be expected to support sustained steady growth in the two leading axes.

1. Economic redevelopment should be strengthened through adjustment and transformation in the Pearl River Delta, the Yangtze River Delta, the Xiamen-Zhangzhou-Quanzhou area in southern Fujian and the areas around Bohai Bay. The government should focus further efforts on the development of the Rizhao-Lianyungang area, the Jiaojiang-Wenzhou area, the coastal area surrounding Fuzhou in northern Fujian, the coastal area around Shantou in eastern Guangdong and the Zhanjiang-Beihai area. These areas can be new growth points supporting coastal economic growth extending out throughout the country. Capital should be raised through various channels to accelerate the construction of expressways and high-speed railways in the coastal region, facilitating regional economic relations.

2. Comprehensive development along the Yangtze axis should be promoted. The more than 3,000-kilometer Yangtze River is China's

main east-west transportation artery. Accelerated economic development in these riverine areas is of great significance to the sustained, steady and coordinated development of the national economy. Today, the Yangtze mainstream must be taken as the central axial line. The large and medium-sized cities in the area, particularly those open cities on the river's banks, should be relied upon to lead development, catching up the surrounding areas in an ever increasing momentum. Pudong in Shanghai is the dragon head on the Yangtze. The open cities along the river shore up the whole. A multi-centered development pattern flowing from east to west and up the river's tributaries will unfold. In the selection of axial lines for priority development at the regional level, areas with best conditions and greater potential for development, such as Shanghai-Nanjing, Wuhu-Anqing, Jiujiang-Nanchang, Wuhan-Huangshi, Yueyang-Changsha-Xiangtan-Zhuzhou and Chongqing-Yibin should be chosen. Industrial corridors running between these paired cities should each have their own characteristics.

3. Development on the Yellow River axis should be accelerated. The Yellow River drainage area abounds in energy and mineral resources. A wide variety of resources can be found here, including ferrous and non-ferrous metals, rare earth and rare metals and non-metallic minerals. The upper reaches have abundant hydraulic energy resources as well as large scale copper, lead, zinc and gypsum mines. On its borders are the Jinchuan nickel mine, Xihe-Chengxian lead-zinc mine and Qaidam Basin. Abundant coal, non-ferrous metals, precious metals, rare earth and rare metals, and salt mineral resources can be found in the middle reaches; 54 percent of the nation's confirmed coal reserves and 95 percent of the confirmed rare-earth reserves are here. The lower reaches are rich in oil and natural gas and agricultural resources. Given this strength in resources, development should focus on the energy power and raw materials industries and processing industries that require larger energy inputs. Particular attention should be given to the coal, electric power, metallurgical and chemical industries. Priority should be given to developing the upper reaches of

the Yellow River, the large triangle formed by Shanxi, Shaanxi and Inner Mongolia (Baotou-Hohhot-Datong), the middle Shanxi region, the Guanzhong and the Shanxi-Shaanxi-Henan triangle (Baoji-Xi'an-Houma) region, the Luoyang-Zhengzhou-Anyang region and the Yellow River Delta (Ji'nan-Zibo-Dongying). These areas should be built into energy and raw materials based industrial zones characterized by coordinated development of various industries.

III. Policies for National Economic Layout and Individual Regions Should Be Gradually Adjusted

1. The policy concerning national economic layout should be methodically adjusted. In the future the government should gradually increase investment in the interior, aiming to increase the interior's share of total investment to 20 percent more than the coastal regions's share during the Ninth Five-Year Plan (1996-2000) and the Second Ten-Year Program. It will be necessary to use economic, legal and necessary administrative measures to ensure the concentrated development of state supported major industries in the areas where they are strong. The continued growth of energy consumption intensive processing industries in the coastal areas should be curtailed, the transfer of such industries to the energy resource rich central and western regions promoted. This goal will require the formulation of a law governing industrial layout.

2. The policy system used for poverty relief should be fully optimized. The State Council decided that beginning in 1994 the nation would carry out an assault on poverty, striving to basically solve the question of adequate food and clothing for the nation's poor by the end of the century. Minimum per-capita net income of 500 yuan in 1990 constant prices will be required. This goal will necessitate the following measures.

(1) The state must reinvestigate the areas it previously designated poverty stricken to ensure that state funds are going to the areas truly in greatest need, those below the newly defined poverty line.

(2) The roles of the central and local governments should be given full support. In principle, poverty-stricken areas should receive aid chiefly from the local governments. The central government should concentrate its efforts on supporting the seriously poverty-stricken areas in the central and western regions.

(3) The experiences of the United Nations Development Program in providing aid to underdeveloped areas can be learned from to improve the government poverty relief fund utilization ratio. Project management should be used in awarding relief. Sate appropriations should be under the direct control and supervision of a special department under the State Council Poverty Relief Office. Low interest loans or discount loans should be supervised by the banks.

3. The transformation of the old industrial bases should be strengthened. In recent years the old industrial bases have fallen into recession and some suffering structural degeneration. Causes vary. First, some industrial cities wholly dependent on mining like Fuxin in Liaoning have declined because the resources they depended on have been exhausted. Second, many old industrial bases are dominated by traditional industries. Their product lines are outdated and their equipment obsolescent. They need to be transformed if they are to be regenerated. From a long-term point of view, the "re-industrialization" of the old industrial bases should pursue economic diversification, structural upgrading, internationalization of sales and multipolar layout. Further extension and expansion should be avoided. This will require appropriate government support through policies and finance.

(1) Special funds need to be established for the transformation of the old industrial bases. These funds can be used for major technological transformation projects, supporting new and replacement industries and training of laid-off workers for reemployment.

(2) Encouragement should be given to the transfer of the equipment used in the heavy chemical industry to the areas surrounding the old industrial bases. This, coupled with an increased emphasis on the development of high-tech industries, will reduce the pressure of rising costs resulting from the exhaustion of resources,

243

environmental pollution and overloaded infrastructure in the old industrial bases.

(3) Old enterprises should be allowed to benefit from accelerated depreciation and reduced taxes or tax exemptions.

4. The development of township enterprises should be accelerated in the central and western regions. In 1993 the State Council issued a "Resolution on Accelerated Development of Township Enterprises in the Central and Western Regions." It decided to grant special loans totalling 10 billion yuan annually to such township enterprises between 1994 and 2000 and gave certain preferential treatment reducing taxes or providing exemptions. All departments and all regions must conscientiously implement this decision and favoring the central and western regions in financial assistance and loans.

(1) Investment from state revenues should be further increased. Between 1979 and 1991 state budget expenditures on township enterprise development totalled 10.9 billion yuan, including 1.37 billion yuan in 1991. More than 50 percent was used in the eastern region, leaving comparatively little for the central and western regions. More state funding should be provided in the future and more of this spending should go to the central and western regions.

(2) Gradually raise the township enterprises in the central and western regions share of all loans granted nationwide. In 1991 agricultural banks and credit cooperatives in the central and western regions lent 44.13 billion yuan to township enterprises, accounting for only 30.6 percent of all loans to township enterprises nationwide. Of these loans, 22.17 billion yuan was lent by agricultural banks, accounting for 41.7 percent of such loans nationwide, and only 21.96 billion yuan by credit cooperatives, 24.1 percent of all such loans. Loans to rural enterprises in the central and western regions should be increased in the future, as should their share of all such loans given.

(3) The construction of small towns should be accelerated and guidance given to the concentrated layout of township enterprises. The central and western regions cover a vast territory and are poorly served by transportation facilities. Infrastructure is underdeveloped, and there

are great shortages of water and electric power in many areas. Therefore, the development of township enterprises, particularly rural industry, must be rationally distributed, concentrated, based in small cities. Facilitating the concentration of township enterprises will require reform of the current residency registration system for small cities and towns. Restrictions on residency should be lifted and peasants, especially peasants from poorer areas, allowed to move to small cities and towns and so as to develop primary and tertiary industries.

Chapter Thirteen   Foreign Trade and the Use of Foreign Capital

In the 20 years since the initiation of the reform and opening policy, the Chinese economy has gone from closed to open. Foreign trade and foreign capital played a very important role in this transition.

Section One   The Relationship Between Exports and Economic Growth

Exports have been intimately intertwined with economic growth in China. This relationship is manifested in three ways.

1. Between 1978 and 1996 the average annual growth rate in foreign trade, calculated in comparable prices, was 15 percent. This not only exceeded the average annual GNP growth rate, but was also far above average international foreign trade levels over the same period. In 1996 the total volume of imports and exports in China was US$ 289.9 billion, more than 14 times the import and export volume of US$ 20.638 billion in 1978.

2. Foreign trade volume was originally targeted to reach US$ 160 billion by the end of this century, but by 1992 it was already US$ 165.6 billion; the degree of dependence on foreign trade was 38 percent rather than the 36.41 percent directed in 1991. This was very high in comparison with other countries. Taking examples from other developing countries, in 1991 the degree of dependence on foreign trade was 12.98 percent in Brazil and 14.25 percent in India. That same year, the degree of dependence on foreign trade was 16.04 percent in the United States, 16.36 percent in Japan, 37.12 percent in

France, 36.85 percent in Britain, 30.7 percent in Italy and 41.89 percent in Canada.

3. China's marginal export propensity indicates that development of foreign trade serves the function of guiding economic growth. Marginal export propensity refers to the proportion of increased GNP correspondiong to increased export volume. Between 1981 and 1991 this proportion's lowest value was 3.98 percent in 1983, and the highest was 60.5 percent in 1990. During these 11 years the GNP added value totalled 1.53845 trillion yuan RMB and export added value was 355.944 billion yuan RMB, a ratio of 1:0.23. This demonstrates that the added value created through exports is the engine driving economic growth.

China's export growth rate by no means lags behind the developed countries. For example, in Japan it took 13 years, (1966-1979), for exports to increase from US$ 10 billion to US$ 100 billion, the former West Germany 17 years (1959-1976), the United States 30 years (1946-1976), and China only 15 years (1978-1993). This gives further proof of China's accomplishments in opening to the outside world.

Section Two   Opening of the Chinese Market and Dependence on Imports

China has a high degree of dependence on foreign trade. This may be seen in increasing exports, but also in the expansion of the domestic market and the growing degree of dependence on imports. Year by year from 1980 to 1991, the degree of dependence on imports was 6.69 percent, 7.7 percent, 6.89 percent, 7.26 percent, 8.91 percent, 14.7 percent, 15.45 percent, 14.28 percent, 14.61 percent, 13.75 percent, 14.55 percent and 17.12 percent. Compared with developed countries and some large developing countries, China's degree of dependence on imports is by no means low. This figure may be taken as an indicator of an economy's degree of openness. In 1991 the degree of dependence on imports in Canada was 20.2 percent, Britain, 19.58

percent, France, 19.29 percent, China, 17.12 percent, Italy, 15.98 percent, the United States, 8.6 percent, India, 7.66 percent, Japan, 7.02 percent, and Brazil, 5.19 percent. This demonstrates China's was already a truly open economy.

Economic growth has been very sensitive to growth in imports. Year by year from 1981 to 1991, the import income elasticity coefficients were 2.95, -0.35, 1.44, 1.93, 2.72, 1.37, 0.51, 1.09, 0.55, 1.51 and 2.23. The coefficient was less than one in only three years. A coefficient less than one indicates a change in the relative GNP rate produced a smaller change in the corresponding relative import rate. The other eight years showed a coefficient greater than one indicating the change in relative GNP rate gave rise to a greater change in the corresponding import rate. In three years, both the marginal import propensity and the import income elasticity coefficient were very high, 22.74 percent and 2.95 in 1981, 39.95 percent and 2.72 in 1985, and 38.18 percent and 2.23 in 1991. In January 1981 China adopted an internal settlement price of one U.S. dollar per 2.8 yuan RMB for foreign exchange earned from foreign trade; non-trade foreign exchange was still settled at the listed bank price of one U.S. dollar per 1.5 yuan RMB. This in fact translated into a 50 percent reduction in the value of the RMB. In 1985 the exchange price of RMB versus the U.S. dollar dropped by 14.29 percent in 10 months. In December 1990 the exchange rate was adjusted from 4.7 yuan to 5.2 yuan. Since April 1991 the RMB has been frequently devalued by small margins. Whenever the exchange rate for the RMB dropped substantially, the import income elasticity coefficient increased to more than two and the marginal import propensity rose to over 20 percent. This demonstrates that devaluation of the RMB could not necessarily effectively reduce imports. For example, when the exchange rate of RMB fell by more than 10 percent in 1991, the marginal export propensity was 39.12 percent and the marginal import propensity was 38.18 percent, the two figures almost the same. Sometimes when the RMB exchange rate fell there was a reverse propensity to export. In 1985, when the exchange rate of RMB fell by more than 10 percent, the marginal export propensity was only 18.82 percent while the marginal import propensity was 39.95 percent. This phenomenon can be explained by China's dependence on imports for the raw materials needed for many of the goods it manufactured. Accordingly, imports did not respond to the devaluation of the RMB.

Section Three   Future Prospects and Policy Choices for the Development of Foreign Trade

The years to come look good for China's foreign trade. Still, some factors have the potential to restrict growth.

1. The Hong Kong factor has a significant effect on China's foreign trade. In 1994 Hong Kong accounted for 26.7 percent of the total export volume and 8.2 percent of China's total import volume. In other words, China's 1994 net export volume to Hong Kong (export volume minus import volume) was US$ 22.9 billion. That same year, the net export volume for the whole country was only US$ 5.4 billion. As these figures make clear, it is vitally important to maintain Hong Kong's position as an international financial, trade, shipping and information center and preserve its economic prosperity and stability.

2. The WTO factor. It is only a matter of time before China is admitted to the World Trade Organization. This will benefit the economy insofar as providing Chinese goods with better access to the international market, but it will also intensify competition between domestic and imported products within the domestic market.

3. The foreign demand factor. Given the increasing regionalization of the international economy, exports of labor-intensive products will be limited and exports of technology-intensive products subject to stiffer competition. The Asian financial crisis forced some countries to devalue their currencies and tighten their economies in 1997. This necessarily affects China's competitiveness in the export market and export volume to a certain degree.

4. The quality factor. The extensive model of export operations has

not yet thoroughly altered. The average annual export trade volume growth rate between 1980 and 1990 was 11 percent, but the per-unit commodity price decreased by one percent every year. It is imperative that this sort of extensive operations strategy be replaced by an intensive model, that success come through quality and technology rather than large quantities of low quality, cheap price goods.

5. The structural factor. Since 1985 China has effectively realized the transition from a primary goods based export structure to a manufactured goods based export structure. However, most manufactured goods exported are textiles, medium and low grade machinery and electrical appliances and other labor-intensive products without much added value. Growth in the exports of such products will be difficult because of restrictions imposed by the market and availability of resources. Accordingly, the export product structure must be optimized through concerted efforts to develop high value added export products and high-tech exports, particularly capital goods and complete installations. At the same time the export of high-tech products should be increased and the export of energy and mineral products should be gradually reduced. Hard work will be required to achieve the transition from the primary or rough processing of export goods to deep processing and fine machining by 2000 and the transition from labor- and capital-intensive export products to high-tech exports by 2010.

In foreign trade development, export-oriented trade should be pursued rather than import replacement. The experiences of Asia's "four small dragons" are worthy of note. In the late eighties, exports provided 130 percent of Hong Kong's GDP, 160 percent of Singapore's, 60 percent of Taiwan's and 45 percent of South Korea's. This may be compared with the 10 to 20 percent averaged during the same period in four Latin American countries, Argentina, Brazil, Mexico and Peru, which followed an import replacement strategy. In 1960 per-capita GDP in Taiwan and South Korea was about US$ 150 compared to US$ 209 in Peru and US$ 346 in Mexico. By 1989, however, per-capita GDP in Taiwan and South Korea was 10 times that of Peru and twice that of Mexico. An export-orientated strategy was the exact cause behind the rapidly diminishing gap between Asia's "four small dragons" and the developed countries. In the sixties per-capita GDP in the United States was 7 to 34 times that in the "four small dragons." By 1989, however, the United States had only double the per-capita GDP of Singapore and Hong Kong and less than four times that of South Korea and Taiwan.

Since the initiation of the reform and opening policy, China has adopted measures intended to promote exports. These measures have achieved gratifying results. In 1994 the 18 countries and regions of the Asia-Pacific Economic Cooperation signed the Bogor Declaration, agreeing that by 2010 the developed countries and by 2020 the developing countries should realize free and open trade and investment in the region. Soon after the signing of the Bogor Declaration, ASEAN expanded its membership from six to ten nations in order to more firmly control over development within the regionalization of their economies. It also decided that the ten member nations, all China's near neighbors, would effect free and open trade and investment by 2005. Given these circumstances, if China is to sustain growth within this rising tide of economic regionalization it must adhere to its export-oriented development strategy. Given the needs of development, China's export dependence rate cannot remain at a high level for an extended period of time, but the absolute volume of exports will continue to rise.

Section Four   The Use of Foreign Capital and Attendant Problems

Between 1979 and 1996 realized direct foreign investment totalled US$ 177.217 billion. This large figure demonstrates the considerable attraction of China's investment environment and investment policies, with investors responding to strong economic growth, constantly expanding market capacity and the ample supply of low-cost production elements. According to the 1993 United Nations World Investment Report, China attracted an average annual inflow of US$ 2.08 billion in direct foreign investment between 1981 and 1991, first among the developing countries. Direct foreign investment has played an active role in promoting economic development in China:

1. The foreign investments have opened international channels for sales and purchase, providing Chinese products with better access to international markets. Foreign-invested enterprises have become an undeniable force in exports.

2. Foreign-invested enterprises have helped optimize the export commodity structure. In 1994 machinery and electrical machinery exports grew at a rate of 40.9 percent, an all-time high and 9 percentage points higher than the total export volume growth rate. Foreign-invested enterprises made an outstanding contribution to this historical leap. US$13.28 billion in machinery and electrical machinery manufactured by foreign-invested enterprises was exported, an increase of 58.1 percent over the previous year, a growth rate nearly 18 percentage points higher than that for the whole machinery and electrical machinery industry. In 1994, 41.5 percent of machinery and electrical machinery exports were manufactured by foreign-invested enterprises, underscoring the value of their contribution to the rapid advances made in the export of these products.

3. Foreign investment has helped increase the competitiveness of Chinese industry, allowing the absorption of advanced foreign technologies and managerial expertise.

4. Foreign-invested enterprises have become one of the pillars of rapid economic growth. For example, in 1994 the state-owned enterprises' share of all exports of machines and electrical machines fell by 5 percentage points while that of foreign-invested enterprises increased by 4.6 percentage points. Exports of machines and electrical machines by state-owned enterprises rose by 30.1 percent over the previous year while that of foreign-invested enterprises by 58.1 percent, 28 percentage points more than the former.

Of course, the absorption of foreign investment involves certain degree of risk, just as would any other investment. In fact, it would be impossible to absorb an unlimited amount of foreign investment. In 1992 realized foreign direct investment rose by 25.3 percent. If growth continued at this rate, the total amount of foreign investment would be US$ 646.82 billion by 2010, almost 2.9 times total global direct investment in 1990. Clearly, this is impossible. If the growth rate is reduced by half to 12.5 percent, by 2010 foreign direct investment will be US$ 92.963 billion, almost 2.9 times direct investment into developing countries in 1990. This goal is attainable. Between 1978 and 1990 the average annual growth rate in external direct investment worldwide was 12.65 percent, resulting in an average annual growth rate of exterior investment in the developing countries during the same period of 9 percent. In the future China should follow certain rule in the use of foreign investment and at the same time pay attention to the quality of the investment. Progress should be pursued, but reliable progress. The blind pursuit of accelerated growth rates is an error.

China has accomplished much using foreign capital, but there remain many problems to be solved. Accordingly, the departments concerned must further tighten control over the use of foreign capital and improve their quality of work.

1. More foreign transnational companies should be attracted to China. Transnationals have abundant financial resources, high and new technologies and advanced managerial expertise. Their investments are more stable and of a longer term than those of medium- and small-sized companies.

2. The industrial structure for foreign investment should be improved and foreign investors encouraged to invest in agriculture and other primary industry, infrastructure including transportation and telecommunications, energy, and the machine-building and electronics industries.

3. The proportion of the paid-in foreign capital should be raised. Between 1979 and 1992 the proportion of paid-in capital in foreign direct investment was only 31.4 percent, 34.8 percent for Sino-foreign joint ventures, 26.2 percent for Sino-foreign cooperative enterprises

and 21.2 percent for wholly foreign-owned enterprises. There was a significant gap between the contracted foreign capital and the paid-in foreign capital. In the future negotiations should be more successful in raising the proportion of paid-in capital from foreign investors.

4. The amount of investment in each foreign-invested project should be increased. At present, investment amounts for individual project are too small. Clearly, the amount of foreign investment is tending to decrease. The average amount of investment per project, in 1992, was only US$ 1.19 million, too small for the construction of major projects or the development of new products.

5. The principle of allowing market access in exchange for technology should be adhered to. The situation wherein the foreign investor refuses technology transfers, particularly of crucial technologies, while the Chinese gives market access should be avoided. Similarly, the situation wherein the Chinese party is obligated to sacrifice a great deal of foreign exchange to import parts for assemblage is to be eschewed.

6. Competition should be encouraged and foreign business people prevented from monopolizing the domestic market.

7. Management should be strengthened and strict appraisals and examinations made of non-cash foreign investment. Any frauds, false losses and tax evasions must be thoroughly investigated and strictly dealt with.

Chapter Fourteen Progress in Science and Technology

In an effort to realize the economic growth targets set for 2010 and upgrade economic operations, China is accelerating work toward technological progress, formulating specific policies to achieve this progress in different industries.

Section One The Role of Technological Progress in Economic Development

Technological progress' role in driving economic development is manifested in two ways. First, productivity is increased, raising efficiency so that an increase in inputs creates a greater growth return in the economy. Second, the economic structure is further improved and the quality of economic growth is heightened, as seen in diversification and upgrading of the industrial structure.

During the last year of this century and the first decade of the next, secondary industry's share of GDP will continue to grow. Faster technological progress and increased productivity will be decisive factors in sustaining rapid economic growth.

1. In 2010 China will be still in the industrialization stage. Investment will still be the primary driver behind economic growth. Even if consumption demand for housing, home electrical appliances, cars, public utilities and so on increases as a share of total demand, that demand will need to be met in part by goods produced by heavy industry. While China has a great abundance of material resources, per-capita resources are in comparatively short supply. Moreover,

rapid economic growth will bring along higher mining and other resource costs. Future economic growth will be severely reined in by limitations imposed by practical availability of resources. There are only two ways to solve this problem. First is to increase imports. Increased imports, however, will be both limited by efforts to balance foreign exchange and affected by international market prices. Export manufactured goods may in effect be exchanged for raw materials. Accomplishing this will require heightened technological levels in products and reduced costs. A second option is to reduce resource consumption, a solution that will also require constantly raising technological levels.

2. Foreign trade will continue to grow as the reform and opening further deepens. However, in commercial transactions with developed countries, China remains in a disadvantageous position in the vertical division of labor regards technology. Chinese products' strong point on the international markets is their low cost, resulting from low labor costs. Most export products are still resource- and labor-intensive with low added value. The exchange of resources for technologies is not fast enough. Changing this situation will necessarily require accelerating technological improvements in the individual enterprises and increased technological content and added value in the products. In this way, China can be in a position in the horizontal division of labor with the developed countries. In addition, different portions of the domestic market can be opened in exchange for technology transfers.

3. Economic development and rising per-capita income will increase the cost of the labor. This puts pressure on enterprises to make technological improvement to cut down on labor costs. Moreover, only if new technologies emerge to promote the growth of new industrial groups, can more job opportunities be created to alleviate the problem of underemployment.

4. Coal, petroleum, power, iron, steel, chemical, non-ferrous and building materials industries' demand for energy and primary materials will reach its peak in the years running up to 2010. These

industries benefit from economy of scale, but are heavyweight consumers of energy and cause serious environmental pollution. If disastrous destruction of the environment as a byproduct of rapid economic growth is to be avoided intensification of production within these traditional industries must be accelerated as they are transformed with high technology.

5. Industrial optimization hinges on scientific and technological progress. Since the eighties, rapid economic growth has been consistently throttled by bottlenecks in transportation, telecommunications, energy and raw materials. The basic way around this problem is to raise technological level in the processing industries, reducing consumption. Improved technology can be used to effect the most rational and efficient allocation and use of resources.

6. This is a peak period of investment growth. Primary industries are characterized by a long investment cycle and high costs. Once investment has been converted into fixed assets there is a substantial degree of difficulty in a second technical transformation. Accordingly, investors must be directed in their selection of advanced technical systems.

7. Important changes will take place in per-capita consumption and the consumption structure. During this period, the Engel's coefficient will gradually decrease and the demand for new fashions and high quality and famous brand consumer goods will keep rising. Technological advances will be essential to rapidly transform the traditional consumer products industries and develop industries producing new products if the people's constantly growing demand for improvements in their material and cultural life is to be satisfied.

Using recently developed research methods, the Institute of Quantitative Economics and Techno-economics of the Chinese Academy of Social Sciences has calculated that in the 26 years (1953-1978) before the initiation of the reform and opening policy, productivity made a negative contribution to economic growth. In comparison, in the 17 years (1979-1995) following the initiation of reform and opening, improved productivity contributing 30.3 percent

257

of economic growth. This indicates the powerful impetus to scientific and technological progress provided by the reform and opening (see Table 14-1).

Table 14-1 Increased Productivity's Contribution to Economic Growth

Year	1953-59	1960-62	1963-66	1967-68	1969-75	1970	1977-90	1991-95
Average annual GNP growth rate (%)	9.93	-13.88	14.21	-7.15	9.6	-2.69	8.5	11.93
Average annual productivity growth rate (%)	-1.45	-17.27	9.69	-10.58	3.69	-7.61	2.71	5.14
Contribution of productivity (%)			68		38.4		31.9	38.9

Source: (1) Li Jingwen and D. Jorgenson, *Study of Productivity and Economic Growth in China, the United States and Japan*, The Chinese Academy of Social Sciences Publishing House, 1993 edition, p.54.

(2) Li Jingwen and Gong Feihong, "Productivity and Economic Growth in China," *Research in Quantitative Economics and Techno-economics*, Issue 12, 1996.

This research has produced a number of results. First, rise in level of technology is invariably accompanied by growth in capital input. Therefore, if technological progress is to be stressed, investment must be increased. Second, only investment that can bring about increased comprehensive productivity can induce economically significant technological progress and more efficient economic growth. Third, technological progress is embodied in new technology or a transformed technological system that can better satisfy the needs of the designer and user in achieving or bringing closer their intended goal. Sometimes, a new technology is put to work and it does not increase output relative to production elements, but it does make things significantly better in an environmental sense, improving working conditions or strengthening the nation. Examples might include power generation through wind or solar energy which reduce coal consumption and environmental pollution, although more costly than thermal power. Similarly, equipment low in efficiency may be less expensive initially, but still undesirable because it consumes more raw materials and energy. A firm grasp of these three points will be of assistance in formulating a rational technology policy.

Section Two Achievements in Scientific and Technological Progress and Problems Remaining

Although China has accomplished much in the fields of science and technology since the initiation of the reform and opening policy, this accomplishment falls short of the demands of rapid growth and of the standard set by the developed countries.

I. Achievements in the Scientific and Technological Arena

With the coming of reform and opening, reforms in the technological and economic management systems have marched in step, propelling technological progress. First, at the macro level, a national technological innovation system has been established and strengthened. (1) This system has promoted the principles that science and technology must be at the forefront of economic construction, that the relationship between technology and the economy is becoming ever more intimate and that the process whereby technical achievements are converted into actual productive forces is becoming shorter. (2) Scientific and technological research has begun to break free from the administrative direction of the planned economy, instead responding to market forces. The number of scientific and technical personnel has quickly grown, joining in the front lines of economic construction. These government workers have been joined by others working in the increasing number of private scientific research institutions.

At the micro level, achievements are still more obvious. In some important areas China has greatly closed the gap with international advanced levels. (1) The hitherto closed military industrial system has been opened and many national defence technologies made available for civilian use. (2) In a number of high and new technologies and projects, the gap with the developed countries has been reduced. Aerospace may be taken as an example. China has mastered the technologies for launching multi-satellite rockets and launching satellites with fixed synchronous orbits and has become a strong competitor with the developed countries in the international commercial satellite launching market. China has also mastered nuclear energy technology and can design, build, install and operate small nuclear power stations. It has made major breakthroughs in the safe management and operation of the nuclear power stations. In the field of power generation and transmission, China can now design and build large thermal power generating units, build and install ultrahigh voltage transmission equipment and medium-sized and small hydraulic power generating systems at the international level of the late 1980s to early 1990s. In the field of machine building, it can independently develop and build different types of large and ultra-large computer-controlled diesel engines for use on ships. In the field of electronics and information, breakthroughs have been made in the development and use of semi-conductors and optical fibers, localization of advanced telecommunications equipment and research and development of products for civilian use. In the field of bio-technology, internationally advanced level results have been obtained in the application of single technologies in biological vaccines for medical use, agro-biology, ecological technology and food bio-technology. (3) Technological levels have generally been raised in a large number of large and medium-sized state-owned enterprises through major technical transformation. Moreover, a number of new large-scale state-owned enterprises employing the latest technologies are up and running. In addition, a large number of small private high-tech enterprises have sprung up as forces to be reckoned with in the pursuit of scientific and technological progress.

II. Importing Technology Is One of the Principal Channels for Technological Progress

Imported technologies have been a cornerstone of enterprises' renovation and transformation since the eighties. The large-scale importation of specialized technologies and production lines for durable consumer goods, such as color TV sets, refrigerators, tape recorders and video recorders, and of technologies and production systems for iron and steel, chemical fibers and automobiles are important factors responsible for the rapidly changing industrial structure, product mix and technological levels. Had China depended entirely on itself for the development of these technologies and equipment, the process would have taken at least 20 years or longer. Through imports, China was able to meet fundamental market demand in ten years and, at the same time, assimilate and innovate, thus speeding the closing of the gap between China and the developed countries.

Technology importation has undergone more or less three stages since the eighties.

During the first stage (1981-1987), growth in imported technology accelerated. (1) Both central and local governments exercised substantial control over the import of technologies, deciding what technologies were to be imported and what projects pursued. Working through the state-owned banks, the central government decided how foreign exchange was to be used and provided necessary guarantees.

The local governments however often did not work in tandem with the central government, pursuing local interests, with the result that much equipment imported was redundant. (2) The amount of money spent on imported technology increased year after year. Transactions between 1981 and 1984 totalled US$ 1.99 billion, rising to US$ 2.96 billion in 1985, and US$ 2.98 billion in 1987. (3) Complete installations and production lines led all imports. In 1985 imports of complete installations accounted for 75.4 percent of all technology imports in monetary terms. This percentage rapidly decreased to 11.8 percent in 1987, while the percentage of all imported technology imported by joint operations rose from 16.5 percent to 70.2 percent, much of which was equipment. This drastic swing over a short period of time is indicative of the seriousness of the problem. (4) Most technology imported during this period came from Japan, the United States and the former West Germany. In 1985, 78.8 percent of the money contracted for imported technology went to these three countries. By 1987 this percentage had dropped but remained high at 55.9 percent. (5) Technology imports were concentrated in the energy, metallurgical, petrochemical, motor vehicle, light and textile industries. General manufacturing received a much smaller share.

Both the positives and negatives were clearly evident during this stage. On the positive side of the ledger, the state pursued a policy of importing priority technologies, assimilating them, then making innovations. It implemented the 3,000 Plan and the 12 Complete and Continuous Processes Plan[1], allowing the quick formation of large-

---

[1] The government used the 3,000 Plan to import 3,000 advanced technologies between 1983 and 1985 for the transformation and renovation of existing enterprises at a cost of US$ 3 billion. In 1986 the central government outlined the 12 Complete and Continuous Processes Plan, designating 12 "leader" technologies to be imported: color television, and electrical and internal combustion engine production lines, synthetic ammonia and coal extraction equipment, technology for cement rotary kiln with a precalcinator, open-end spinning machines and arrow-shaft looms, garment-making production lines, beer production lines, and a series of projects in lean pork production. Research institutes, universities and production enterprises were organized to work together on importing and assimilating these new technologies.

scale production capacities and making a major contribution to meeting market demand. On the downside, the central government lacked the effective control measures and policy guarantee. As a result, there was redundancy in imports at the local level and excess capacity in imported color television, refrigerator, marble processing and other imported production lines.

The second stage (1988-1991) saw a temporary sag in the nation's economy. The scale of technology imports contracted and the overall structure moved increasingly to imports of complete installations. Imports in 1991 were below the 1988 level; complete installations accounted for 84 percent of all imported technology as opposed to 93 percent in 1989. This was a period of economic reconsolidation and priority in technology imports was given to the energy, petrochemical and chemical industries. These three industries accounted for 56 percent of all such imports in 1989. Changes took place in the sources for imports. More were imported from the former Soviet Union and Italy than from the United States, Japan and the former West Germany. As this was a period of economic adjustment, the central government still exercised strong control over technology imports.

The third stage, beginning in 1992, saw rapid economic growth. The reforms gained in presence and the enterprises had more and more decision-making power over production and business operations. The government moved away from direct control over projects and the allocation of funds, relying instead on policies at the macro level and management of property rights. Enterprises themselves increasingly became the main actors in the importation of technology. While the economy grew rapidly technology imports declined, dropping from US$ 1.712 billion in 1992 to US$ 1.39 billion the following year. Imports of technologies used in the manufacture of electronics, textiles, automobiles, machines and other light industrial products increased as a share of all imports, and 82 to 89 percent of all technology imported was equipment.

III. Key Problems Retarding Technological Progress

Although great progress has been made many problems remain.

1. There is no effective mechanism at the macro level for encouraging technological progress throughout society. China has relied more on moral suasion than the profit motive. First, enterprises, particularly state-owned enterprises, are motivated by short-term considerations, (e.g. the short-term contract system). They pursue short-term interests at the expense of technological progress that would provide benefit in the long run. Second, distribution of income on the basis of labor contributed has in fact changed to distribution on the basis of length of service and the rate of attendance. Technicians and research scientists cannot expect rewards commensurate with their contribution. In many cases manual workers earn more than mental workers. Not surprisingly, this discourages enthusiasm for the hard work needed for technological innovation and progress. Moreover, technological innovation, particularly the creation and application of new technologies in today's world, holds the potential for great profit but is also freighted with great risk. Society should supply a certain portion of assurance and compensation for the risk involved in technological innovation. All developed countries have a mechanism for offsetting the risk inherent in the research and development of new technologies, such as government subsidies or banks dealing in venture capital. With the exception of the tax reductions or exemptions available in high-tech zones in keeping with international practice, China has no such risk compensation mechanism.

2. The relationship between technical transformation, technology imports and domestic research and development has not been handled well. Imports have been stressed at the expense of domestic research and development. More attention has been paid to constructing new enterprises than refurbishing old enterprises. Investment in research and development or innovation in products currently imported has been consistently low. Imports are relied upon for many parts and accessories used in manufacturing. The ratio of investment capital

used for technology imports to investment capital used for domestic assimilation is 1:3 in Japan and South Korea and less than 6:1 in China. As a result, production cannot reach designed capacity, production costs remain high and products are less competitive in both domestic and international markets. This is particularly true, as most technologies imported on a large scale are not up to the latest standard in the developed countries. Following installation and a period of use, the quality of the products produced may have fallen behind the most current international market requirements.

3. There is not a strong, effective national system for promoting technological innovation, nor are there set targets or precise strategies. Japan's success in this respect has been attributed to its consummate national technological innovation system, an organic combination of production, government and schools and its implementation of systematic and sustained industrial and technological policies with definite goals. There, economic and technological development are closely linked, interdependent and mutually promoting. After 1966 in China scientific and technological development was separated from economic development, all the more so after the 1980s. Technological policy drifted away from economic policy. The role of economics was decidedly weak. Today, the system for technological innovation is not only much less than consummate, it still has not completely entered the economic system.

4. The technological structure is far behind the times, development is extremely unbalanced, and such technological advances as are made are still not rapidly disseminated to industry. China's level of basic research is by no means substandard, but, viewed in its entirety, the technology structure lags 20 or 30 years behind the times. For example, the overall level of technology used in agriculture, including mechanization, electrification and economies of scale is less advanced than that in the United States in the sixties. Likewise, the motor vehicle industry matches US levels of that time period at best. In the iron and steel industry, only the Baoshan Iron and Steel Company has reached Japanese levels of the early eighties, while most in the

industry have only reached the level of the United States in the sixties or seventies. With the exception of a small number of single use of technologies imported in recent years, most railway transport technologies remain at the pre-1960s levels of the United States, Japan and Western Europe.

5. Insufficient competition and excessive competition exist side by side. Some important sectors remain under exclusive monopoly. This is detrimental to technological progress.

Section Three Goals and Directions for Scientific and Technological Progress

Scientific and technological development in the years up to 2010 will be oriented toward a number of intentions. The general requirement of sustained, steady, rapid, highly efficient economic development is to be met. Scientific and technological progress is to be used to promote economic development, social progress and steady, rapid growth of the productive forces, thereby attaining the second strategic goal of socialist modernization. Technological safeguards to effectively alleviate population pressures, conserve resources, improve environmental conditions and increase the effective supply capacity will be pursued. High priority new and advanced technology industries will be systematically developed and breakthroughs and innovations achieved in high technology and basic research so as to further approach international advanced levels, achieving the standards of the developed countries in the mid nineties. The extensive economy characterized by high consumption and low profits will be transformed into an intensive economy characterized by low consumption and high profits. Productivity's contribution to economic growth can be taken as an indicator of technological progress. This figure is expected to rise from 30 percent in early 1990s to 35 percent by 2000 and 40 percent by 2010.

I. Agriculture

Marked progress was made in agricultural development in the 1980s, but there were also grave problems and a hidden crisis. Farmland decreased by an average of 600,000 hectares annually while population grew by more than 16 million a year. If the per-capita grain output and output of other farm crops of the mid-1980s are to be duplicated in 2000, per-hectare yield will need to increase 2.3 percent annually. This will be extremely difficult. Current production methods cannot meet future demand. The key to more rapid growth in agricultural output will necessarily be scientific and technological progress.

Several ideas are essential to technology aimed at developing agriculture. (1) Reasonably develop and use and protect the agricultural natural resources. (2) New varieties of crops, livestock, fowl and aquatic products must be selectively bred and systems to establish this goal adopted. (3) Food sources must be expanded and the urban and rural food structures improved. (4) Farmland construction must be strengthened and high-yield, flood- and drought-free farmland established. Techniques for increasing outputs from farmland, animal husbandry and fishery should be developed, combining high yields, high quality and high efficiency with low consumption. (5) The use of regional, comprehensive development and management technologies should be popularized. (6) Research in storing, transportation, processing and packing technologies and agricultural mechanization and engineering should be encouraged. (7) The use of advanced technologies in agriculture, including computers and biological technology must be strengthened. (8) The study of modern agricultural economic and scientific management should be improved.

II. Important Industrial Sectors

Generally speaking, modern science and technology, especially microelectronics, new materials and new energy sources, are needed to transform industry. The industrial structure must be adjusted for optimum functionality and new technological principles and design methods adopted. Product lines and technological processes must be renovated, new manufacturing technologies and resource exploitation technologies developed, automation increased in the production process and intellectual standards raised. The portion of domestically manufactured complete installations and advanced technology used in key industries must be increased and management over technology and safety levels improved.

1. Technological progress must be made in the energy industry. Problems to be confronted include expanded energy production, resource exploitation and the development and effective, rational use of new energy sources. In this latter case, the goals should be improved efficiency in use and reduced harmful impact on environment. With this in mind, efforts toward improving technology used in the energy industry should zero in on heightening the quality of technology used in key equipment, developing energy conserving and environmentally friendly technologies. Domestic demand for oil is ever increasing, but any increase is limited by the supply of resources, a situation that impedes rapid growth or production breakthroughs. In the future, particular attention should be given to solving the technological problems interfering with the location and exploitation of oil and natural gas in desert and offshore areas and the development of better technologies for better recovery ratios in old oilfields. The coal centered energy consumption structure will remain in 2010. One major area for technological improvement remains mining technology and utilization of coal resources. Semi and fully continuous coal mining technologies and equipment must be developed and technologies for coal transportation improved. Industrial development and rising living standards will produce ever increasing demand for electricity. Advanced, large-capacity thermal power and ultrahigh voltage power distribution technologies and technology for the construction of large advanced hydraulic power stations must be developed. New energy sources with potential include renewable

energy sources such as solar energy, photocells and biological energy, nuclear energy and environmentally friendly technologies such as fluidized-bed combustion. Chemical fuel energy, energy saving and storage technologies also hold potential. Although none of these can obviate the need for conventional energy sources in the immediate future, work must begin now to harness their potential. Particularly deserving of attention are research and development of large-scale, advanced nuclear energy technology and nuclear safety technology, development of economical, practical new energies and rural energy sources and the popularization and application of advanced, energy-saving technologies.

2. Electronics and information industry. The electronics industry is in fact a group of industries, embracing electronics materials, equipment manufacture and components. Frequently, electronics are integrated with other technologies in other industries to form new technologies or new products. For this reason, electronics play an exceedingly important role in the current technological system and economic development. The electronics industry is the foundation of the information industry. The information and electronics industries overlap to some extent, but differ in nature. The information industry in other countries, particularly in developed countries is on the rise, gaining in importance within the various national economies. The changes this has brought about is sometimes referred to as a fourth industrial revolution. The information industry, including modern telecommunications, information processing and transmission and information consultancy and services, will be one of the fastest growing industries in China in the years leading up to 2010. Although it will be impossible to build a nationwide information superhighway by 2010, transregional or inter-city networks will be attainable. The electronics and information industries should be targeted as leading industries in the Program Up to 2010.

In the immediate future during the Ninth Five-Year Plan Period (1996-2000) technological progress in the electronics industry should be aimed at production technology systems for key equipment and components and the realization of scale production. Technological work in the information industry should be directed toward networking, digitalization and integration in the collection, processing and transmission of information. At the same time, more effort should be made in software development. Strong policies should be used to steer the infusion of the electronics and information industries into traditional industries. For example, research and development of technological systems integrating electronics with machines, computer-aided design, computer-aided manufacturing, flexible manufacturing systems, computer-aided management systems and computer-integrated manufacturing systems should all be accelerated. This should form an essential part of national technological policy.

3. Technological progress in raw and semi-finished materials industries. Traditional raw materials, including iron and steel, cement and other building materials, basic chemicals, and non-ferrous metals, and new materials such as semi-conductors, photoconductors and super conductors, and new structural and building materials are the products of primary industries essential for sustained, steady high-quality economic growth. Increased production and technological levels in these materials can significantly improve the quality of goods and services provided through the various economic sectors and the different departments of the national economy. They are the material foundation for current technological progress. Without high-quality raw materials, technological progress will remain beyond reach. In this respect, accelerated technological improvement in the raw materials industries is the foundation for updating the entire national economy. The traditional raw materials industries are the principal consumers of energy and producers of environmental pollution. Major problems currently present in these industries include economically inadequate scale of production, backward testing methods, substandard batch manufacturing technology, limited product variety, uncertain quality and serious environmental pollution. If these problems are to be addressed, work on improving technology in the raw materials industry should be directed toward research and development in

increased scale of large-scale complete set technology systems, automatic monitoring systems, energy conservation systems and quality guarantee systems. The widespread introduction of modern electronics and information technology can be sued to transform the traditional materials industry.

4. The manufacturing industry. The manufacturing industry, including the production of all kinds of machinery and equipment, instruments and meters, and electrical appliances, is the nation's provider of equipment. Manufacturing technological levels, to a large degree, determine the production technologies used in other industries and the performance of those technologies. China has a complete range of manufacturing. The most serious problems plaguing industries are backward testing methods, low automation levels, inadequate integration of electronics into machinery, lack of flexibility, insufficient product quality and reliability and low return from scale. Efforts to correct these and other problems should be steered in the following directions.

(1) The industrial technological policy for the motor vehicle industry has already been formulated. It remains for it to be fully implemented. Research on electric automobiles should be intensified.

(2) The process whereby international standards (ISO) become commonly used in China should be accelerated. China has already joined the ISO. It should be more rigorous in adhering to ISO systems so that product technological systems will be in line with international practice.

(3) The popularization and improvement of manufacturing automation technologies should be accelerated, particularly regards products produced on a large scale or in common use. Automation can be used to improve product consistency. The increased use of computer-aided design and the use of electronics and computers in manufacturing should be encouraged.

(4) Product design is the soul of manufacturing. Outdated design technology lengthens the amount of time necessary to create new products and does not allow the production of modern advanced

products. This has been an important factor behind the low efficiency in the production and delivery of manufactured goods. If this problem is to be corrected, design technology should be made a key target for technological improvement.

III. Other Industries

1. Transportation. The transportation industry is one of worst bottlenecks strangling economic growth. The energy problem is to a certain degree a transportation problem. Every year, large quantities of coal spontaneously combusts because overcrowded transportation facilities lacked the capacity to deliver the coal to would-be consumers. The principal cure for transportation shortfalls is accelerated railway construction and full use of all forms of transportation. Technological improvement in the transportation industry is also an important tool. Given China's current level of transportation technology, work in developing technology should build on the basis of the coordinated development of all forms of transportation, focusing on greatly increasing the level of networking and increasing comprehensive efficiency. Accelerating the establishment of a comprehensive transportation system is essential. Management and operations must be further modernized. Technological standards used in railway construction should be suitably raised. Average speeds on trunk railways and through important railway hubs should be increased, engine tractive force increased, trains capable of carrying heavier loads developed and electrification accelerated. Highway construction should be directed toward creating an expressway network. Every effort should be made to open more transportation channels.

2. Environmental protection. Environmental protection has become a common concern of every country as the 20th century draws to close. In the past, China's environmental protection policy was centered on the premise that the potential polluter was responsible for bringing pollution under control. Inevitably, pollution came first and limiting pollution only later. This was reasonably effective regards big

polluters, much less so with the many individual small polluters. This policy resulted in pollution control being too scattered and decentralized, too expensive and difficult to monitor. The concept of environmental protection needs to be rethought. The principle that the individual polluter is responsible for exercising control over the pollution it creates should continue to be adhered to, but environmental protection should be regarded as an industry in and of itself. The socialization and industrialization of environmental protection should be promoted and comprehensive, concentrated control over pollution strengthened. This will benefit research and development of environmental technologies, and their popular application. In the long term, work in environmental protection technologies should be directed toward the creation and gradual optimization of an efficient system for recovering the "three wastes," waste gas, waste water and industrial residue.

3. High-tech industries. (1) Microelectronics and information technology, automation technology and associated industries. (2) Biotechnology and associated industries. Work should concentrate on cultivation of high-yield, high-quality, anti-degenerative and disease-resistant new varieties of animals and plants, new biological vaccines, biological products and medicines. (3) The development and multiple application of reusable or renewable resources to ease shortages in resources. (4) Research and development and the popular application of new materials.

Section Four The Thought Behind Policies for Accelerated Scientific and Technological Progress

China's general strategy for accelerated technological progress is based on the principle of "walking on two legs." The first of these is reliance on market forces. Reform of the economic system pushes enterprises into a competitive environment where they are pressured to improve the technology they use to increase their competitiveness. The second is the use of suitable macro and micro economic policies and moderate intervention to create an environment conducive to technological progress. A sound and effective mechanism for technological innovation will be put into place and enterprises actively guided toward the pursuit of technological progress. Proceeding from this basic idea, the general strategic framework should entail grasping the key areas and accelerating reform, moderate intervention, a combination of rewards and punishments, the creation of conditions wherein competition can thrive and increased investment so as to build the nation through technology.

1. Grasping the key areas and accelerating reform. The state has limited financial and material resources. This strategy calls for the use of these limited resources in a limited number of key advanced technologies in the hope of making breakthroughs. Outside of these key areas across the broad range of industry technological progress will come through market competition spurred on by increased economic reform. Key areas could include microelectronics technology and associated materials, bio-engineering, the development and application of new energy sources and information technology. The exact areas to be designated can be determined by experts and economists based on the degree of correlation to the technologies. The concept of key breakthrough need not be limited to research in key technologies; it may also include the import, development and application of these technologies in traditional industries to truly achieve industrialization and innovation. Accelerating reform is an essential condition for accelerating technological progress. This means that the market mechanism and heightened competition must be also brought into play in the development of these key technologies. The old road of planned management and uncompensated investment should be abandoned. Organizational forms intended to develop and propagate new and advanced technologies such as the 863 Program, the Spark Program and the Torch Program should continue to be

strengthened. But they should be still further improved by introducing the competitive mechanism to ensure their success.

2. Measured intervention should include a combination of rewards and punishments. It means to perfect the effective social incentive mechanism. The government's timely formulation of industrial and technological policy supported by appropriate financial policies can accelerate the improvement of the industrial organization and the technological structure. The government does not directly participate as an actor in specific activities of the industrial and technological projects, but gives guidance to enterprises and helps them pursue large-scale activities aimed at progress in technology which they would be unable to accomplish on their own. This help would come in the form of various economic and legal measures, such as tax reductions or exemptions, economic safety nets for risky endeavors, low-interest loans, licensing import and export business and providing information and consultancy services. Tools such as these can provide enterprises with the impetus to realize major technical innovations. If this process is to be brought about, time cannot be wasted in formulating and optimizing detailed regulations for the implementation of a law supervising technology and quality, strengthening law-enforcement institutions and ensuring the strict enforcement of current laws relating to technological progress.

3. Conditions should be created wherein competition can fully play its role. A healthy social environment and good conditions for the supply of resources will serve technological progress. A healthy social environment would included an awareness and appreciation of technology and healthy cultural quality on the part of the entire citizenry, equal competitive opportunity among all enterprises and individuals. Competition would proceed in an orderly, standardized fashion. Society would recognize positive innovations and accomplishments by groups and individuals, providing suitable rewards. The most important resource in the pursuit of technological excellence is technically skilled, high quality personnel. Over the long term, the importance of education in further fueling technological

progress is not to be underestimated. This includes normal higher education, but also secondary technical education, on the job technical training, popular education in science and technology, indeed all kinds of education at all levels.

4. Investment should be increased and the country built through technology. The concept of technology should infuse development strategies and the formulation of policy. Accelerated technological progress will be the source of the nation's coming wealth. Science and technology should be regarded as the engines driving economic growth and state investment in this field should be increased. Awareness of science and technology should be increased throughout society and respect for its preeminence and for scientists and technicians propagated. Increased investment in technological progress should include more than just direct financial assistance from the government. In a broader sense it embraces a bias toward technology in the disposition of the national income. First, investment in education should be increased to improve awareness of technology throughout society. Second, investment in technological research and development should be increased to increase the popularization of new technologies and their broad use throughout industry. Third, intellectual property rights should be protected and the rights of scientists and technicians to benefit monetarily from their intellects respected. Technological innovation should be encouraged through legal, administrative, economic and moral measures. Income engineers, technicians or scientists earn from innovations they have created receive tax reductions or exemptions.

Drawing up a specific policy to promote technological progress is an exceedingly complicated, systematized project inseparable from economic policy. Technological policy must be recognized as an integral part of the economic policy system in future economic plans and policies.

Chapter Fifteen   Population

China has more than 1.2 billion people, and will have around 1.3 billion by the end of the century. Overpopulation is a very difficult problem to solve and remains a major hurdling block to economic development.

Section One   Population Control Targets and Strategies and the Continued Improvement of the Population

I. Population and the Economy, Coordinated Social Development

For many years, two views regarding the impact of population growth on economy have stood in direct opposition. One side welcomes population growth, saying that human labor is the greatest resource; the other claims that increasing population is a time bomb, ticking away, which may explode destroying the very foundation of human existence. This issue is fraught with complications. Beginning in the sixties, the concept of population growth as a threatening explosion gained in circulation drawing common concern. The international community has come to realize that development and progress should be judged not only by changes in GNP, but also by infant mortality and literacy rates, housing conditions, equitable income distribution, life expectancy and employment rates. The United Nations Development Program (UNDP) has proposed a human development index (HDI) based on three factors: average life-expectancy, literacy rate and purchasing power. Hermann Derek and John Colbert have outlined an index of sustainable economic welfare (ISEW), which takes into account air and water pollution, decrease in arable land, worsening environmental conditions, income distribution and even automobile accidents, all factors affecting human well-being. In the United States in the early 1950s improvement in ISEW matched increase in GNP, but after the 1970s, while GNP continued to rise, the ISEW stalled and then began to fall gradually. Researchers in China have also proposed comprehensive indices of excessive social development and population plays an important role in their calculations. Population growth affects economic growth both positively and negatively. An American science report on the population growth and economic development finds six reasons for optimism and three reasons for pessimism.

1. Resources thought to be exhausted may be able to be exploited for a period of time. The relationship between population growth and resource consumption may be less intense than previously thought.

2. Pollution can be alleviated through proper government policies. Population growth is not a cause of pollution.

3. In the past it was thought that rapid population growth would lower the savings rate. Currently, that situation seems to have changed. Within the short term the impact on investment has decreased.

4. The influence of investment in education on investment in production is not very clear. Reductions in investment per student can be used to fund increases in investment in human resources.

5. Urban sprawl can be restricted through appropriate policies as has already been proven.

6. The urban unemployment is not brought about by urban population growth. A reduction in the urban population growth rate will not in itself improve the quality of services. However, excessive urban population growth will aggravate the urban problems; therefore, it should be kept within proper limits.

Three conclusions were more disturbing.

1. The population growth has played a very negative role in the

deterioration of resources, particularly renewable public resources such as rain forests and fish, which have been extremely adversely affected.

2. Excessive population growth leads to increases in the size of individual households, reducing per-child expenditure in health care, nutrition and education, clearly reducing the children's opportunities for future development.

3. Generally speaking, the positive effects of economy of scale, resource utilization and technological progress brought about by population growth are not enough to offset the direct negative effects.

These conclusions accord with those obtained by Chinese researchers. Their research has shown that limiting population growth is playing an important role in economic growth and the improvement of the standards of living, and the policy coordination is needed on all sides. The relationships between population and the economy, environment and resources demand population control.

II. China's Greatest Sustainable Population, Optimum Population and Realistic Goals

As has been confirmed by a multitude of studies, China's population load is already very close to the maximum that could be supported by existent resources.

The most acute shortage is of fresh water. China ranks sixth in the world with 2,800 billion cubic meters in fresh water reserves, but 88th per capita. Continued population growth in the next century will reduce China's rank below 100th. Currently, 108 cities suffer from serious water shortages. Excessive tapping of ground water has led to surface subsidence and the funneling down of the water surface. Such water resources as exist are unevenly distributed across the country. The distribution of the water resources is not in concert with the distribution of the land. South of the Yangtze River can be found 83 percent of the nation's water resources, but only 38 percent of the farmland, while the 9 percent of water resources in the basins of the

Yellow, Huaihe, Haihe and Liaohe rivers must support 42 percent of nation's farmland. There is also a great contradiction in the timing of supply and demand. In the season when waters are abundant they rush straight down to the sea even spilling over the river banks causing disastrous floods; in a dry spell, the Yellow River may even stops its flow. Constructing water reservoirs or diverting water from the south to the north is a major expense. Only three years in ten comes good weather for crops. In other years there are disasters, large or small, often droughts or floods. By the end of this century, total demand for water in a moderately dry year is predicted to be 600 billion cubic meters, 100 billion cubic meters in excess of water supply. Clearly, the shortfall is quite serious. Given available water resources, China's maximum population capacity would be 1.6 billion. Assuming an average life-expectancy of 80 years, after the population stabilizes there will at most be 20 million new births annually. Considering population inertia and the influence of past high birth rates, new births per year should fall to around 15 million within a number of years, ensuring that the population will not rise above 1.6 billion.

Farmland and energy are the two indispensable nonrenewable resources. Excessive rapid population growth may lead to two undesirable economic consequences: progressive reduction in remuneration and excessive resource consumption. The contradiction inherent in China's enormous population and scarcity of farmland is common knowledge. Of all the heavily populated countries only Japan has less per-capita farmland. China is also among the countries with the least farmland per adult of working age. Energy consumption is also a serious problem. Current per-capita consumption of standard coal is 0.7 tons per year, far less than the 9.4 tons of standard coal per capita consumed in the United States. Even in Japan, a nation long conscious of energy conservation, per-capita energy consumption is the equivalent of 3.5 tons per year. Further social and economic development in China will surely bring very substantial increases in per-capita energy consumption. A shortfall of 200 million tons of standard coal is expected by 2000, a shortage that will be still greater if population growth is not held in check. The needs of economic development, the demand for energy and the limited availability of farmland all necessitate the population being held to below 1.6 billion.

Agriculture is an essential pillar of sustained development. Economic development, improving living standards and population growth create growing demand for farm products. Since 1978 per-capita urban consumption of pork has nearly trebled and that of sugar nearly doubled. Increased meat consumption has greatly increased demand for fodder grain. Currently, half of increased production of grain and meat is consumed by the individuals representing increase in overall population. Even so, China's per-capita meat consumption is only one tenth of that in the economically developed countries. Accordingly, demand for grain and other farm products will continue to rise, and the contradiction between growth in grain production and growth in demand become increasingly pressing.

The problem of overpopulation is even more salient regards economic returns. There are 120 million surplus workers in the countryside. This has negatively affected the adoption of advanced technologies and intensive management in agriculture, resulting in a failure to achieve economy of scale. In state-owned enterprises 20-25 percent of staff and workers are superfluous, the hidden unemployed. Surplus workers increase the burdens on enterprises, increase costs, and make it difficult for them to adopt new technologies. Light industry is underdeveloped, leaving agriculture to bear the brunt of the burden in supporting industrial development. Rises and falls in agricultural production are to a large degree responsible for rises and falls in industrial production. The enormous surplus of rural labor power has greatly hindered structural change.

Overall national strength and quality of life are factors to be considered in determining strategic population goals. More attention should be given to the people's wishes and enforcement capability in deciding policy. A number of studies have come to the same conclusion: China's maximum population capacity is approximately 1.6 billion. In terms of economic development, a population of 700 million to one billion would be ideal. To quickly reduce the nation's population to this level would require births to be limited to 10 million a year, an unattainable goal at present. A more realistic strategy would be to make every effort to limit the birth rate to such a level that population not exceed 1.6 billion in the long term, gradually smoothing out the age structure.

Section Two   Population Growth Forecasts

Population systems are governed by inertia. Change come slowly, a cycle taking approximately 70 years. A high tide in the birth rate in the sixties has resulted in a second high tide of births as the earlier generation came of child-bearing age. During the nineties 22 million new births per year were expected. If this birth rate continues and life expectancy averages 80 years in the new century, total population will reach 1.76 billion before it stabilizes, a figure in excess of the maximum capacity suggested above. However, current family planning policies will gradually reduce the proportion of women of child-bearing age in the total population beginning in the late nineties. In the first part of the next century, the number of women of child-bearing age will begin to decrease in absolute terms. This should result in fewer new births each year. However, the present enormous population will almost necessarily continue to engender great population growth, the so-called inertia mentioned above. If this tendency is to be overcome, low birth rates must be maintained for a period of time. Ideally, the number of new births each year will be approximately the same. This will better serve society regards employment and social stability and the construction and use of kindergartens, schools and other service and welfare institutions. Gradual change will be best for society. These ideas should provide the groundwork for further consideration of long-term and immediate population goals.

Expected changes in China's population (not including Hong Kong, Macao and Taiwan) in the nineties and the first half of the next century are shown in Table 15-1.

Table 15-1   Changes in the Population

Unit: million

Year	Total population			Sex ratio* (%)	Births	Deaths
	Total number	Male	Female			
1991	1158	597	561	106.49	23	8
1992	1172	604	568	106.42	22	8
1993	1185	611	574	106.35	22	8
1994	1200	618	582	106.28	23	8
1995	1215	626	589	106.21	23	9
1996	1229	633	596	106.14	23	9
1997	1242	639	603	106.07	22	9
1998	1255	646	609	105.99	22	9
1999	1268	652	616	105.92	21	9
2000	1279	658	621	105.84	21	9
2005	1332	683	648	105.44	20	10
2010	1381	708	674	105.02	20	10
2050	1582	796	787	101.17	18	19

*male : female, female=100.

Section Three   Economic Results from Controlling Population Growth

I. Economic Development, Labor Supply and Demand and Population Movement

One quarter of the agricultural workforce is surplus labor. The marginal output of the rural labor is very low. This enormous redundancy in the rural workforce has been given vent in a huge itinerant population. In 1996, reportedly, 6.54 percent of the total population, 80 million persons, were living away from their homes; 44 million had temporary residency permits issued by the local public security bureau and 30 million were temporary workers floating from province to province. These figures, however, very likely substantially underestimate the extent of the problem. The floating population probably exceeds 100 million.

Most of this floating population can be found in the economically developed coastal provinces, 11.3 percent of the provincial population in Zhejiang, (the highest), 8.2 percent in Guangdong and 8 percent in Fujian. The most populous province of Sichuan makes the greatest contribution to this army of transient workers, 7.1 percent of the provincial population.

Most of these transient workers are young or middle-aged, 57.2 percent between 15 and 30 years in age. Not well educated, 31.9 percent have only reached primary school level and 38.6 percent junior middle school level.

During the 1982 and 1990 census, the nationwide working age population increased by 138 million, up 2.58 percent per annum, much higher than the 1.48 percent annual population growth rate averaged over the same period. The employed population increased by 125.69 million during this time, up 2.41 percent per annum. Growth in light and tertiary industries and township enterprises played a tremendous role in absorbing surplus labor power. In 1995, 52.9 percent of those employed worked in primary industry, 23 percent in secondary industry and 24.1 percent in tertiary industry. The greatest portion of surplus labor was still to be found in primary industry, greatly reducing this sector's efficiency. From early on, primary industry's marginal output has been zero or even negative. At present labor supply still exceeds demand. The only hope for striking a balance between labor supply and demand during the first two decades of the coming century will be a successfully realized family planning policy.

II. Economic Results of the Family Planning

Family planning is a vital tool in reducing the birth rate. There is a negative correlation between savings and investment and population growth. A decline in population growth leads to increased savings and investment. Between 1971 and 1993 family planning resulted in 270 million fewer new births. This saved society the 3.5 trillion yuan that would have gone to caring for the babies. The savings went in part to increased consumption and in part to increased savings and investment.

A reduced birth rate is also beneficial in easing pressure on poverty-stricken areas, making it easier for the poor to reverse their circumstances and helping shift the distribution of income more toward low income households. The birth rate in the poorer provinces and autonomous regions is twice that in those more wealthy. The vast majority of these more wealthy regions now have relatively stable low birth rates and have the conditions necessary for increased investment in child education and accelerated economic development.

A reduced birth rate also has indirect economic effect. When workers have fewer children, they need less time for child-care and thereby improved their efficiency in the work-place. Women workers have less of a burden in nursing babies and more opportunity to receive professional training, thus further tapping production potential.

Thus can be seen, a reduced birth rate is beneficial in improving population quality and promoting economic development.

Section Four   The Aging of the Population and Social Security for the Elderly

I. An Increasingly Aged Population

China's population is still very young compared to those of the economically developed countries. A one percent sampling in 1995 indicated 10.17 percent of the total population, 120.9 million people, were 60 years or older. Of these, 61 percent were in their sixties. This state of affairs should continue into the early part of the next century. The aging of the population structure will greatly accelerate after the 2020s as the many babies born during the sixties enter the ranks of the aged.

Three quarters of the elderly live in countryside. However, because the birth rate in the cities began to fall in the sixties, reaching very low levels in the eighties, the urban population will age much more quickly than its urban counterpart. Shanghai already has an elderly population structure. Beijing, Tianjin and the more heavily urbanized provinces will all sooner or later evolve in the same way. This huge elderly population will affect social and economic development in many ways.

Mid-level forecasts foresee 134 million Chinese aged sixty or above by 2000, 10.48 percent of the total population. This percentage will increase to 16.84 percent by 2020. There will be 468 million elderly by 2050, 27.77 percent of the total population. The elderly within the non-agricultural population will increase by 2 percentage points. The ever growing numbers of elderly puts increasing burdens on the government, enterprises and society. In 1978 expenditure on old-age pensions accounted for only 3 percent of all wages paid, rising to 16.9 percent in 1991 and to 19.03 percent in 1995. This figure continues to rise.

Retirement pay has also increased greatly and will account for 20 percent of total wages by 2010 and over 30 percent by 2050.

II. Social Security for the Elderly

Old-age retirement pay systems typically take three forms: current receipts funding current payouts, a fully funded system and partially funded system. The first of these is the system presently used in China. The funding required for retirement pay in a given year is collected that year. This has the advantage of relative simplicity but forces workers to carry the costs of the retired, dampening their enthusiasm for production. A fully funded system is a personal retirement fund system based on compulsory savings, with the worker preparing for his or her own support after retirement during the period of his or her own employ. A critical defect in this system is its vulnerability to inflation. Singapore provides a successful example of a fully funded system. A partially funded system combines features of both other systems. In principle, revenue is determined by expenditure, a slight surplus is maintained, accumulation is gradual and increases to the fund offset payouts. Reforms in many countries are moving in this direction, but operating this system is relatively difficult. This would seem the most viable alternative for China. Of key importance in the partially funded system is the question of how to schedule stepped increases in the collection rate. If there is a higher rate of collection before the high tide of aging arrives, of course, there will be less of a burden when the time for greater payouts arrives. However, this creates a greater burden on present workers who must provide the funds both to support the elderly today and to provide for their own future old age support. Conversely, a lower rate of accumulation will help alleviate this double burden but may leave the system underfunded during the peak aging period. Appropriate levels of collections must be begun immediately. Funds accumulated during the earlier period can be used to make up for the shortfalls to be expected in time of greatest expenditure. Actual rates used should be based on price indices, increases and decreases in the value of the fund and other factors. Model calculations suggest that 20 percent of total wages be collected to fund the system. This burden would be borne in set proportions by the state, enterprises and individual workers. A three trillion yuan shortfall is anticipated between 2030 and 2060, but at the 20 percent rate this can be offset by funds collected but not paid out prior to 2030 plus interest which should come to 3.5 trillion yuan (in 1990 constant prices). Thus the shortfall can be met, with a surplus as a cushion.

Section Five   Regional Population Distribution: Urbanization and Adjustment of the Industrial Structure

The huge surplus rural workforce effectively precludes scale operations. Labor productivity in agriculture will lag behind that in industry for many years to come. In 1992 industrial workers were 13 times more productive than agricultural workers. Accelerated urbanization is an inevitable part of industrial structural adjustment and economic and social development. Township enterprises will play an important role in this process. The rise in their share of the total industrial output value from 9.09 percent in 1978 to 55.78 percent in 1995 gives a clear demonstration of their expanding vitality.

Different provinces, autonomous regions and municipalities have widely varying levels of population urbanization; 58 percentage points separate the most heavily urbanized of these, Beijing, from the least, Yunnan. Yunnan is almost entirely rural with less than 15 percent of its people living in cities. Liaoning, is the only governmental unit at this level with more than 50 percent of its population urbanized, in addition to Beijing, Tianjin and Shanghai, the three municipalities directly under the central government.

The urbanization process depends to a large degree on changes in the industrial structure. The first step is to transfer a large number of workers from primary industry to manufacturing. The second step is to greatly expand the service industries, substantially increasing tertiary industry's contribution to total production. The State Planning Commission and the State Statistical Bureau have determined that 30,000-40,000 yuan will be needed to arrange a new job in the city. Given current financial capability and level of economic development, the cities can absorb 4 million rural workers a year, in addition to supplying jobs for new city born workers. Accumulatively, by 2000, urban jobs can be found for approximately 24 million peasants.

Generally speaking, the process of urbanization has lagged behind economic development. There are historical reasons for this. In China agriculture was used to support industry. The economic system left tertiary industry woefully underdeveloped. Population in excess of demand for labor has created employment and social development obstacles to urbanization. Changes in the urban structure lag behind changes in the production structure, seriously impacting economic development. Township enterprises have long operated in an environment of low efficiency and are heavy polluters. This has been detrimental to the transformation of the overall economic structure to socialized production and the formation of a standard market mechanism and has impeded the concentration of farmland in the most capable hands and the adoption of new technologies and advanced machinery and equipment.

The urban structure also has a significant impact on economic development. A city's small size results in a small market, a situation not beneficial to economic growth. The minimum population for a city to begin to benefit from scale is generally put at 250,000-300,000 people. Oversized cities suffer from many complications with urban transportation, garbage disposal, housing, energy supply and water supply. Urban populations above two million find these problems difficult to solve. Half of China's city population and one quarter of its urban population live in "super-cities" with populations over one million. Cities with an average of 2.12 million in non-agricultural population and cities with an average of non-agricultural population of 720,000 or more account for 80 percent of the total urban population. In comparison, medium-sized and small cities averaging less than 70,000 people, far fewer than the 300,000 necessary to drive economic growth, remain underdeveloped. Such a state of affairs is detrimental to economic development. To correct this situation, the size of large cities should be limited, medium-sized cities developed appropriately and small cities actively developed.

Section Six   Improving Population Quality and Promoting Coordinated Social and Economic Development

Prior to the founding of the People's Republic in 1949, 80 percent of the Chinese population was illiterate. The so-called "sick man of East Asia" was weak and divided. In the nearly fifty years since China stood up, great progress has been made in education and improving cultural levels. Average life expectancy has increased from 35 to nearly 70 years. The infant mortality rate, an effective barometer of social and economic development level and living standards, have fallen from 200-250 per thousand to 35 per thousand.

Education levels of those employed have grown consistently higher. The 1990 census reported that 1.4 percent of the population had a college level education or higher and 8 percent had a high school education; 16.9 percent were semi-illiterate or illiterate. Much progress has been made, but a substantial gap remains between China and even those nations ranking in the middle range in terms of education. Only 20.42 percent of the administrative personnel in government institutions between 15 years and 29 years in age have received higher education, and half are only at the high school level. Only one in four technicians between 15 and 29 years in age have received higher education, and 18.38 percent have received only a junior high school education. Few of the 120 million urban workers are highly skilled. Even in Shanghai, only 5.52 percent of workers are highly skilled. Needless to say, this is hardly conducive to the development of a market economy or increased production and technical levels. Clearly, great efforts are called for to accelerate educational development. At the same time, the current personnel management system needs to be altered to give full play to the capacities of currently available personnel.

Since 1949 the people's physiques have improved. Another measure of improved health other than falling infant mortality is the increased heights, weights and chest measurements of those between the ages of 7 and 25. However, in terms of per-capita doctors and hospital beds, China still lags far behind economically developed countries like the United States, Japan, Germany and France. Inadequacies in the health care system are most apparent in the countryside. A sampling taken in 1987 indicates that 18.11 percent of Chinese households include a disabled person, implying more than 50 million disabled nationwide. Quality prenatal and natal health care should be encouraged as should health care for the young child so as to reduce the incidence of disability. Activities to encourage recovery from disability should be developed and the disabled helped to recover full health or improve their ability to care for themselves. Those disabled able to work should be given job training and jobs. This work can be another effective tool for improving the quality of the population.

Chapter Sixteen   Employment

In the 18 years since the initiation of the reform and opening policy, 230 million new jobs have been created, approximately 30 million more than in the preceding 30 years. However, as the reform has deepened, the labor and employment issues have become ever more problematic.

Section One   The Current Employment Situation and Attendant Issues

I. Pressures from Three Kinds of Surplus Labor Power

Reform and development have not altered the situation with surplus labor. The supply of workers will grow rapidly in the coming years as a result of natural growth as a large portion of the population comes to working age. During the first five years of the nineties the labor pool was increased by 12.5 million persons per annum. Between 1995 and 2010 this annual rate will increase to 14.5 million.

The introduction of the contract responsibility system linking remuneration to output in the countryside in the late 70's and early 80's resulted in increased labor productivity in agriculture and the emergence of a surplus rural workforce. The actual number of agricultural workers demonstrated to be redundant by this new policy is estimated to be 90-120 million. Township enterprises and growth in the urban and rural economies have helped reduce potential surplus labor pressure by two thirds, but a very substantial number of surplus workers remain, joined each year by new workers coming of age. In the years running up to 2010, new jobs will need to be found for 35 to 40 million otherwise surplus workers, an average of 2.3 to 2.7 million new jobs a year.

Moreover, deepened reform of state-owned enterprises will reveal large numbers of redundant workers. When they are trimmed from the enterprise payroll they are left unemployed. This is yet another source of the expanding supply of labor. At present, more than 150 million people work in state-owned units. If employment in these units is to be reduced by a factor of 0.1, new jobs will have to be found for approximately 12 million newly unemployed in the years running up to 2010, 800,000 new jobs a year. If employment in these units is reduced even more, by a factor of 0.2, more than 24 million new jobs will have to be created for those laid off, 1.6 million per year.

Increases in the labor supply from all three sources are laid out in the following chart.

Unit: million

	Population increase	Surplus rural labor	Workers laid off from state-owned enterprises	Total
Annual demand for new jobs (1995-2010)	14.5	2.5	1.6	18.6

Thus 18.6 million new jobs will have to be created annually in the years before 2010, 3.5 to 6 million more new jobs to be created annually than during the eighties.

II. Structural Imbalance in Employment Distribution

The seriousness of the problems involving labor and employment go beyond the great numbers involved. The situation further suffers from an imbalance in the distribution of human resources. Since the initiation of reform and opening the rapid flow of labor has been very one sided, from the less developed regions to those more developed, from the west to the east, and from the inland to the coast, from the countryside to the city, from industries less market oriented to those more market oriented, and from the state-owned sector to the privately-owned sectors. Areas experiencing an outflow of workers will undoubtedly enjoy increased capital infusions as income earned elsewhere returns and increased job opportunities created by this inflow of capital. But the areas receiving an inflow of workers suffer from increased employment pressures and problems arising from social instability.

III. Contradictions in the Changing Employment Model

Difficulties are presented by the transition from the former employment model which was based on vast numbers of workers to the more efficient model necessitated by the requirements of market development. The current mode of agricultural production based on the individual peasant household remains a diffuse, small-scale mode of production. In the future, farmland will be concentrated to better take advantage of the economy of scale and further raise labor productivity in agriculture. This will require more surplus agricultural workforce to leave the land. The change will come about naturally as peasants act in their individual best interest, inevitably increasing considerable employment pressures on the whole of society.

China will also face the task of technological upgrading in the years before 2010. Fierce market competition will drive enterprises to actively select combinations of capital and labor with more technological content, increasing the technological composition of their capital, and using new technologies in place of manual labor. Again, this creates more surplus labor.

China, then, is confronted with a contradictory situation. It would like full productive employment, but this goal is unattainable before 2010. At the same time, the establishment of an efficient employment system will result in fewer workers per unit capital, further distancing demand for labor from supply. Given this contradiction, the government must make some serious policy choices, take advantage of more employment sources and create more jobs.

Section Two   A Multiple Strategy for Solving the Employment Problem

There are two principal ways to alleviate the strains between labor supply and demand. Growth in the number of new workers can be controlled or new jobs can be created.

Since the government adopted its family planning policy in the middle seventies, natural population growth has markedly decreased. The natural growth rate is currently approximately 1.2 percent, 0.9 percent in the cities and slightly over 1.2 percent in the countryside. If continuity in the population control policy is maintained, the natural growth rate in the rural areas will tend to fall to a certain degree in response to rising incomes and the development of a social security system. If rural natural population growth approaches the urban standard of "1+1=1", (one couple producing one child), or even is actually limited to "1+1=1.5" (two couples averaging three children), rural natural population growth will be further reduced. At present, there is concern that 90 million surplus rural workers who have moved to the city have not been counted in national population statistics. A proper count of the working-age population is essential.

Short-term methods for reducing the labor supply include the introduction of a paid holiday system and the encouragement of women, where appropriate, to return to their households. Labor inside and outside the household are of equal importance in the modern concept of labor. Household work can be done by the housewives themselves or in the company of others in specialized household service companies. In this way, a portion of the female workforce can exit the ranks of workers in the broader society, reducing pressures created by competition for jobs. Opportunities are also created for women from low income households to find jobs.

I. Sustained Growth and Increased Demand for Labor

In terms of development, the fundamental technique for alleviating the contradiction between supply and demand of labor is to generate more demand, create more job opportunities and raise the macro employment level. This calls for an appropriately rapid economic growth rate, 8 to approximately 10 percent.

II. Adjustment of the Employment Structure and Peasant Cities

If there is an excess of workers, more labor-intensive businesses need be brought to the fore and capital replaced with labor. This strategy can also serve to ease shortages of capital. The key to effecting this change is accelerating the growth of tertiary industry, increasing its role in the national economy. Approximately 56 percent of employment is in agriculture, but agricultural output value accounts for less than 22 percent of GNP. Long-term programs and government policies should enable the increase of tertiary industry's contribution to GNP from the current 20 percent to 25 percent by 2000 and nearly 40 percent or higher by 2010. This coming trend will be of great importance in reducing employment pressure in years to come.

As development of township enterprises slows down and the increase of urban laid-off workers and staff, more rural workers find themselves out of work, new channels for the transfer of rural workforce must be found. One possible solution would be the development of towns and small cities for the peasants. These would benefit the expansion of rural non-agricultural employment, raise overall employment levels and accelerate industrialization and urbanization, without increasing the burdens on existing cities. The government should create a good policy environment for the development of towns and small cities in rural areas.

III. Choices in Reform: Two Available Roads

Recently, peasant incomes have risen year after year. Outside of expenditure on very simple farm production, most of the income has been used for consumption. Capital accumulation in agriculture is extremely inadequate. This is primarily the result of the lack of a long-term policy for the protection of the peasants' individual capital. City dwellers also have a lot of money. After expenditure on food, clothing, housing and travel expenses, bank savings deposits, and non-industrial investment in treasury bonds and stocks, however, a good portion of their income is spent on luxuries. This money has not been invested in industry and creates no jobs. This is a very serious waste of resources. This state of affairs also results from uncertainty over long-term legal protection for private capital. Controls over individual and private businesses are excessive. More job opportunities can be created if the government removes the obstacles hindering the development of the private economy, especially small and medium-sized businesses principally financed by individual families. This can be done by providing legal protection and removing restrictions and encouraging individuals to accumulate capital or themselves fund the opening of a store or a factory.

Redundant employees currently on the payroll of state-owned enterprises will be a source of future surplus workforce. However, changes in the enterprise system and the invigoration of state-owned assets can be used to generate more demand for labor. For example, the government can auction off some state-owned assets and invest the earnings in building railways and water conservancy projects, which, in turn, will absorb otherwise surplus workers. The buyers can put their newly acquired assets into operation using a new combination of capital and labor, again creating new jobs. In this way new jobs generate still more new jobs. In fact, the auction of state-owned assets not only helps increase employment, it also helps increase taxes and accelerate reform of the social security system. Non-state-owned institutions pay taxes. This revenue can be used for public investment and the establishment of social security funds.

IV. Selection of Trade Strategies and Professional Training

Trade strategies will have a great impact on employment. Many more workers can be employed if exports are principally of manufactured goods than if exports are mainly of resources for import replacements. Exports of primary products should continue to be reduced. This will help avoid the depletion of resources resulting from rapid growth and increase employment by increasing exports of manufactured goods. The manufactured goods export structure can also be further adjusted. Small industrial products and traditional agricultural products still have international markets and their export should be encouraged; processing and services associated with these products can provide more job opportunities. In addition, during the course of making import substitutions, imports of products that represent excessive labor savings or have little practical application should be reduced.

Although China has a surplus of labor power, this does not mean there is an acute shortage of jobs. In fact, there is a shortage of intellectual and professional people in many industries, especially in industries with a fairly high level of modernization, which require more highly skilled workers. This calls for the vigorous development of the educational work and professional training.

In short, only by adopting multiple strategies to accelerate demand for labor and increasing workers' levels of practical skills can the employment problem be alleviated.

Section Three   Future Employment Policy Goals

I. There Is Always Unemployment in a Market Economy

A full employment policy does not require a zero unemployment rate. In fact, zero unemployment rate is neither desirable nor possible.

This is true for the following reasons. (1) Unemployment at an appropriate scale provides a pool of reserve labor for adjustment of the economic structure and new combinations of capital and labor. (2) Workers change their work preferences from time to time. There is always some voluntary unemployment in the labor market. (3) The fixed capital renewal and replacement cycle results in cyclical fluctuations in total employment, producing cyclical unemployment. A "full employment" policy that achieved a zero unemployment rate would result in reduced efficiency in the use of capital and labor. Government policy should not be geared to completely eliminating unemployment. Rather, it should take effective measures to create more job opportunities and work hard to reduce the actual unemployment rate.

II. Macro Policy Goals: Control Unemployment and Inflation

Reaching the low unemployment rates targeted in full employment should not mean a complete relaxation of the money market and the adoption of a loose monetary policy. Two principal fiscal policy forms of regulation can be used regards full employment goals: budgetary regulation and tax regulation. If a portion of the funds budgeted for construction are diverted by the government from the competitive sector to the public sector, leaving the competitive sector to non-governmental institutions, the government can increase employment in the public sector using that portion of the budget. Tax regulation can be used to increase employment in two main ways. First, excise taxes can be collected. Second, income tax hitherto evaded and used for consumption can be collected. After collecting in taxes money that would otherwise be spent in non-production areas, the government can use a part of the revenue for public production to provide more job opportunities and another part as an equilibrium fund to be used to reduce taxes as is appropriate on some products, thereby increasing employment.

III. Anti-Recession Policies and Stemming Increases in the Unemployment Rate

Long-term analysis indicates that the Chines economy tends to move in five-year cycles. When the economy is at its lowest point unemployment is higher, with surplus rural workforce returning to the countryside, more workers laid off in the state-owned sector and fewer jobs available in the non-state-owned sector. If this trend is not drastically altered, over the next ten plus years there will possibly be three periods of high unemployment. If the government hopes to reduce unemployment during these recessions, it must formulate an explicit policy to combat recession, fine tuning the economy if an effort is made to slow it down when overheated. A long-term tightening of demand is not desirable during a downturn in the economy, a radical long-term reduction in demand will result in increased unemployment. If large numbers of people lose their jobs in a recession they will have less money to spend, presenting an inestimable danger to society. Avoiding excessive economic decline and keeping unemployment to a minimum during a recession are of decisive importance to economic development and to social stability.

Chapter Seventeen   The Environment

This chapter discusses the role of the environment in rapid sustained economic development. What is China's resource carrying capacity.

Section One   The Environmental Situation Since the Initiation of the Reform and Opening Policy

I. Economic Growth with Relative Stable Environmental Conditions

Since the initiation of the reform and opening policy, rapid economic growth and a marked improvement in living standards have been achieved while maintaining comparatively stable environmental conditions. In the 16 years after 1978, forested area nationwide increased from 118.73 million hectares to 133.7 million hectares, and reserves of standing timber rose from 10.7 billion cubic meters to 11.785 cubic meters. The number of nature preserves has increased from 34 to 766 and where they once accounted for 0.13 percent of the nation's territory, they now accounted for 6.8 percent. More than 6,000 species of animals and more than 1,000 species of plants are under state protection.

The total quantities of industrial waste water discharge, heavy metals in industrial waste water and industrial smoke and dust have all dropped in absolute terms. Although the absolute quantities of waste gases, solid waste materials and the sulphur dioxides in waste gases have risen, they have risen at a rate far lower than the GNP growth. "Three wastes," (waste gas, water and industrial residue), per billion yuan GNP have been more or less halved. The standard waste water discharge rate has risen from 26 percent to 54.9 percent, and the solid waste disposal rate from near zero to 25.8 percent. The comprehensive utilization rate has been raised from 20 percent to 41.9 percent. Solid waste accumulation has begun to decrease.

The proportion of urban households using running water has risen from 81 percent to 90.6 percent, and those using liquid gas from 13.9 percent to 47.1 percent. The Ten-Year International Potable Water Supply and Public Health campaign helped raise the proportion of rural households using clean drinking water from 20 percent to 66 percent, benefiting 71.8 percent of the rural population. Today, 49 percent of small rural townships and 9.9 percent of villages, representing a total population of 215 million are using running water.

However, desertification which claimed an annual average of 1,560 square kilometers during the fifties, sixties and seventies, claimed an annual average of 2,100 square kilometers in the eighties. There are 1.79 million square kilometers of water-eroded land and 1.88 million square kilometers of wind-eroded land. Other data also shows worsening environmental conditions. Taken together these indicators give voice to the grim aspect of the Chinese environmental situation. Environmental quality in China is far behind that in the developed counties. Moreover, it is far short of its own environmental development target.

II. Analysis of the Factors Necessary for the Maintenance of Relatively Stable Environmental Quality

Investment in the environmental protection has steadily increased since the beginning of the reform and opening period. During the Eighth Five Year Plan (1991-1995) it was the equivalent of 1 percent of GNP. Constantly increasing investment in environmental protection has promoted better management of the environment. Overall, the key factors affecting sustained stability of environmental conditions are strategic readjustment, transformation of the mechanism and rearrangement of the system.

1. The strategy prioritizing the development of heavy industry should be changed to encourage a fairly high growth rate in light industry. The impact of light industry on the environment is much less than heavy industry.

2. Policies and organizational systems distorting prices for resources and products should be abandoned and resource utilization rates greatly improved.

3. The environmental protection system should be gradually optimized. For example, a system for the design, construction and operation of pollution prevention and control facilities accompanying major parts of all new, reconstruction and extension projects. Industrial and mining enterprises that discharge waste beyond the standard can be charged for doing so and this money used elsewhere for pollution control. An environmental impact evaluation system should be introduced and the possible impact of a project to be constructed on the environment can be scientifically demonstrated and evaluated. Before groundbreaking, all construction projects would be required to submit a report on how they planned to control environmental impact. An environmental protection targets responsibility system should be adopted. Leading government officials at all levels should be held responsible for local environmental quality and entrepreneurs held responsible for the prevention and control of pollution at their own enterprises. A quantitative check system for overall control of environmental conditions in the cities should be established, as should a permit system for discharged pollutants. A concentrated pollution control system and a system for the control of the pollution sources over a given period of time should be set up. An enterprise environmental protection check system under which product quality, consumption of materials, economic returns and environmental protection are all considered in the evaluation should be put into place. Environmental monitoring and statistical work should be improved.

China currently has a national environmental network of more than 4,000 environmental monitoring stations which supervise and limit environmental problems such as acid rain, air pollution, earthquakes, and pollution of major river systems and the marine environment.

No environmental protection work was being done in the first developed countries back when their per-capita GNP was several hundred U.S. dollars. Yet China, at this low income level, has already established a fairly complete legal system for enforcing environmental protection. This is an important factor in maintaining relatively stable environmental conditions in China despite rapid economic growth.

4. Scientific and technological progress should be encouraged. The role of the price mechanism and system arrangements have promoted rapid progress in technologies aimed at the economical use of scarce resources and these resources are now more effectively utilized.

5. Family planning should be realized. The natural population growth rate has stabilized at 11 to 14.4 per thousand, below the world average. Over the last 20 years there were 200 million fewer births than there would have been had the birth rates of the seventies continued. This decrease played an important role in reducing consumption of resources and lessening pressure on the environment.

6. Public works intended to better the environment should be actively developed. (1) The "three norths" forest shelterbelt system is an important project underway in western Northeast China, northern North China and Northwest China stretching across 13 provinces and autonomous regions. Between 1978 and 1992, 13 million hectares of forest belt were added and 12.67 million hectares were planted with trees using aerial sowing. More than 3 billion trees were planted, increasing the percentage of forest cover in these regions from 5.05 percent to 9.09 percent. (2) The forest shelterbelt system along the upper and middle reaches of the Yangtze River was started in 1989 and has been implemented in nine riverine provinces. By 1992, 670,000 hectares of forest had been added. (3) After more than 40 years of effort, more than 8,000 kilometers of forest belts along the shore have been added to the coastal forest belt system and 5.5 million hectares of

wind and sand shelter forests have been added, sheltering 1.33 million hectares of farmland.

Section Two   The Growth of Township Enterprises and the Environment

The vigorous growth of township enterprises has forcefully accelerated rural industrialization, becoming an important revenue source for the central government and the main power within the expanding national economy. The question remains how this rapid growth has adversely affected the environment.

1. Township enterprises for the most part produce labor-intensive products. Only 7.7 percent are pollution sources.

2. The negative impact on the environment caused by township enterprises is concentrated in a small number of industries, principally paper-making, printing, electroplating, chemicals, food, building materials, coal products, and mining and dressing of non-metallic ores.

3. Those industries which do pollute produce substantially more pollution than their urban counterparts.

4. The intensity of pollution generated by township enterprises negatively correlates with economic density (output value per square kilometer).

5. Environmental management of township enterprises is unsatisfactory.

There are three causes of township enterprise pollution. First, a small number of free or low-price resources create enormous waste and serious environmental pollution. Second, there is lack of cooperation between the governments at different levels in the prevention and control of environmental pollution. Local governments sometimes relax supervision over enterprises that pollute. Third, township enterprises are insufficiently concentrated geographically, seriously limiting the development of environmentally friendly production.

Section Three   Changing Environmental Trends

The growth rate in heavy industry was very high from the fifties when China began to industrialize to the eighties. But this came at the cost of serious pollution. Since the initiation of the reform and opening policy, environmental conditions have not significantly worsened, but the environmental pollution already present has continued.

China suffers losses of around 100 billion yuan every year due to earthquakes, typhoons, windstorms, floods, droughts, insects and other natural disasters.[1] Some of these calamities are unavoidable, but some can be eliminated or mitigated through human effort. All of these natural disasters are connected with the quality and stability of the environment. The higher the quality and the more stability of the environment, the smaller the losses from natural disasters. China's tremendous losses from natural disasters are an indication of the nation's low-quality, unstable environment.

China's ecological system is deteriorating because resources are being utilized in excess of their carrying capacity. Between the early fifties and late seventies, excessive harvesting of forests, destruction of woods and grasses for use as farmland, reclamation of the wet lands, the building of dykes to reclaim land from lakes and seas, and excessive hunting and fishing have led to a reversal in the succession of ecological communities found in forests, reduced organic content in farmland, aggravated soil erosion, regional expansion of the desertification and salinization of former farmland, a near exhaustion of forest and fish resources, and a reduction in the size of the natural habitats of endangered species and in the species communities themselves. About one third of farmland is subject to soil erosion, and approximately 5 billion tons of soil are lost every year; 3.93 million hectares of farmland and 4.93 million hectares of pasture are menaced

---

[1] Deng Nan, "Some Questions Concerning China's Agenda in the 21st Century," *Population, Resources and the Environment in China*, No. 3, 1994, p. 1.

by desertification. The sharp increase in the use of chemical fertilizers and insecticides has had a negative effect in aggravating eutrophication in lakes and coastal waters, worsening the habitat for marine resources. Since the eighties, China has made great efforts to limit logging, plant trees and grass, returning farmland to forest and prairie, establish natural preserves and protect endangered species. Still, it remains far from attaining its goal of effecting a comprehensive reversal of the worsening of the nation's ecological systems.

The distribution of the water resources in China is extremely uneven. About 81 percent of the nation's water resources supply only 36 percent of the nation's farmland in the Yangtze River Basin and south of the river. Approximately 64 percent of the nation's farmland is located in the Huaihe River Basin and further north. This region has only 19 percent of the nation's water resources. Inadequate water supplies have compelled many areas in northern China to reduce area irrigated and the number of effective irrigations, resulting in losses of more than 5 billion kilograms of grains that could have otherwise been produced. Per-capita water resources nationwide are very low. There are acute water shortages in North China, eastern Shandong, central and southern Liaoning, and Northwest China. More than 300 of the nation's 500 cities do not have enough water; 40 suffer serious shortages. Losses in potential industrial output value resulting from the water shortage near 100 billion yuan every year. Water pollution is also very serious. Of the 123 key sections of the seven major river systems and other inland rivers, 25 percent have satisfactory water quality in compliance with the standards set for categories one and two by the Surface Water Environmental Quality Standards, 27 percent are rated in the third category and 48 percent in the fourth and fifth categories. Water quality in the mainstreams of six major river systems, the Yangtze, Yellow, Pearl, Huaihe, Songhua and Daliaohe, is basically good, but where the rivers flow through cities they are clearly polluted. Polluted groundwater under cities is increasingly higher in nitrogen content and hardness of water. One third of well water is blow standard for drinking. Waste of water resources is very common. The industrial water recycling rate is only 25 percent in large cities, with the highest rate only 49 percent, far below the 70 to 90 percent averaged in the developed countries.

For many years efforts have been focused on increasing output value and environmental protection has been ignored. Almost every city has been adversely affected by pollution from a large number of enterprises. Environmental quality is bad. These enterprises have been working since the eighties to limit pollution. Some resource utilization technologies have been strictly controlled. However, with rapid expansion in the scale of industry, the total quantity of pollution has not been reduced, with the result that the quality of the urban environment has not improved. Investigations by the environmental protection authorities in recent years revealed that few of the nation's more than 500 cities have reached the national grade one standards for air quality. Atmospheric dust and particulate matter and sulphur dioxide in every northern city exceeds standards. In the south the situation is little better with nearly 100 percent of cities failing to meet the standards. While atmospheric nitrogen oxide levels do not exceed standards, concentrations are increasing and the prospect is by no means optimistic. Concentration levels of fine particulate matter in some cities are more than ten times the standard laid out by the World Health Organization. China's main source of energy is coal. About 75 percent of the fuel used in industry and for motive power, 65 percent of the chemical raw materials, and 85 percent of the fuel used by individual urban households is coal. This heavy reliance on coal is determined by the nation's energy resource structure. The situation is unlikely to change. As the economy and population grow, more and more coal will be used each year. If no major breakthroughs are made in the technology used to burn coal or in replacement of energy sources, air pollution will be extremely difficult to control and in all likelihood will worsen.

Almost all of southern China suffers from acid rain. Monitoring in recent years has found acid rain in Guangdong, Guangxi, the Sichuan Basin, and most of Guizhou. The annual frequency of acid rainfall in Guangdong was 48.1 percent in 1991, 5.7 percentage points higher than in 1989. The lowest pH value of the rainfall was 3.02. The frequency of acid rainfall in Guangxi's principal cities, Nanning, Liuzhou, Guilin and Wuzhou, was 73.5 percent, 89 percent, 68.1 percent and 82.7 percent, respectively. The frequency of acid rainfall in Sichuan exceeded 50 percent, and that in Guiyang approached 100 percent. Annual economic losses caused by acid rain have reached 14 billion yuan. If this problem cannot be effectively controlled, great damage will be done to the agriculture, livestock breeding and fishing industries.

Noise pollution is also a very serious problem in China. The average equivalent acoustic level in 39 cities was 51.7—72.6 decibel in 1993, and in five over 60 decibels. Approximately 30 percent of workers are estimated to be working under excessively noisy conditions and around 40 percent of city dwellers live in places surrounded by noise pollution.

Unburied solid wastes produce secondary air and water pollution. Although disposal rates have improved in recent years, thousands of tons are still piling up.

Historical reasons and restrictions imposed by the level of economic development led to the use of technologies from the fifties and sixties in most industrial construction projects undertaken prior to the eighties. Most had no facilities for pollution prevention and control and were inefficient regards energy and resource consumption. They remain major polluters. Eliminating pollution at these industrial enterprises would require at a minimum an estimated 200 billion yuan. Comprehensive transformation of these enterprises would require still more money. They are currently burdened with aging equipment, relatively low returns on production, the enormous expense of supporting retired former employees and an acute shortage of the financial resources necessary for technical transformation. It will be difficult for them to solve the problems that remain from history if they are left to rely on their resources, but if these problems are not corrected they will limit any improvement in environmental quality.

Some specialists in China have drawn upon the experiences in the developed countries to try to calculate nationwide losses from environmental pollution. Their figures show annual losses around 40 billion yuan from water pollution, 30 billion yuan from air pollution and 25 billion yuan from solid waste and insecticide pollution, a total of approximately 95 billion yuan, about 6.75 percent of GNP. According to United Nations Environmental Program figures, economic losses from environmental pollution are the equivalent of 3 to 5 percent of GNP in the United States, Japan and other developed countries. Clearly, China's pollution problems are more severe than those in the developed countries. During the Eighth Five-Year Plan (1991-1995) 135 billion yuan was lost annually due to pollution.[1]

An analysis predicting China's environmental conditions up to 2010 based on the available data indicates the following probable developments.

I. The Negative Impact of Poverty on the Environment Will Decrease While That of the Growth Will Increase

The adverse effect of irrational agricultural techniques necessitated by poverty will be lessened when all peasants have enough food to eat and clothing to wear, reclaimed farmland has reverted to forest or grassland and ecologically coherent agriculture adopted. On the other hand, so long as the effect of technological advances and environmental management on reducing industrial pollution remain insignificant, as will likely remain the case, total quantities of waste waters, gases and materials are not likely to decrease, indeed may increase, with rapid industrial expansion.

---

[1] Qu Geping: *The Environment and Development in China*, The Chinese Environmental Science Publishing House, 1992, p. 47.

II. Ecological Systems Benefiting from Technological Progress and the Rearrangement of the Systems Will Tend to Improve While Those Not Benefiting Will Continue to Worsen

For example, the weak ecological systems in Northeast, North and Northwest China have benefited as forest cover there has been increased from 5.05 percent to 9.09 percent. Special arrangements have been made and local governments made responsible for the afforestation of waste land and barren hills. Guangdong and 11 other provinces have all fulfilled their assignments in completing this task. As China's water and soil conservation technology is becoming among the best in the world, the negative impact from soil erosion on environment will be reduced. Total water and soil loss is projected to be 10 percent less in 2000 than in 1990. However, no technological advance has been produced that can counter the creeping desertification of farmland. Control over the three industrial wastes likewise awaits a solution. Technological progress and rearrangement of the system effected by the government should gradually alleviate these problems.

III. Resource Systems with Clearly Defined Property Rights (e.g. Farmland) Will Tend to Improve While Those Without Will (e.g. Grasslands) Tend to Worsen

IV. Urban Environmental Pollution Will Slowly Improve While That in the New Towns Built in the Countryside Will Gradually Worsen

V. Global Environmental Changes Will Have an Increasing Effect on China

This will be principally seen in two ways. First, the warmer climate will aggravate problems with desertification and soil salinization, degenerating grasslands in North and Northwest China. The frequency and intensity of typhoons will increase in the coastal areas, creating still greater problems with wind, rainstorms and flooding for the southeastern coastal areas. Summers will be hotter, increasing plant diseases and insect pests. Second, rising sea levels will seriously menace economic development in the coastal areas. Oilfields and salt-fields will suffer. Farmland will be in threat of increased salinization and difficulties in water drainage.

Section Four   Measures to Counter Environmental Problems

I. Developing the Market System

1. The market for production elements should be developed. For example, price subsidies for coal and irrigation water should be removed to encourage enterprises to limit consumption and reduce pollution. (Data collected by the World Bank shows that the price of electricity is only 38 percent of production cost, coal 85 percent and irrigation water only 20 percent.)

2. The market for pollution emission rights should be nurtured. This system is intended to limit emission of pollutants and facilitate the trading of the right to produce certain quantities of pollutants. At present, the system only serves to meet the first of these two goals, but, in fact, the second is more important. The trading of the "right to pollute" is an important tool for solving environmental problems. If some pollution is inevitable, the market mechanism can be used to keep that pollution to a minimum. Development of this market should be accelerated, based on experiments of trading of pollution emission rights.

II. Strengthening the Government's Role in Environmental Management

1. The law and necessary administrative measures should be developed to protect the environment. A basic legal system for the

protection of environmental resources has been established. In the future stress should be shifted to the enforcement of the laws while continuing to complete the system. (1) Rural areas should implement strict environmental protection system. (2) Concentration limits for pollutants should be changed to total quantity limits and discharge limits to final release limits. In this way the pollution produced during production process can be reduced timely as required by the standards set for each stage of production. (3) Charges for emission of pollutants should be increased to encourage enterprises to reduce pollution. (4) Compensation charges should be initiated for use of renewable resources, encouraging the economic use of resources by enterprises. Compensation charges for the use of renewable resources should be introduced to foster the production of such resources.

2. The responsibility for supporting the development of the environmentally responsible industry must be undertaken. (1) Work in the environmental statistics and monitoring system should be strengthened, and a national environmental information network established. (2) The environmental protection investment growth mechanism should be optimized. The key here is guaranteeing that a set proportion of investment in an enterprise goes to environmental protection and that investment in environmental protection goes up as the enterprise's profits go up. (3) The development of environmentally responsible enterprises should be very actively supported through preferential treatment in taxes, loans and pricing.

3. Environmental costs should be included in the prices of resources in the accounting system.

4. Allocation of research resources should be increasingly directed toward appropriate technologies beneficial to the protection of the environment and resources.

III. Zones Should Be Set Up for the Development of Township Enterprises

Special areas in the countryside should be set aside for the establishment of township enterprise development zones. This will beneficial to the relocation of the rural surplus workforce, the acceleration of rural industrialization and urbanization and concentrated control over pollution from township enterprises. Unified planning should be adopted and implemented as early as possible.

图书在版编目(CIP)数据

走向 21 世纪的中国经济:预测与对策:英文/李京文主编 . —北京:外文出版社,2000
ISBN 7 - 119 - 02029 - 3

Ⅰ.走… Ⅱ.李 Ⅲ.①经济发展 - 研究 - 中国 - 英文 ②经济预测 - 研究 - 中国 - 英
文 Ⅳ.F120.4

中国版本图书馆 CIP 数据核字(1999)第 03655 号

责任编辑 吴灿飞
英文编辑 朱惠明
封面设计 王 志

外文出版社网址:

http://www.flp.com.cn

外文出版社电子信箱:

info@flp.com.cn

sales@flp.com.cn

走向 21 世纪的中国经济 —— 预测与对策
主编 李京文

*

©外文出版社

外文出版社出版
(中国北京百万庄大街 24 号)
邮政编码 100037
北京外文印刷厂印刷
中国国际图书贸易总公司发行
(中国北京车公庄西路 35 号)
北京邮政信箱第 399 号 邮政编码 100044
2000 年(大 32 开)第 1 版
2000 年第 1 版第 1 次印刷
(英)
ISBN 7 - 119 - 02029 - 3/F·59(外)
05500
4 - E - 3284P